THE CRAFT OF INTERVIEWING

The Craft of Interviewing

JOHN BRADY

Writer's Digest Books

DAVID GLENN HUNT
MEMORIAL LIBRARY
GALVESTON COLLEGE

Library of Congress Cataloging in Publication Data

Brady, John Joseph
The craft of interviewing.
1. Interviewing (Journalism)
I. Title.
PN4784.I6B67   070.4'3   75-33133
ISBN 0-911654-44-5

Second Printing
©Copyright 1976, John Brady

Writer's Digest
Div., F&W Publishing Corporation
9933 Alliance Road
Cincinnati, Ohio 45242

Speech is the index of the mind.

—Seneca

Out of thine own mouth will I judge thee.

—Luke 19:22

"You can tell your paper," the great man said,
"I refused an interview.
I have nothing to say on the question, sir;
Nothing to say to you."
And then he talked till the sun went down
And the chickens went to roost.

—O. Henry

Acknowledgments

I never use the word very. It's always superfluous. Except now. These people are special. Very. My warmest thanks and gratitude to them for being themselves and for being there along the way.

Rose Adkins
Sister Alice Regina, O.P.
James Ballowe
Mary Barrett
Jeanne Brooks
Christopher Buckley
Ric Calabrese
Al Candia
John Christie
Mae Dick
Eugenie Beck Dowling
Lynne Ellinwood
Murray Fisher
Barker D. Herr
Robert Holibaugh
Pete Johnson
Richard Loomis

Charles Matusik
Susan May
Reya Maxymuk
Phil Moffitt
Kirk Polking
Bob & Manya Prahl
Rex Reed
Dick & Lois Rosenthal
Allan Scott
Art Spikol
Philip Spitzer
Gay Talese
Leon Taylor
Bob Thomas
Bill Truskoloski
Joe Wambaugh
Skip Weiner

for

Lilia & Leona
the women in my life

Contents

Getting an interview with someone is like asking your good-looking cousin to go out with a friend of a friend on a blind date: you must approach the subject Just So. Fortunately, there are *so* many ways of approaching him. You can phone him, write him, telegram him, stalk him, badger him (even if he's a Sonny Liston), plead with him, pay him, or woo his secretary. And you needn't be a celebrity to interview a celebrity — no more than you need be a cab driver to interview a cab driver. What you *do* need for celebrity or cabbie (a fetching introduction, an interview appointment), and what you should brace for (ground rules, cash requests) are laid out in this chapter. Among plenty else.

You can tell when some writers are about to embark on research. Their eyes freeze over, like a winter windshield. They look stooped and fatigued. They become, in short, martyrs, and it's not necessary, because research can be fun: gold-digging in almanacs, wooing the librarian, getting the goods on your interviewee from his old schoolteachers. The thrill of discovery, and the feeling of being truly prepared for an interview is exhilarating. Anyway, it sure beats asking Vivien Leigh what part she played in *Gone With the Wind,* and watching her turn Scarlett.

3. Face to Face

At last, the long moment of truth: meeting the interviewee head-on. Now is the time to hone your horns, paw the ground, and mark off your turf, no? No. Now is the time for *rapport.* For friendly — even if pointed — conversation. Role-playing helps. So does sensible dress. Gabbing, however, is risky. "The observation may be elementary, but it is important," says John Hohenberg. "No talking reporter ever held a decent interview."

4. Popping the Questions

Many writers seem to have studied interviewing at medical school. "But . . . but . . . how do you *feel,* Mr. Beethoven? About being a genius and all. How do you *really feel?*" Reprieve, please. Lead us not into dull interrogations. Provoke your interviewee with open-ended questions of issue and controversy; then provide the reader with color by egging your subject into anecdotes. Plan your questions — a little. And make that opener a winner. Hal Higdon once started an interview with, "Why don't you tell me a little bit about what you've done?" "If you don't know," retorted the subject, "what are you doing here?"

"OK, fella. No more glib answers, or I'm going to rinse out your bridgework. Now just how do I get tough in an interview?" "With — *glurg* — moderation. Getting tough does not mean getting mean. It means persisting — politely, even gently, if the interviewee is inexperienced. Blame someone else for the question. Start it off with some praise. Study Barbara Walters. Above all, be a professional about it, and I don't mean a — *bleg* — professional wrestler!"

Vexation is a cop who provides a bevy of anecdotes about sex on the waterfront, then leans back and says, "Uh, that's off the record, of course." You *should* throttle him. But you can also outfox him — by confirming the stories elsewhere; by bargaining with him for a veiled attribution; or by damning his torpedo eyes, and running the stories with full speed and attribution. 'Tis a case of conscience. Let your reader — and this chapter — be your guide.

An interviewer without notes is like a comedian without writers: naked and defenseless. Yet poor notes — cuneiform style — can backfire; and excessive notetaking can pry loose the writer's grasp on the essential points. Herewith are tips for those interviewers with palsied script, mortal memory, and the best of intentions: on reaching casually for the notebook; on shorthand and instant editing; on capturing color; on "doing a Capote," with coaching from a certain Truman.

your editor because the profile was due yesterday. But the secret of written and phone interviews is this: they are strongest when yoked together. Read all about it.

Bringing the interview to an artful close is an art in itself. You want to leave your interviewee with the impression that *he* is doing the closing. And even after the last good-bye, you must still verify the facts in the interview, untangle conflicting stories, get your source's approval of the transcript (if you *really* need it), and cultivate him with an eye toward future stories. A writer's work is never done.

Writing may be the arduous aftermath of interviewing; but it is also the most rewarding phase of a job well done. For the writer loves two worlds — a world of clatter and conversation, and one of solitude and words. Empowered by his craft, he shuttles between them freely. But he is not free to ignore the rigors of writing — of grammar, accuracy, style and life. They receive a once-over here. Tightly.

A brief foray into bloodlines that account for the interview as we know it today.

Introduction

The nineteenth century was the era of the novelist.
The twentieth is the era of the journalist.

—James Reston

There are writers who will say that interviewing is simple, as simple as inviting a stranger out to lunch; that it is only a well-prepared, lively conversation, with the quieter conversant recording tape or taking notes. That it is easy. That it is certainly no book.

And, in a sense, it isn't. It is taking care of an itch—as simple and natural as that. You don't need a college degree. You don't even need a degree of gregariousness. You only need an abiding curiosity about people and, perhaps, a cautious faith in them.

But like most pursuits of curiosity, interviewing is a craft and a profession; rarely a science, sometimes an art. Like so much in journalism, it can be learned by trial and terrifying error; but there are shortcuts, too, and this book explores some of them. One hopes that they will make you a better-organized interviewer; that they will dispense with the clutter of your work; that they will enable you to master interviewing as a craft, so you are free to pursue it as an art.

For no matter how fine a writer might be, he is crippled if he is not an effective interviewer. The most valuable and original contributions in journalism today are usually obtained in interviews. "These days, more than at any other time, our most vivid impressions of our contemporaries are through interviews," says Denis Brian, author of *Murderers & Other Friendly People*—a book of interviews with—who else?—interviewers. "Almost everything of moment reaches us through one man asking questions of another. Because of this, the interviewer holds a position of unprecedented power and influence."

And he is in unprecedented demand.

Today's reader wants more than bare facts—he wants to know why an event occurred, what feelings it incited, how it might have been avoided. Editors demand journalists who know more than just the card tricks of writing, who know how to probe their interviewees for the telling detail, the taut quote. Many editors consider the best interviewers to be, inescapably, the best writers. In nonfiction, anyway.

And nonfiction is what counts today. While fiction was in strong demand a generation or so ago, the market has reversed dramatically. Americans today seem to prefer fact over fiction in their reading. Most magazines use articles exclusively. Of some 30,000 new books published in 1975, only 2,407 were fiction, according to *Publishers Weekly*. And even novelists among us are turning increasingly to the techniques of nonfiction. Bestsellers like Truman Capote's *In Cold Blood*, Joseph Wambaugh's *The Onion Field*, James Michener's *Hawaii*, and Arthur Hailey's "research" novels—*Airport*, *Wheels*, et alia—required months of fact-gathering interviews.

Even obituaries can require interviews. Alden Whitman, the former chief obituary writer for the *New York Times*, made his wary rounds from year to year chatting with elder statesmen and celebrities, taking notes, absorbing impressions that would appear only—and promptly—after a subject died.

In broadcasting, the interview is likewise ubiquitous. Quiz shows, game shows, and talk shows all derive their format from the Q&A exchange. News shows, of course, would be stranded without interviews. "The interview is a basic tool of our business," says Reuven Frank, former president of NBC News, "and we could not survive without it." Interviews present abstract ideas in human terms. "No important story is without them," adds Frank. "They can be recorded and transmitted tastefully. Integration, Algeria, Skybolt, nuclear disarmament, flood, automation—name me a recent news story without its human involvement." The rather abstract concept of inflation was dramatized on television by an interview with an unemployed itinerant who described how he had to scavenge leftovers from fine restaurants at which he had formerly dined.

We Americans like interviews so much that we *create* them. Daniel Boorstin has called the interview a "pseudo-event," artificial news, in which things happen not of their own volition—as do fires, floods, acts of God and rage—but of *our* volition. We bring people together.

We insert questions. We oversee. We edit. We print and read the results. We judge the participants. We talk endlessly about them—about Kate Hepburn on the *Dick Cavett Show,* G. Gordon Liddy on CBS's *Sixty Minutes,* Tennessee Williams on the *David Frost Show*—and in our homes, in our easy chairs, we interview each other about the interviews.

"Sometimes I think it's another sign of the sad necessity of our crowded, lonely lives," suggests George Garrett, "an urgent, hopeless reaching out to touch something real, a deep hunger for something authentic when everything seems false, a desire to believe at least in the possibility of the naked truth. And we seem to know, to realize . . . that these people, the characters we encounter in the various forms the interview takes, are . . . really very much like us, not any wiser or braver or more virtuous, not even smarter or more skilled at whatever it is they do, but maybe more clever, certainly luckier than the rest of us."

Interviewing is travel, meeting all kinds of people, quenching curiosities. Interviewing is a celebrated, enigmatic woman sitting back and saying, "OK, go ahead. Ask me anything." Interviewing is someone you have never heard of (but of whom your editor has said: "Get him!") saying, through the coolness of a call from his secretary, "Mr. Hagendorf is too busy to talk with you today, and he's leaving for the Philippines tomorrow." Interviewing is, above all, the unexpected. Its joy is not unlike what Gloria Steinem once said of writing in general: "It's the only thing that passes the three tests of métier: 1) When I'm doing it, I don't feel that I should be doing something else instead; 2) it produces a sense of accomplishment and, once in a while, pride; and 3) it's frightening."

The interviewer seeks truth—but his work does not require the creative surges of art, nor does it possess the certitude of science. And, unlike the scientist, the interviewer has no "rules" that aren't broken daily by fine writers getting great quotes. "There is no clinical skill, really," says Alex Haley, *Playboy* interviewer and author of *Roots* and *The Autobiography of Malcolm X.* "I just use all the things I can think of from my experiences."

The only rule to remember is this: be flexible. Asking questions is, after all, an unpredictable and exhilarating pursuit. What follows is intended as a literary stretch sock—its ideas should fit each reader comfortably, yet in a different manner. Suggestions are intended as guides, never as restrictions. Any suggestion, mechanically followed, is bound to defeat the purpose.

Mostly, I think, successful interviewing is a matter of professional—and, one hopes, genuine—curiosity overtaking the writer's innate shyness. It was for me; and most writers that I have met are likewise private people. But the urge to communicate is too strong, and we become interviewers in spite of ourselves. And for ourselves.

In interviewing, you will have a modest feeling of power. Not the power of manipulation, but the power of knowledge—of holding a handmade key to a secret room of the subject's mind. The feeling is ephemeral, but sturdy and true. Afterward, when the interview is in print, you will realize that the secret has ended, but has touched other lives.

For some readers, this book is a beginning. For others, it may be a refresher course. But all, I hope, will find it helpful in resolving a writer's riddle: how to win friends and interview people.

—*John Brady*

1. Getting Interviews

*Well, yes, you do have great big teeth; but,
never mind that. You were great to at least
grant me this interview.*

—Little Red Riding Hood

When Henry Stanley of the *New York Herald* finally caught up
with his subject somewhere in deepest Africa in 1871 and inquired
"Dr. Livingstone, I presume?", the good doctor's response was *not*
"No interviews at this time, please." Such reports are highly exaggerated. Still, some Pollyanna-like thinking is to be found in a remark
once made by A. J. Liebling, the legendary *New Yorker* columnist.
"There is almost no circumstance under which an American doesn't
like to be interviewed," he said. "We are an articulate people, pleased
by attention, covetous of being singled out."

Even in this land of milk and honey, getting interviews can be
tough. Or easy. Or, at best, uncertain. Perhaps the uncertainty of
it all is what keeps a good interviewer going: the thrill of the chase.
Barbara Walters, for example, puts considerable effort into obtaining
difficult interviews. She worked for two years trying to get former
Secretary of State Dean Rusk on the *Today Show,* and ended up
scoring a coup when Rusk gave her his first interview after leaving
the cabinet post. "First of all, there's a challenge in getting the people
who don't do interviews," she says. "NBC would never have given
me a Dean Rusk interview. Even if he had come into the studio,
the interview would probably have been done by Hugh Downs. If
H. R. Haldeman had agreed to be interviewed on *Today,* Frank McGee
would have done it. But if I go out and get these people for *myself,*

then they're *mine*. This is my motivating thing and I work extra hard at it."

Slipping Up

Interviewing has been compared with the fine art of salesmanship — and the first thing that a salesman needs is a list of potential customers. "The reporter and the salesman have much the same problems," says one interviewer. "Both must be able to reach their man, to gain and hold his attention, to direct his mind along the way they want it to travel, and finally to show that it will pay him to talk."

There are a few shortcuts to tracking down people for interviews. Names and phone numbers of many well-known Americans are available in the various Marquis *Who's Who* volumes. If a subject has published a book, his publisher will have his address — and will be willing to forward a letter, if not reveal the address. If the subject lectures or performs, a lecture or performing bureau will know where to find him. If he has had a recent article published, the magazine might give you his address, or at least forward an inquiry. If he is known in a particular field, a newsletter or organization in that field may know where to find him.

People of similar interests tend to flock together. Sometimes a preliminary interview will serve as a lead to other sources. "In research for one of my articles," says freelancer Mike Edelhart, "my first interviewee gave me the names, addresses and phone numbers for virtually every other major name in the field." Regardless how one acquires a list of potential interviewees, once that is done, the job of selling the subject on the interview begins.

You can often slip up on a subject on his doormat. Ask Carl Bernstein and Bob Woodward. The *Washington Post* reporters who investigated Watergate worked 12 to 18 hours a day, seven days a week; and in four months, they interviewed over 1,000 people. "You knock on a lot of doors and you make a lot of phone calls, and people put you on to other people," Bernstein told journalist Timothy Crouse. "Nine times out of ten, people wouldn't let us in the door. But sometimes it worked. The theory was that there were a lot of people who worked in places where the last thing in the world they would want was a visit from somebody named Woodward or Bernstein.

And if you call them on the phone, they're gonna say no."

"But instead you show up at their homes and show that you're well-dressed and civilized," adds Woodward. Bernstein: "And you convince them that you're interested in the truth and not in any preconceptions. You tell them that if you've been in error, they're in a position to show you where you went wrong. We didn't think we were in error very often, but it's an effective introduction."

Hunter and the Hunted

Investigative work represents but a tiny tip of the interviewing iceberg. Most writers on routine assignments know that in order to procure interviews, they must be polite, precise and punctual. Getting an interview means making an appointment to see the subject, identifying yourself and the nature of your research, and showing up on time for the interview itself.

Making an interview appointment is usually done by writing or phoning at least a week in advance. If an editor wants the story yesterday, the one-week rule may have to be waived; but a waiver is the exception. "It is not a good idea, when avoidable, to drop into somebody's life by phone and abruptly ask him to give you half an hour or more of his time right then and there," says Max Gunther in his *Writing and Selling a Nonfiction Book*. "Daily newspaper reporters often have to do this, but as a book writer you lack the excuse of daily deadlines. The source can reasonably assume the interview will be as useful to you next week as this week, and if you ask him to do it right away he may be irritated."

Another reason for making an appointment in advance is that the subject has time to collect his thoughts. If the topic is a sensitive one, this can be especially helpful. In *Writing the Modern Magazine Article*, Max Gunther tells of the time he was researching an article on child suicide for the *Saturday Evening Post*. He did not know where to go for information, so he talked to the director of a psychiatric hospital. "Well, you're welcome to come and see me," the man said, "but I really don't think I'll be able to help you much." When the writer turned up three days later, though, the director was beaming with success. "During the three days, he had talked to other doctors and had collected a whole list of sources for me," says Gunther. "What's more, he had even done some of my library work for me.

He handed me a sheet of paper listing references to medical journals in which cases of child suicide had been written up. None of this could have happened if I'd phoned him and tried to interview him on the spot."

When should you call for an interview? If you phone when a subject is sleeping, eating, bathing—or worse—you may find it difficult to get him to agree to *anything*, much less an interview. Timing is all. Bear in mind, too, the difference in time zones for long-distance dialing. If you are spending a day at the phone doing interviews, you would do well to begin in the morning in New York, and then to work your way across the country to the Golden Coast.

For Gonzo journalists, of course, all bets are off. When Hunter Thompson arrived in Washington as the *Rolling Stone* correspondent in 1971, he found "it was a nightmare at first, nobody would return my calls." One problem was that nobody had heard of the magazine. "Rolling what? ... Stones?" was a typical attitude: "I heard them once; noisy bastards, aren't they?" "Anyway, it didn't take me long to learn that the only time to call politicians is very late at night," Thompson told *Playboy* interviewer Craig Vetter. "*Very* late. In Washington, the truth is never told in daylight hours or across a desk. If you catch people when they're very tired or drunk or weak, you can usually get some answers. So I'd sleep days, wait till these people got their lies and treachery out of the way, let them relax, then come on full speed on the phone at two or three in the morning. You have to wear the bastards down before they'll tell you anything."

J. Dickey

While the Fear and Loathing Theory of Interviewing has its advocates, most writers are more diplomatic in their dealings with subjects—even politician subjects. On the phone, for instance, if someone answers and says that your subject is unavailable, be polite yet persistent in conveying the importance of your assignment. That sense of urgency is likely to be passed on to your subject. Most people answer their own phones, of course. Even Robert Townsend, the author of *Up the Organization*, answered his phone as president of the Avis Rent a Car Corporation—a policy he recommends for executives in his book. So accessibility is often there, even at high corporate levels. At home, it's even more likely. While doing research for her famous exposé of the Famous Writers School for the *Atlantic,* Jessica Mitford got on the phone early one Sunday and began calling the school's "Famous Faculty." "I got their phone numbers by looking them up in *Who's Who,* to get their married names and hometowns," says Mitford. She reached Faith Baldwin, Phyllis McGinley and others in this manner. "They spoke very freely, and were quite frank about admitting they were just figureheads."

Never let up. Mike Edelhart was working on a piece on whitewater canoeing for *College* magazine, and his editor suggested strongly that an interview with James Dickey, author of the canoeing novel *Deliverance,* would be a big plus. Therefore Edelhart had to find, make an appointment with, and interview Dickey—whom he had never met—in the three weeks before his deadline. "Actually, it was easier than you might think," recalls the writer. "If I have discovered one thing from my interviews, it is that people, even famous ones, are more available and more talkative than you might suspect. Of course, this varies enormously from person to person, and is dependent on your persistence and credibility on the phone; but usually it's not hard to find your subject, or at least to find out if he's available."

In the case of James Dickey, Edelhart knew he was poet-in-residence at the University of South Carolina from the dustjacket of *Deliverance.* He got out the Columbia, South Carolina, phone book (most large libraries carry a generous supply of major-city phone books) and looked up the number for the university English department. "He wasn't in his office, so with my pitch firmly in mind I tried the only J. Dickey in the phone book," recalls the interviewer. "It was him."

Edelhart explained the nature of his assignment. Dickey agreed to the interview, but asked if the writer could call him back in about ten days—"after school lets out and I have more time," said the poet. Edelhart called again ten days later in the evening, and was told by Dickey that breakfast time the next morning was *the* time. The next day Edelhart, who was in San Francisco, got up at 6 a.m. to reach the poet in South Carolina at nine. "This time my patience and perseverance were rewarded with a fruitful 20-minute conversation that proved invaluable to the article."

The lesson here is obvious: never assume that well-known people are more difficult to find than anyone else who is likely to be busy. It's often harder to reach your family doctor. Another point to remember is the preliminary phone call for an appointment. "If I had greeted James Dickey with 'Hi, I'm Mike Edelhart, and I want to interview you,' I would have gotten a quick slam and a dial tone for my trouble," says the interviewer. "Instead, I said something like this: 'Good evening, Mr. Dickey, this is Mike Edelhart from *College* magazine. We're planning a piece for our spring issue on whitewater canoeing. Your novel *Deliverance* has had a tremendous effect on the popularity of whitewater, and you've expressed some distress about the injuries that have resulted from unprepared people taking to the rapids. We wondered if we could make an appointment to talk about some of these things whenever you're free.' "

Please Deposit $3.25

This introduction is precise, and doubtless was effective on someone like Dickey, a master compressor of words. It's important to make your initial contact with experts or famous people in terms they are familiar with. Project yourself as a kindred spirit. You might even write out what you are going to say on the phone, if you think you are likely to become wordy or awkward in ad-libbing it. Identify yourself fully; tell the subject what you are working on and where he fits in.

Freelancer Mort Weisinger has developed what he calls "a sure-fire gimmick which works nine out of ten times" in getting through to an inaccessible VIP or celebrity. "I simply ensconce myself in a public telephone booth and fortify myself with a stack of quarters and dimes. Then I phone the celebrity at his office, person-to-person." In order to minimize the chance of a secretary road-blocking a call, Weisinger calls during lunch hour, when secretaries are likely to be out. "I have found that most famous folk, particularly women, are so busy they usually send out for their lunch and eat at their desk," he observes. When the interviewee-to-be has been reached and the operator says "I have your party. Please deposit $3.25," Weisinger goes into his ritual of inserting 13 quarters. "Can you imagine the reaction of the subject at the other end?" he asks. "When I identify myself as a freelance writer, he knows I have invested $3.25 of my own hard-earned money (not a big magazine's) and he immediately feels obligated. . . . He regards me as an underdog and becomes quite loquacious." In fact, when Weisinger phoned Robert F. Kennedy, the late Senator asked the operator to charge all overtime to his own phone.

Getting Ike's Advice

Phrasing is important, too. With *some* subjects, you can perhaps be euphemistic with effect. "Never ask to 'interview' a busy person," suggests author Philip Marvin. "Rather, ask for an appointment to get his 'constructive criticism' of the background information you have already gathered." Columnist Sheilah Graham got a revealing interview with Jackie Chan, the actress who had been Anthony Armstrong-Jones's favorite girl until shortly before the announcement of his engagement to Princess Margaret, by asking her to have lunch and to discuss her career. "If I had said 'to discuss Tony,' she would not have agreed, as she did, to have lunch with me," Graham recalls in *The Rest of the Story.* "We *did* discuss her career, and I later interested Ross Hunter in offering her a role in *The Flower Drum Song.* During our lunch, oh so carefully, I brought up the name of Mr. Armstrong-Jones. To my surprise she discussed him very frankly. And I had another scoop."

If an interviewer's phrasing is intriguing enough, it may get him an interview from someone who didn't want to give one at all. When General Dwight Eisenhower was traveling from Kansas to Europe (where he was to take over NATO), he told Robert M. White of the *Mexico Ledger* in Missouri that he would give no interviews. "I understand, sir," said the reporter. "I have only one question: What is your advice to young men today?" Ike couldn't resist. "That question was a direct shot at a great heart," wrote White afterward. "He couldn't keep from answering, even though he had made up his mind that he would not let anyone have an 'interview.' " As matters turned out, White got the *only* interview Ike gave on his trip, all because of a carefully phrased question that pried open a subject.

Double Time

When making an appointment for an interview, specify the amount of time you will need. Once the questions have begun, however, few subjects remain clock watchers. The late Richard Gehman always rose to go when the requested time had elapsed. Usually the subject was just getting warmed up, though, and would ask Gehman to stay.

"Arthur Godfrey is a notoriously difficult interview," Gehman recalled. "Once, doing a piece on Pat Boone, who was singing on his show, I asked Godfrey's secretary for ten minutes. ... I was ushered into the great man's presence. He was affable and voluble; it was one of his good days. At the end of my ten minutes, I stood up. 'Where are you goin'?' he asked, in surprise. 'Sit and chat for a while.' I was with him for more than an hour."

Such largesse may not always be the case, however; the interviewer should suggest how much time he will need, and be prepared to complete his interview within the time allotted, though the subject may talk longer.

A Bead on Reed

If the subject is difficult to reach by phone (and if time allows), you might request an interview in writing. Some writers feel that is more dignified. In addition, if the letter goes unanswered, you have a foot in the door for a follow-up phone call.

Asking for an interview by mail is like querying an editor on a story idea. You should identify yourself and your proposed article idea, and try to sell the idea and yourself to your reader. Be polite. Be flexible in arranging an appointment. Be professional — right down to your stationery. An interview request written on pink, dime-store stationery — or on one of those egregious "From the desk of" memo pads — may diminish the tone of that important first impression. Remember: even the beginning writer is competing against professionals. Letterhead stationery, like a good typewriter, is a valuable investment for the beginning writer. For the professional, of course, it is standard.

No matter how attractive the stationery, unless the letter is convincing, the request for an interview may fail. Here is a letter I sent to Rex Reed, which resulted in an interview for *Writer's Digest:*

Dear Mr. Reed:

In addition to being an admirer of your work, I am a freelance writer who does interviews for *Writer's Digest.* The editors of the magazine are most anxious to feature you in an upcoming issue. Would you be available for an interview?

Enclosed are a few samples of my work. I realize that you are quite busy, but as you can see, I use the Q&A technique, and 90 minutes over a tape recorder is all I need. Two hours, tops.

If the idea is agreeable to you, I can make my travel plans at your convenience. I hope you will be able to find time for this endeavor, and I look forward to hearing from you soon.

Sincerely . . . .

Wanted: Interviews

Occasionally a writer can obtain an interview with a hard-to-get subject with a letter of introduction from some other prominent person who will vouch for the interviewer's work. Louis Sheaffer, for instance, was able to interview many of Eugene O'Neill's friends for his two-volume biography because he was armed with a letter of introduction from Brooks Atkinson, the *New York Times* critic.

Some writers find the telegram advantageous as a means of getting interviews. Certainly it raises one's request above the crowd of routine mail that a national figure receives daily. "No one ignores a telegram," freelancer William Lynch Vallee once observed. "It not only gives the interviewee a chance to think about matters, but it gives you the opportunity to express your needs succinctly." When Hal Higdon was having difficulty reaching the Rev. Jesse Jackson for a *Chicago Tribune Magazine* article on Martin Luther King, Jr.'s death, he got around the secretarial barriers at Jackson's office by sending a telegram to the minister's home. Within hours the man who was talking with King at the time of his death responded to Higdon, and an interview was arranged. The writer had wasted a month trying routine channels without luck.

You can also advertise for interviews. We have all seen letters in the back of literary journals or book-review sections of newspapers in which a writer announces that he is working on, say, a biography of Jack Benny. The writer then solicits any information, letters and leads that readers might know of in the field. When Jessica Mitford was in the preliminary stage of her exposé of the Famous Writers School, she took an ad in the *Saturday Review,* saying: "Wanted: Experiences—good, bad, indifferent—with Famous Writers School. Write Jessica Mitford. . . ." She received a number of responses, all negative, which led to interviews and further leads for the piece. For *American Journey: The Times of Robert Kennedy,* coauthors Jean Stein and George Plimpton wanted to get the impressions of people who stood by the tracks watching the funeral train carrying Robert Kennedy's body from New York to Washington, D.C. They placed advertisements in local newspapers along the train route, asking for interviews. Many responded; and when the book was completed, interviews with onlookers along the railroad tracks comprised the first segment of each chapter.

Charm 'Em

Another way to the interviewee's heart is through his secretary. Veteran interviewer Alex Haley claims that only secretaries "know the idiosyncrasies of the man which are important to me. And they are glad to contribute. They can also tell you how best to approach their boss — how he flows best." In John Behrens' *Magazine Writer's Workbook,* Haley expands on the Wooing Theory of obtaining interviews:

> If a man has a secretary, particularly if she is the older, trusted secretary genre, I will always go in and work on her like Rudolph Valentino in a quiet, subtle way. My expense account in such situations invariably is around $100. I will wine and dine them as long as I can keep it just this side of overt courting for a purpose. I buy lots of flowers and perfume—sometimes I go out with her. From my standpoint, if I had the choice to get friendly with the wife or the secretary to get information, I'd take the secretary every time. They know much more about the man—for the interviewer, anyhow.

Vera Glaser—who writes the syndicated column Off Beat Washington with Malvina Stephenson—once got an exclusive interview with Frances Knight, the U.S. Passport Director. At the time, rumors were circulating that Knight was going to be fired, and she had been forbidden to give interviews. So Glaser began working on Knight's secretary. "Vera told the secretary that Miss Knight was being persecuted from all sides, that she should let someone tell her story, and that she, Vera, was the one to tell it," recall the authors of *Don't Quote Me!* "Miss Knight called her back within a few hours and Vera went to her office."

Talk Football

Occasionally an interviewer can get an interview by appealing to a subject's offbeat interest. Hunter Thompson recalls covering the 1968 Presidential primary in New Hampshire and parlaying an interest in professional football into an interview with Richard Nixon. Nixon's aides knew of Thompson's football knowledge, and at the end of the campaign, when Nixon was about to take a 90-minute drive to an airport, Thompson was invited along. "The boss wants to relax and talk football," Thompson was told. "You're the only person here who claims to be an expert on that subject, so you're it. . . . No talk about Vietnam, campus riots — nothing political; the boss wants to talk football, period."

More often, of course, it is the serious issue rather than the frivolous one that gets the attention of the interviewee. The late Lowell Limpus got an interview with General Tomoyuki Yamashita just before he was to be hanged as a war criminal in 1945 by appealing to the General's sense of historical accuracy. Limpus sent him a letter saying "that he was Japan's outstanding commander and owed it to his professional standing with posterity to clear up certain moot technical points about his campaigns while there was still time to do so." The idea evidently intrigued the General, and he started sending Limpus questions concerning the kind of points he had in mind. "I secured expert advice and carefully framed answers, which almost demanded detailed explanations on large-scale maps. After a long series of exchanges, he invited me to his cell, where he and members of his staff could go over these points with me." The rest is, quite literally, history.

No Zingers, Please

You may have to arrange or agree to ground rules as a basis for a subject's consent to an interview.

They are generally confining for the interviewer and self-serving for the subject; but if the interview is important enough, the interviewer has little choice but to agree to them. Shortly before the 1972 Presidential election, Jack Horner of the *Washington Star* had become a favorite writer of the White House, and was fed exclusives by Ron Ziegler because he worked for the *Washington Post*'s competitor. At one point, in fact, he was granted what he called the biggest beat of his life—an exclusive interview with Richard Nixon. There was but one ground rule: Horner could not print the questions he asked. Only the answers. This sounds innocuous enough, but, as Timothy Crouse points out in *The Boys on the Bus*, it "meant that Nixon could virtually ignore Horner's questions and simply spew out his carefully prepared remarks. Horner was being used as a funnel, but he did get his scoop. As he sat there in the Oval Office, feeling the delicious whirr of the little tape recorder that he always carried strapped to his waist like a pacemaker, Jack Horner must have thought to himself: 'What a good boy am I.' "

In 1970 *Esquire* magazine did a parody of the *Playboy* interview. The subject was Hefner. "The *Esquire* interview with Hugh M. Hefner," wrote Rust Hills, the interviewer, "was conceived with the idea of satirizing—or, let's face it, the hope—of making something of an ass of the *Playboy* publisher himself." Hills adds: "But while the *Playboy* staff may seem to some of us, uh, say *misguided,* they certainly aren't *silly*—or at any rate they aren't silly enough to let a retired fiction editor of *Esquire* fly out to Chicago, tape an ingratiating interview with Hefner, return to N.Y. & C., and edit the bejesus out of the transcript, quoting the man out of context to make him look silly, then run it in the magazine with a headnote that undercuts anything sensible that might have been left in." Which is exactly what Richard Rosenzweig, Hefner's assistant, suggested on the phone to Harold Hayes, then *Esquire*'s editor. "How can you possibly think we'd do anything like that?" asked Hayes.

"Oh, come on," said Rosenzweig. "We know you guys."

Thus, elaborate ground rules were drawn up for the occasion. *Playboy,* according to Hills, insisted on "complete approval" of the interview—"that is, not just 'approval for accuracy,' which is to check the transcript against the tape to show that Hefner actually did say something or other, but approval of the interview-as-a-whole, 'including editing for space requirements.' They tried to think of everything, including approval of the headnote ... and provisions designed to prevent what was informally called a 'zinger' (some stab-in-the-back reference to Hefner planted elsewhere in the issue) .... Their original justification for all this was that the subjects of *Playboy* interviews are given such approval and assurances; but later they'd just justify these precautions on the ground of common sense."

When Hills arrived at Hefner's Chicago mansion, he was met by Rosenzweig who showed him a letter of agreement which had been drawn up. It struck Hills as seeming "to specify a lot of things I wasn't sure Harold Hayes had agreed to.. But I signed it cheerfully." *So* cheerfully, in fact, that Hefner's aide looked at the interviewer sharply and sighed, "What difference does all this paper make anyway? You guys can still kill us if you want to, can't you?"

"I certainly don't see how," said Hills. "You've covered yourself very carefully." Then he grinned. "Besides, you know we wouldn't want to." Rosenzweig sighed again.

The interview went remarkably well, and was the brightest feature in a Christmas issue of *Esquire* that easily outshone the heavy "holiday" issue *Playboy* put forth that December. "In fact, what happened was far more a conversation than an interview," said Rust Hills afterward. "I've never liked *Playboy,* but I did like Hefner, and I rather fancy he liked me—so we just slung the shit without shame, more or less as if the tape weren't running. The conversation lasted more than three hours." Thus, ground rules, while often necessary to *get* an interview, do not necessarily hamstring the interview itself.

Hubert Horatio Who?

Be careful in what you tell subjects. "If you are doing the piece on speculation, don't say so unless you have to," says Joseph Trento. "No press man worth his salt will waste his boss's time in order to 'take a chance' on a promising freelancer. If you have appeared in magazines before, then drop a few names. If you haven't, then get the interest in your idea for a specific publication that the VIP can't afford not to be in." Getting a firm assignment from an editor is certainly a door opener for many interviews. "Nothing paves the way for a talk with a busy or famous person more quickly than being able to say that an editor has indicated interest in having the proposed article," adds George L. Bird.

Joseph N. Bell finds that a photocopy of a letter from his magazine, saying that he had been assigned to do a story, is a timesaver in arranging particularly sticky interviews.

Obviously, a writer of reputation gets interviews more readily than someone who is merely ambitious. John Gunther was in his Minneapolis hotel room one morning in the 1940s when the telephone rang. The morning newspaper had printed a small item announcing he was in town. "I had not done my homework carefully, and did not identify the name of the caller," recalled Gunther in his *A Fragment of Autobiography.* "His voice boomed cheerfully into the telephone, with the words that he would drop in to see me at five that afternoon. I did my best to avoid this commitment, on the assumption that an interview with this unknown would be a waste of time." Gunther told the voice that he had another engagement—but his efforts were in vain. "Finally I said that I would call him back—and asked for his name and number."

"Why, I'm Hubert Humphrey—I'm the mayor!" said the voice on the phone. At five o'clock the mayor and a few assistants arrived. They stayed for more than three hours. "I have never had a more acute and provocative briefing," conceded John Gunther afterward. All because he *was* John Gunther.

Beginner's Luck and Pluck

While acknowledging that "in many cases the established writer has a distinct advantage," William Rivers, author of *Free Lancer and Staff Writer,* says that "the beginner who tries to pass himself off as a writer who is virtually certain of publication is virtually certain to fail." He adds:

A beginner should make it clear that he is speculating, if he is, even though many sources will probably give him less time and attention than they would give a well-known free-lancer or a staff writer on assignment. Honesty offers several compensations. If the writer has admitted that his article may not be published, the source is not as likely to call periodically to ask when the article will appear. Also, some public officials who are inclined to guard information are more relaxed with beginning journalists (especially students) and tell them more than they would tell established writers. Finally, some sources will try to help beginning writers by giving them much time and attention.

Joe Marshall could second that notion. When he was a journalism student at Columbia University, one of his assignments was an honors project, and Marshall wanted to do his on sportscaster Howard Cosell. The problem for a beginning journalist with no assignment from a magazine, of course, is to get the cooperation of someone like Cosell. Marshall got his story. "Howard was just great," he said later. "He is concerned with being a journalist rather than just a TV personality, and he was very helpful to me as a journalist. He helped me get the facts I needed, and whenever I would run into walls because I didn't represent anybody, Howard opened the doors for me. For example, I called the secretary of an important executive of ABC radio and she was pretty cold on the telephone. She'd say, 'Who are you doing this for?' and I'd tell her it was my Master's thesis, and of course that got me nowhere. Finally, Howard simply walked me right across the floor at ABC into this executive's office, introduced me and got me an appointment."

When the piece was finished, Marshall sent it to *Esquire,* where it was published. "I didn't then realize that the piece could be sold," said the young writer. "At Columbia we heard constantly about the six years we must spend getting rejection slips and starving as we learn to write." To Marshall's credit, "Howard Cosell Is Just Another Pretty Face" is, I think, the best article ever written on the sportscaster America loves to hate. And Marshall? He ended up working at *Sports Illustrated.*

Writer As Actor

According to Jessica Mitford, having a household name can some-times even be "a hindrance." Because of her reputation as "queen of the muckrakers," Mitford admits that she sometimes has to employ others to do her dirty work—"to go in and say 'I'm a graduate student doing a thesis,' or whatnot, and find information that way."

Sometimes the best policy is dishonesty, according to Mitford: "Very often, the *only* way you can get information" is by falsifying your reason. While researching *The American Way of Death,* for example, she did not always tell the people that she was gathering information for a book on the funeral industry. She also encouraged one of her university students (in a Techniques of Muckraking class) who was investigating the sale of prison hardware to write manufacturing companies that he was a on "a citizens' committee for more secure jails." He was swamped with material.

One of the earliest devices for falsifying your motives in an interview is the telephone. A colleague of Harry Romanoff on the old *Chicago*

Herald-Examiner said Romy could "play the phone like Heifetz playing the violin." When the wire services reported that boxing promoter Tex Rickard was seriously ill, Romanoff reached for the phone and called Rickard's wife. "This is Governor Len Small of Illinois," said the reporter in a soothing voice. "I am distressed to hear of the illness of my old friend, Tex. Tell me, Mrs. Rickard, how is he?"

"He's dying, governor," said Mrs. Rickard tearfully. And the *Herald-Examiner* had another scoop.

Not all of Romy's performances were convincing, however. Once, when he learned of a South Side shooting in which some policemen were hurt, he phoned the switchboard at St. Bernard's hospital where the injured were taken. "This is the police commissioner," he said. "Connect me with one of my men there." He was connected with the sixth floor, where a quiet voice said, "Yes."

"This is the police commissioner," repeated Romy. "What's going on out there?" His subject gave a detailed report that was so impressive, Romy asked "Who is this, anyway?"

"This is Police Commissioner Fitzmorris, Romy," said the quiet voice. "I knew you'd be calling."

Give Me an Estimate for That Quote

The only method lower than lying to get an interview is paying for one. Increasingly, though, subjects ranging from psychologists to politicians are trying to sell interviews. Many celebrities and newsmakers are reluctant to grant interviews because they know that some publications and syndicates will offer handsome prices for exclusive rights. Thus, the battle for an interview can become a bidding war.

Life magazine signed up the astronauts for what one wag called "an astronomical amount of money," and other magazines have paid for the exclusive rights to stories about quintuplets and whatnot. The Associated Press once paid for the story of a trapped miner in a shaft, and heart-transplant patients have been known to sell their stories. Philip Blaiberg, for instance, sold photo rights to a publication as well, and at one point during his post-operative period he wore a paper bag over his head rather than allow street photographers to take pictures of his walking in Johannesburg. "There is, among magazines, an informal agreement not to pay subjects unless they are involved in what are called 'signers' or first-person articles," observed the late Leonard Shecter. "What the magazines do about that is cheat. If they want the article badly enough, they will pay." And if the interviewee needs the money badly enough, he will sell. In 1957 baseball star Jackie Robinson sold the news of his retirement to *Look* magazine. He even agreed to withhold the information from his team, the Dodgers, as well as the Giants (to whom he had been traded that winter) as well as the working press that had covered him throughout his colorful career. "I think they will understand why this was one time I couldn't give them the whole story as soon as I knew it," he said. "He is probably correct," observed Red Smith. "Those who feel he has flim-flammed them will understand that he did it for money."

Bill Surface ran into the say-for-pay fray while researching an article on the high cost of getting elected. "I noticed that the logical source of information was a U.S. Senator who had decried the growing possibility that only multimillionaires could afford to seek Presidential nominations," recalls the writer. When Surface approached the senator's executive secretary, however, he was told that while the senator "felt strongly" about the subject, "how much can the senator get from this?" Surface replied that magazines seldom pay for a person being interviewed unless it's a bylined story. The secretary told the writer that the senator would prefer that the article appear under his byline. Negotiations collapsed. "About four months later I did see the same article," says Surface, "under the senator's byline, in a magazine which an editor said paid a 'higher-than-usual fee.' "

Paying for The Prize

Editors should be told when a subject demands payment for an interview. "We've had some of that," says Murray Fisher of *Playboy*, "and the policy is generally no. But it depends on how much we want the subject, and who it is. Usually it's not a demand for a fee, but for a donation to some personal cause, which we don't mind doing in some cases. We don't make a policy of giving an honorarium, though. We feel that the interviewer is the one who does the work, and that the subject is simply giving his time and getting an awful lot of free space out of it."

I once did an article for a religious magazine, which then sent a copy of the piece to the subject for approval. The subject then approached the magazine's editor for payment. Shocked, the editor phoned and told me what had happened. "You'll get your fee," he said, "but we're not going to pay the subject; in fact we are killing the article. If that's the sort of person he is, we don't want to waste our pages on him." Freelancer Sol Stern ran into the same problem when he wanted to do a story for *The New York Times Magazine* on Frank Wills, the security guard who first discovered the Watergate break-in and called the cops. Stern was introduced to a lawyer who was trying to turn Wills into a "hot property," and who acted as agent/overseer for all the young subject's public appearances, endorsements and interviews (for 25 percent of all fees). The lawyer had charged TV reporters up to $300 for an interview, but Stern was able to get two hours with Wills for $50. The interview took place, appropriately enough, in the lawyer's office where a quote beneath a picture of Abraham Lincoln observed: "A lawyer's time and advice are his stock in trade." Unless he has 25 percent of a hot property, that is.

Many writers pay for interviews and consider it a good investment. The best material that Irving Wallace got during the early period of research for his novel *The Prize* came from professional newspapermen in Sweden who were filled with information they had never been able to use in their annual coverage of the Nobel prizes. Wallace paid for this information, and bragged about it. Many of the anecdotes he obtained were priceless for his purpose: a blockbuster novel.

Some celebrities value privacy so much that they put a high price on themselves to *discourage* requests for interviews. It is said that Winston Churchill once turned down $100,000 rather than be interviewed by Edward R. Murrow of CBS. Frank Sinatra can be an expensive interviewee when he wants to be. Television producer David Susskind once sent the singer a telegram inviting him to participate in a discussion of "Sinatra and the Clan" on Susskind's *Open End* program. Sinatra wired back that his fee was $250,000 an hour. Susskind sent a telegram in reply: "Presume stipulated fee is for your traditional program of intramural ring-a-ding-dinging with additional fillip of reading musical lyrics mounted on Tele-Prompter. Please advise price for spontaneous discussion." Sinatra responded: "The $250,000 fee is for my usual talent of song and dance. However, now that I understand the picture a little more clearly, I must change it to $750,000 for all parasitical programs."

Reluctant Debutantes

Sometimes it's the obscure person who balks at an interview. "Public figures of stature are accustomed to contacts with newsmen, and usually they have confidence in the treatment they will receive and an understanding of the importance of sound relations with the public through the news media," notes Mitchell Charnley in his journalism text *Reporting*. "The man who has never before been asked for an interview, the one just promoted to his first executive position — or just elected dog-catcher — is more likely than the 'arrived' business or political or professional figure to be suspicious, over-cautious or self-important." But an inexperienced and reluctant subject can usually be brought around. "The trick is to be sympathetic and make friends," observed Lowell Limpus. "You can risk more flattery here than with the experienced type. An appeal to sympathy often works; tell 'em you may lose your job if you don't bring back something."

Businessmen are especially busy, and, according to trade-magazine writer Omer Henry, some "are not at all eager to cooperate with writers. Therefore, one should be prepared to point out certain positive results which may accrue to the company from the publication of the article." Henry suggests that the writer tell the subject that an article "may demonstrate the firm's management expertise and cement relations with other companies," that it may create a demand for the firm's products, and that the article can be distributed to customers, stockholders and business colleagues in reprint form.

Scholarly types are often reluctant interviewees; they do not want the censure of colleagues who view publicity as unprofesssional. "The writer will be better able to put the scholar at his ease and lessen his dread of the criticism of his fellow scientist if he shows the learned man the importance of helping mankind," suggests Helen Patterson in her book *Writing and Selling Feature Articles*. "The writer's own sincere enthusiasm about the expert's discovery will entice even an introvert into showing some interest in sharing his knowledge with nonscientists." The message is the medium.

George Bird suggests a similar approach for physicians. "Most individuals are ready enough to give an audience to a responsible writer, because the published article may be a help in their careers," he says. "This is true of almost everyone in the public eye, except the physician, who has to be handled more carefully. Frequently the latter can be persuaded to talk by showing the need for public information on a certain subject, and by promising to keep his name in the background."

Loose Jocks

Sports interviews are usually easy to obtain because sports heroes are dependent on public favor. There are exceptions, of course. "I find interviewing works best on the road," says Peter Carry, *Sports Illustrated's* pro basketball writer. "In a plane you have a captive audience. Players are usually pretty bored, and reluctant interviewees simply cannot jump out of moving planes and buses." He points out some interesting distinctions between athlete types, too. "Basketball players are pretty accessible. They are not as harassed by the press as football and baseball players. And the latter play far from the spectators, heavily clothed and indistinguishable without their num-bers — basketball players perform in what amounts to underwear, close to the crowds, and their mistakes are more obvious. As a result they are looser, more willing to discuss problems and generally have more open personalities."

Barnacle Idlers

Generally. Unfortunately, there are oyster-tight celebrities in every profession. Blessed, then, be the PR reps—for they can help pry pearls from the mouths of oysters. "I think press agents are a much-maligned profession," says Bob Thomas, veteran Hollywood correspondent for the Associated Press. "I respect press agents and enjoy their friendships and their service. They can be of great service to a writer, particularly in this town—where everybody's telephone number is unlisted and you can't keep track of where everyone is at all times. They are *very* helpful in reaching stars, personalities, and arranging interviews. Sometimes they come along, but I have never found them to be intrusive. Sometimes they can be a *help* with a shy, untalkative personality."

When Mike Edelhart was asked by *The Graduate* magazine to interview singer John Denver, he was given a two-week deadline, which is tight for a piece on someone who would be difficult to locate and talk with at length in the midst of a heavy schedule. Edelhart called the concert promoter in a city where Denver had recently given a concert. From here he was referred to a big booking agent in Nashville. The agent there had dealt with the William Morris Agency (the largest talent booker in the country) in New York. There Morris's folk music agent said he had dealt with a lady who was Denver's personal booking agent. She in turn gave the writer the name and phone number of the singer's press agency and of his New York press agent. "The press agent finally gave me something solid," recalls Edelhart. "He liked my proposal and said a copy of the magazine and a letter stating my intentions would be helpful in persuading Denver's people. He said he saw no trouble, if times could be arranged."

Meanwhile, John Denver was filming a TV special and had not been in touch with his press agent. Edelhart kept calling the agent, trying to line up a time for the interview, but then the writer had to go on the road himself for other story assignments. He ended up in Los Angeles, where he got in touch with the local branch of Denver's press agency. By then the singer had the flu and couldn't talk at all. Finally, with his deadline two days away, Edelhart's phone number was conveyed to John Denver on the set of his TV special. Whenever Denver got a break, he'd phone. Edelhart settled down for a nap by the phone. At 3:30 p.m., after two weeks of suspense, the phone rang and a voice said, "John Denver here!" Says Edelhart: "An hour later, mission accomplished."

Occasionally, a PR rep's fervor for protecting a client does the individual more harm than good. The client may not even be aware of the reckless goings-on. "My advice to every aspiring article writer is to avoid press agents at all cost," said Richard Gehman in Fred Birmingham's *The Craft of Writing*. "Even the best are troublesome. Their only usefulness lies in their ability to set up appointments, and often they are not useful at all in that function." Gehman ran into Frank Sinatra at a party while he was researching an article on literary agent Irving "Swifty" Lazar. "He was most anxious to talk to me about his friend Lazar," said the writer. "But that collection of assorted idlers who stick to him like barnacles, answer his telephone, etc., never gave him any of my messages, and after seven attempts I gave up."

Johnny On the Spot

Richard Warren Lewis once did an article for *TV Guide* on comedian Johnny Carson entitled "Whe-e-e-e-ere's Johnny?" Most of the article dealt with the difficulty in getting to talk to Carson, who has what Lewis calls a "well-known, near-pathological aversion to interviews." When Lewis called the NBC press department to request "an audience with the Prince," a pessimistic voice told him, "I'll have to get back to you. He hasn't been doing interviews."

Months went by. Then the NBC press officer called. "Johnny will be available next Tuesday, at 3:30," he told Lewis. "I have a list of six areas that Johnny's willing to talk about."

"You're kidding!" said Lewis. "An agenda? This isn't Kissinger meeting with the Syrians. I mean, that's incredible." He describes the remainder of the conversation this way:

There was a long pause, followed by a sigh. "You might want to write this down," the voice wearily continued. "Number one: Is comedy changing? Two: Are audiences changing? Three: Is humor becoming more national? Four: What makes Johnny laugh?"

"Swell," I thought.

"Five: What is Johnny's own personal type of humor? Six: How has *The Tonight Show* helped the careers of new performers and become a true showcase for entertainers?"

"That's it?" I asked.

"That's it."

"You mean Carson won't talk about what he and Euell Gibbons *really* do after the show with those hickory nuts?"

"Don't try to be funny."

"This doesn't seem terribly promising," I complained. "Especially since the editors want a piece emphasizing Johnny's California life style."

"One other thing."

"I can't wait."

"Johnny wants to approve a copy of the article before you submit it to the editors. You don't have to tell *them* about it. It'll just be between us."

"In that case, there'll be no interview," I said, invoking the spirit of John Peter Zenger.

There was another pregnant pause on the other end. "I'll have to get back to you," said the voice.

Some three weeks later, what Lewis calls "a détente" occurred. He was told that Carson had reconsidered. Lewis: "He would both grant a meeting and waive his request to review the article. I was told that he trusted me." In fact, when he finally sat down to talk with Carson, and he asked which of the six prescribed questions the comedian would like to deal with first, Johnny said: "Talk about anything you like. Just let's wing it."

Thus, Richard Warren Lewis got his interview, and a freewheeling one, in spite of all the precautions and paranoia. Patience, persistence, and press agentry paid off in the end. Well, patience and persistence, anyway.

Reaching the Boss

Increasingly, even noncelebrities have to be reached through PR representatives. The problems are familiar. Hal Higdon was doing research for his book on the management-consulting profession, *The Business Healers,* and he tried to reach James L. Allen, the manager of the largest consulting firm, Booz, Allen & Hamilton, Inc. "Booz Allen gave me grudging cooperation," recalls the writer, "but dodged the issue of my seeing the boss. When I asked the firm's public relations man for an interview, he wanted to know my deadline." Two months, said Higdon. "Mr. Allen is going to be tied up for the next two months," he was told. The writer then mailed a rough draft of the section of his book on Booz Allen to the manager at his home address, with a note saying he was sorry to have to publish the book without his contribution. "I didn't know you were reaching for me," Allen told Higdon at the outset of their interview.

Mildred Tyson, who has written more than a thousand features for trade journals and business magazines, avoids the public relations department altogether, even at large corporations. "I always make my initial approach with a letter addressed to the president of the company," she says. "This method has never failed to bring a response." The letter Tyson uses goes something like this:

Dear Mr. Jones:
Such and such magazine would like to do a feature article about

your 15 stores, if you can give us enough information to produce such an article.

There is no cost to you other than the 1½ to 2 hours time required for such an interview, and no advertising tie is involved.

Perhaps the attached Xerox copy of a feature I have done recently about a company in your business category will give you an idea of the information I need.

If you will let me know if you are interested in the idea, and when I may see you, I will appreciate it.

Cordially,

"Not more than one percent of all my queries to businessmen result in 'turn downs,'" adds Tyson. Within a week or two the subject generally replies by phone, pleased that he has been asked for an interview. An appointment is set up. Tyson says she is successful with this approach chiefly because of the Xerox enclosure of a published article. This persuades the subject with two key points. "He can visualize exactly how his company will look in print if he grants the interview," says the writer. "As a successful businessman he will also see the value of being published in a national trade journal, and ways he can further promote the published piece." If a writer lacks publishing experience in a certain subject, he can send along an article that demonstrates his skills in a nearby topic. The point is to demonstrate that you are professional, and worthy of the interviewee's time.

The Goon Show

Some subjects may be protected by bodyguards as well as PR types. *New York* magazine sent Christopher Buckley to Las Vegas to do a story on Frank Sinatra. One night at Caesars Palace, Buckley noticed Debbie Reynolds talking in whispers with singer Tom Jones at a table in the private dining room. Jones had just completed a two-week engagement at the hotel and was in the midst of a "surprise" birthday party arranged for him by the management. Yet everyone's nerves "were a bit edgy," according to Buckley, because the word was already out: Frank Sinatra would not show up for the party. He was asleep.

When Reynolds noticed the writer taking notes, she motioned to Chris Hutchins, Tom Jones's PR man. He signaled to someone sitting directly below Buckley. The goon stood up and put his arm over the writer's notebook and gave him a cool stare. "Am I making you nervous?" asked Buckley, trying to look him in the eye.

"Hey, he's taking notes," said the bodyguard—who once played the title role in some grade-C Italian *Hercules* movies. Then, to Buckley: "Hey, they don't like you around here." No interviews.

An interviewee who is physically intimidating *without* bodyguards can be a problem, too. Sonny Liston, the former heavyweight champion, was once described by Howard Cosell as "a cheap and ugly bully without morality." Liston had a record of more than 20 arrests—and he hated interviewers. In September 1962 he was training for his first title fight with Floyd Patterson at Aurora Downs outside Chicago. Cosell was scheduled to do a radio broadcast of the fight, along with former heavyweight champion Rocky Marciano.

Cosell and Marciano, accompanied by Oscar Fraley—the UPI sportswriter (and coauthor of *The Untouchables*)—drove out to Liston's training camp to do an interview for the prefight show. There they found an armed guard patrolling behind a barbed-wire fence and, ultimately, five people standing around watching Sonny Liston shadow box to a recording of *Night Train*. "The whole thing was eerie," Cosell told a *Playboy* interviewer. No one made a sound. Suddenly, the fighter's wife came into the room, climbed into the ring with Sonny, and started doing the twist. "And all this time, no one has said a word," says Cosell. "I'm telling you, the scene was *weird*. I pulled Marciano aside and said, 'Look, as soon as the Listons finish dancing, the smart thing for us to do, champ, since you were the greatest, is for *you* to do the interview.' Rock looks at me and says, 'I want no part of it. You think I'm nuts?' So I turn to Fraley and before I can say anything, he says, 'I wanna go home.' "

Meanwhile, Liston's manager tells the fighter about the visitors. Liston gives them a sinister stare, then shouts: "Goddamn it, I ain't talking to no one! No one, you understand?"

"We understood," said Cosell afterward, "but we had to get that interview. When his workout was over, Liston finally allowed Marciano to approach him, but the Rock was so shook he virtually couldn't speak. So I said, 'Now look, Sonny, you're going to be the heavyweight champion of the world and it's not going to take you long. You're going to have to present a whole new image to the American public, 'cause you got a lot to make up for. I don't give a goddamn if you hate me; I don't like you either, and I just met you. But you gotta do this interview."

Later, Cosell did not know why he spoke so forcefully to Sonny Liston. But it worked. The fighter gave Cosell a big smile, and, recalls the interviewer: "Suddenly I realized that the son of a bitch was really just a big bully. And he finally did quite a pleasant interview. When we left, they were playing *Night Train* again."

Helplessness Helps

Getting a hostile or balky subject to agree to an interview can be downright difficult. "I usually don't press," says Nat Hentoff, "because I recognize the right of anybody not to be interviewed. However, if the subject is crucial to a story about someone else (I would not do a piece in which a hostile interviewee was the main subject), I do make some attempt. My usual procedure is to tell him that since he will be in the story anyway, for the sake of accuracy I would much prefer to get his statement firsthand." It is also standard operating procedure at publications like *Time.* When the magazine did a cover story on author John Cheever, for instance, the subject objected. "I tried to stop the story," Cheever told Bruce McCabe of the *Boston Globe* recently. "It was at that time in my life that I thought publicity was abominable. I've since changed my mind. I said, 'I don't want the story,' and they said, 'We didn't ask.' They ask you to pose for a portrait, but if you don't there are files and files of photos they can use. You do what you want and they do what they want.... I went skiing in Stowe and I was followed down the slopes by a *Time* editor, researcher and a photographer.... The FBI is nothing compared to being on the cover of *Time.*"

In 1966, when James Reston was contemplating quitting the *New York Times* — and joining the *Washington Post* and *Newsweek* magazine — because he was unhappy in that newspaper's Washington bureau, Gay Talese tried to interview him for his biography of the *Times,* called *The Kingdom and the Power.* "He'd been on the *Times* since 1939," reflected Talese afterward, "and it was not easy for him to quit, and before doing so, before even submitting his resignation,

he talked to Walter Lippmann." Talese found it impossible to get
a candid account of this great meeting of minds. "I wanted to know
what they said. So I went to Washington to find out. And Reston
wouldn't talk; no comment. Lippmann? I didn't get to Lippmann.
I went to Katherine Graham, the publisher of the *Washington Post,*
and she wouldn't talk about it." Adds Talese: "I was fascinated,
because it reminded me of a few years ago when the *New York Post*
was on strike, or there was some walkout, and I went to the *New
York Post* and tried to see Dorothy Schiff, and I couldn't get in.
And finally after waiting and waiting and waiting: no comment. And
I felt then, and feel now, that reporters and publishers shouldn't be
allowed to say 'no comment,' they shouldn't be allowed not to report
on themselves."

Perhaps writers who are accustomed to wrestling for good copy
are afraid that they themselves might not make good copy. They
do tend to clam up. Todd Everett, a West coast music freelancer,
was reluctant to even talk with me when I told him I was doing
a book on interviewing. Finally, he agreed to lunch, but throughout
the meal remained cautious, volunteering nothing about his experiences doing interviews with rock stars. On the way out of the restaurant
I confessed, "Well, Todd, you haven't said a thing worth quoting.
You haven't helped me at all." I laughed, but this admission of
helplessness struck home. Everett could empathize with my feeling.
He relaxed and opened up with ancedotes about The Carpenters,
Anne Murray, Jethro Tull and numerous other personalities on the
interview/concert tour. A few days later he phoned with some
additional information he had forgotten the first time we spoke. "You
were very helpful the other day," I said. "I took several pages of
notes from our conversation afterward." "Really?" said Everett. He
seemed relieved.

The Long Way to Indianapolis

If helplessness fails, writers have been known to use other devices
for getting interviews. Like hanging around a lot — which is how
I got an interview with Jessica Mitford. The author of *The American
Way of Death* was on campus at Indiana State University in Terre
Haute several years ago, where she gave an address and conducted
seminars for two days. Mitford had just completed *The Trial of Dr.*

Spock, and hardly a minute of her two-day visit was her own. Even lunch and dinner breaks were spent with political science students, and members of the university faculty. I asked her if she would be willing to give me an interview for *Writer's Digest.*

"Yes, I would," she replied, "but I don't see how it's possible. I'm so busy, I don't think I have a half-hour free between now and my flight tomorrow."

"How are you getting to the airport?" I asked. She would need a ride to the Indianapolis airport, some 75 miles away.

"I'm not sure. The university has made some arrangement."

"Would it be all right if I drove you?" I asked. "We could talk on the way."

"Delightful," said the author. I made a few phone calls to cancel the university car, loaded my cassette recorder with fresh batteries, and wrote out my questions on index cards. The next day I took the *long* way to the Indianapolis airport, with Jessica Mitford graciously holding the recorder while I peeled index cards off my lap and kept an eye on the traffic. I'd ask a question, drop the card on the floor, and Mitford replied into the mike. The interview came to a successful conclusion at the airport cocktail lounge some two hours later.

Hanging Around is also Alex Haley's foremost technique for getting interviews. "Alex more or less lives with someone until the subject feels completely comfortable and starts acting natural and opening up," says Murray Fisher, who has edited Haley's interviews for *Playboy,* as well as his manuscripts for *The Autobiography of Malcolm X* and *Roots.* It took Haley two weeks to get close enough to Dr. Martin Luther King, Jr. to "get a word worth using out of him," recalls the interviewer. "He was so busy I couldn't get to him, really. . . .and as eloquent as he was onstage, offstage he was like the sphinx." At the end of two weeks, on the advice of King's secretary Dora Williams (Haley's tips on Secretary Wooing appear earlier in this chapter), he hung around at a picnic that King was attending. The two men chatted a bit. "He was surprised I was still there," recalls Haley. "Finally, he said 'Look, let's go over to my office.' When we got there he put his feet up on the desk — something he just doesn't do — and I think we talked for four hours or so. That's when I got the interview." "The thing that finally swayed Martin Luther King, Jr., and made him accept Alex as a friend," adds Murray Fisher, "was that Alex donated his fee for the assignment to the Southern Christian Leadership Conference. That act of Christian sacrifice earned King's attention and respect. That's the kind of guy he was, and that's the kind of guy Alex is."

What Makes Sammy Talk

If hanging around fails, hang tough. Sheilah Graham once got an interview with Richard Burton by threatening the publicity man for the movie *Cleopatra* that she would write a story about the wasted millions of dollars going into the film's wretched excesses — such as 81 stand-by cars. "I think the shareholders will be very interested in my story of how their money is being spent," Graham intoned over the phone, after getting the run-around for several days. That evening, in a private room on the ground floor of the Grand Hotel, she had an exclusive interview with Burton on the subject of an actress named Elizabeth Taylor.

Alex Haley used a flanking maneuver to break through Sammy Davis's entourage for *Playboy*. "All performers are egocentric," the interviewer told John Behrens. "They can't stand somebody upstaging them. They are very, very sensitive about what people say and think about them. Sammy has an entourage of about six or seven people and I would get in a physical situation where I would talk to a few of these individuals where Sammy could see us but not hear what was going on. I'd tell them a funny story guaranteed to make them laugh suddenly. Sammy would hear and see this laughter; and being hypersensitive, he thought we were talking about him. Now he's paying these people and this bugged him no end. Finally, one day he came over and asked, in a less than pleasant way, when I was going to ask him questions. We started and he began rolling. I turned on the tape recorder and he was on. I have a beautiful tape of Sammy because of that incident."

A Friend Sent Me

Another side-door approach is to talk with friends of the prospective subject; such activities will come to his attention. Of his experience as a subject for *Time's* cover story, John Cheever recalls: "Some boys I played marbles with when I was little called me from Wilmington, Delaware, and said: 'What have you done wrong? Two people from

Time magazine are coming up to see us in 20 minutes.' " A Hollywood reporter did this to obtain an interview with Marlene Dietrich, generally regarded as one of the most unapproachable film stars. His phone rang one day and Dietrich said, "I hear you have been asking questions about me. What do you want to know?" He interviewed her that afternoon.

"Ask the person closest to the celebrity where he will be at a certain time," suggests Bill Surface. "When, for example, Brigitte Bardot was standing up writers with firm appointments, I was in Paris and went to a man who was close to Brigitte. 'No problem,' he said, 'let's go talk to her right now.' I got a pleasant interview with Brigitte." On another occasion an editor gave Surface an assignment to profile a politician, with the warning that two previous writers had failed to get to see the elusive subject. "When I called one of the politician's female friends, she instantly replied, 'He'll be at this spot at four.' I was at that spot at four. 'Joyce sent me,' I said. He talked for about an hour."

Hanging Around Hangers-on

Even if a subject doesn't give an interview, it is possible to do a good story using a subject's friends as mirrors. Nathaniel Benchley, oddly enough, could not persuade Greta Garbo to talk to him; so he went to more than 30 people who knew the actress and did a fine article about her. Likewise, Sue Sheehan saw some 100 friends and acquaintances of Jacqueline Onassis for her *New York Times Magazine* profile. "Jackie wouldn't let me interview her, but in retrospect I'm glad she didn't," Sheehan explained to colleagues. "I was able to see her entirely as others see her, without my own reactions getting in the way." She adds: "The important thing is to get the OK from the press secretary — in Jackie's case, Nancy Tuckerman. Without that, people like artist Bill Walton, a close friend of hers, would never have had me for tea and scones and very high-level gossip."

Gay Talese profited from a cold shoulder, too, when researching his famous *Esquire* cover story, "Frank Sinatra Has a Cold." An interview with Sinatra had been arranged for Talese through the singer's public-relations office. The writer flew from New York to Los Angeles, thinking he would spend some time with Sinatra and interview him on the occasion of his fiftieth birthday, which was to be the slant of the piece. "When I got there, Frank Sinatra was not feeling well and everyone was very nervous — 'everyone' meaning those people who work for Sinatra, like the publicity man and a dozen other people who have various roles," recalls Talese. "And Sinatra had a cold." The writer was told that whenever Sinatra had a cold he became extremely irritable. So Talese hung around. He was never able to sit down alone with the singer for an interview. "But this wasn't very important, because if I *had* been able to sit with Frank Sinatra, this man who for 30 years had been in the public eye, and if I had been able to ask him questions, I don't think I could have asked him — nor do I think he could have answered — those questions in any way that would have been as revealing of himself as I was able to gather by staying a bit of a distance away, *observing* him and overhearing him and watching those around him react to him."

For six weeks Talese was accepted by the Sinatra staff because the boss had a cold and the interview was postponed. During this period Talese got what he would later call "a better story than an interview. I was seeing the reactions. I was able to see the publicity man at work on other things having to do with Sinatra's life. I was able to learn a lot about the Hollywood press agent — that type, that high-priced, very successful, very nervous kind of man such as Frank Sinatra had hired. There were also people in the record business. I was able during this delay to really get onto another story which was far better."

Finally, if someone refuses to grant an interview for reasons that seem self-serving, it may be easiest to work around that subject, finish your research, then tell the reader what happened. *Newsweek* once did a feature on the bands that provide musical backdrops for TV talk shows. The magazine got cooperation from the studio bands for Dick Cavett, Merv Griffin and David Frost — but not from Doc Severinsen of the *Tonight Show*. The article ran across two pages, with plenty of photos and lively anecdotes. But the most memorable feature of "Music to Talk By" was a tiny three-line footnote in the lower left-hand corner of the first page: "Through a network press agent, Severinsen declared he had no time to be interviewed unless the resultant story was exclusively about his band."

Well, now. Refusals like that can *help* a story, not hold it back.

2. Doing Research

Be Prepared

—Motto,
Boy Scouts of America

Item: When Vivien Leigh arrived in Atlanta for the premiere of the reissue of *Gone With the Wind,* a reporter asked her what part she had played in the film. Scarlett informed the writer that she did not care to be interviewed by such an ignoramus.

Item: A beginning reporter's first question of naturalist John Burroughs was, "By the way, Mr. Burroughs, just what do you do?" End of interview.

Item: Shortly after author Bernard De Voto arrived in Hartford, Connecticut, a reporter asked, "Can I interview you?"

"Splendid," said De Voto.

"I'm sorry," began the reporter, "I really didn't have time to look this up. Just exactly who are you, Mr. De Voto?"

"Young man," replied the author, "if you don't have the time to look it up in a *Who's Who* or in your own library and find out, I haven't any time for you." He dismissed the reporter.

The episodes could continue, but three will suffice. Few things are more infuriating for a subject who is busy (or who believes himself to be busy) than to grant an interview to an unprepared writer. "The worst thing is the interviewers who haven't got a clue as to what they're interviewing you about," laments Jessica Mitford—a skilled interviewer herself. "I guess rock bottom was hit on the tour for *The American Way of Death* when we went to a radio station in Tulsa. A rather unpleasant blonde was the interviewer. Just as we went on the air she leaned over and whispered to me, 'What is it you've done?' "

Ten to One

Experienced writers agree that for every minute spent in an interview, at least ten minutes should be spent in preparation. Interviews that follow (rather than precede) careful research are nearly always more productive. "The first time I interviewed President Kennedy, I was supposed to see him for ten minutes," recalls William Manchester, author of *The Death of a President*. "The interview lasted three and a half hours. It was exciting and it led to further meetings." What accounted for this Presidential generosity? Research.

"I think it is very important for a person to do his homework," explains Manchester. "There's nothing more insulting than to ask a man, like a President of the United States, a question that he's answered many times before. Then he's quite likely to dismiss you. So what you want to ask are the questions he's never been asked before, questions that show that you have a great familiarity with his life. And then he's likely to respect you and be interested in the exchange, the colloquy." In preparing for his initial interview, Manchester went through a list of the appointments that President Kennedy had made with special assistants and cabinet advisers. He found that over 80 percent of them were within a few years of the President's age. So he asked Kennedy if he were a "generation chauvinist." "Now, he'd never thought of this," says Manchester, "but he liked the idea and he played with it, and it was entertaining for him. A really first-rate interview with an articulate man can be fascinating for him. And if he is fascinated, then it will go on and you will learn more from him. It all depends on how much time you spend in advance."

Mike Wallace Gets Stuffed

Better to be *over*-prepared than to be caught without enough advance preparations for an interview. Associated Press correspondent Eugene Lyons once had an interview with Joseph Stalin, which he was told would last two minutes. "At the end of two minutes I found that Stalin was in no hurry," recalls Lyons, "and there I was without a program of interrogation. I remained in Stalin's office nearly two hours and forever after would reproach myself for having failed in the excitement of the thing to ask significant questions." On another occasion, Lyons was told he could interview the Shah of Persia, but could only ask five prescribed questions. These took but a few minutes, and the Shah seemed to enjoy the novelty of being interviewed. He smiled and invited the reporter to ask more. "It was there, in the Shah's workroom, that I made a solemn vow," lamented twice-burned Lyons afterward. "Never again, I pledged in my secret mind, would I come into the presence of the great of this world without scores of questions carefully prepared in advance for an hour or two of interview—even though the arrangements call for only a few minutes of it."

For hard-nosed reporting, research is particularly crucial. Political writer Richard Reeves: "In dealing with people who you have reason to believe will try to deceive you—and I would take that to be every politician—you should look very carefully into what they've said on subjects in the past, and without letting them know you know they've answered this question before, ask them the same question and see how the answer differs."

Still, the best of preparations can go for naught. Mike Wallace certainly did his homework before his infamous paid-for interview with H. R. Haldeman on CBS television. "Wallace was stuffed, like a Strasbourg goose, with papers and facts and questions and quotes," observed *Esquire* columnist Nora Ephron. "He spent 55 hours in preliminary talks with Haldeman—a period of time so long as to make me suspect he left the fight in the locker room—and when he sat down to tape, for over six hours, he found out firsthand why H. R. Haldeman used to be called the Berlin Wall." Says Wallace: "The amount of preparation I had done on that bloody interview was monumental. But because he was willing to show his teeth and smile, and he was tan and good looking and bland, he wound up conveying the impression that he wanted to convey."

When preparing for an interview with a political figure, the writer must research current events—right down to the morning paper. A reporter once asked former Secretary of Agriculture Orville Freeman how he planned "to open Eastern markets to Minnesota milk." Replied Freeman: "If you had been reading the papers, you would know very well how I plan to do it." Embarrassing.

Keep on Truckin'

The lengthier the interview, the greater the research. Preparations for a *Playboy* interview are legendary. When Eric Norden went to

interview ex-Reich minister Albert Speer at his villa a few miles from
Heidelberg, he had already spent six weeks studying Speer, "poring
over his book [*Inside the Third Reich*] and published interviews, as
well as the voluminous reviews and polemical articles in the American
and European press." The interview extended "into almost ten days
of relentless day-and-night question-and-answer sessions," adds Norden, "ending with both Speer and myself on the brink of exhaustion."
The point of research beforehand is not to impress the interviewee,
but to talk intelligently on the topics he takes up. This is especially
important for the beginning writer who is seeking an interview with
a specialist who balks at talking with an unpublished writer. "The
magic door opener is research," advises Beatrice Schapper, a teacher
and freelancer. "Few people will refuse to be interviewed by someone
who shows he has spent time on a given subject, is familiar with
its importance, and aware of the trends and personalities in the field.
Writers, even beginning ones, should not underevaluate their contribution. They are a conduit from the expert to the public. Often the
expert cannot communicate with the public directly and welcomes
the *informed* questioner."

"Never interview anyone without knowing 60 percent of the answers," was one of eight "Ryan's Rules of Reportage" penned by
Cornelius Ryan shortly before his death. "Do your homework—you
can bet the person you are interviewing has, and is prepared." Actor
James Dean used to research the *interviewer* before each interview,
getting a run-down on him and his special interests from film press
agents. "Then he would proceed to charm the interviewer by trans-
forming himself into whatever he thought would appeal to them,"
recalls Dean's friend Joe Hyams. Such research in reverse is common
when the subject is in the entertainment business, where fans often
use ploys such as an "interview" to gain access to someone they admire.
When I phoned two writers for *All in the Family* to ask for an interview,
I was asked to call back in a week for an answer. When I phoned
again, I was told, "Fine. Let's do the interview. We've checked you
out, read your stuff, and we're looking forward to meeting *you*." That's
showbiz.

Serious research usually begins at the library—a labyrinth more
intimidating than the toughest interviewee for some writers. (There
are 80 miles of bookshelves in the New York Public Library's central

building alone.) "I am hopeless at libraries, since I don't understand how they work," confesses Jessica Mitford. For an hourly fee, the queen of the muckrakers says she finds it "much better to have somebody do your research than to have to go through the frustration of visiting a library, parking your car, waiting around and all that." Mitford does begin a project "by looking everything up in the *Encyclopaedia Britannica,* to find a certain amount of historical background on any subject." But since hers is the 1911 edition—it's onward to research assistants in the library for an update.

Ron Frederick, a freelancer who is also a trained librarian, is more comfortable doing research. "The interview may be the primary source of good quotes and anecdotes for an article," he says, "but I think that library research is *more* important than the interview because in order to ask good questions, you've got to know the background of your subject. Virtually any library has more information than most writers realize, and it's all just sitting there: public property. I think that writers should use libraries the same way that truckers use public roads—that is, as public resources for creating private income."

Information-to-Please Almanacs

What follows is not intended as a sure cure for library fatigue, but rather as a method for streamlining the library stint when a writer is in a hurry to get on with the interview(s). By knowing how to get around in a library, a writer not only saves time; he saves (Jessica Mitford, please note) money.

For openers, the Mitford method is a sound one: use encyclopedias as general background reading. *Britannica* (1974, not 1911) is excellent, but don't stop there. Try the *Americana,* or any other encyclopedia that features signed articles. Encyclopedias vary in their coverage of the same topic—for better and for worse. Then look for a more specialized encyclopedia in your field. There are excellent encyclopedias in religion, mythology, psychology and criminology—to name but a few categories. Jot down the names of authors of encyclopedia essays; they are potential interviewees.

Statistics are important, too. We live in an age of computers, pollsters, bookies, percentages—numbers everywhere. Government sources and atlases are essential to the interviewer who wants to dig in. And almanacs are like cluttered attics—sometimes exasperating for tracking down specific facts, but always delightful for rummaging. Ron Frederick notes that "almanacs will give enough statistics for most folks, and are not nearly as difficult as the *Statistical Yearbook of the United Nations*." Some useful titles are the *World Almanac & Book of Facts, CBS News Almanac, Information Please Almanac,* and—honest—the *Reader's Digest Almanac. The U.S. Fact Book* is the statistical abstract of the United States (prepared by the Bureau of the Census), and is doggone intriguing.

The Statistical Yearbook of the United Nations is a compilation of statistics from countries throughout the world, on a wide range of subjects, such as population, agriculture, national income, education and culture. *Statistics Sources* likewise is "a subject guide to data on industrial, business, social, educational, financial, and other topics" in the United States and abroad. *The Rand McNally Commercial Atlas* is good for locating economic data from particular locales, especially states and cities.

Government agencies are roundly damned for their excesses, but the writer can take advantage of their relentless flood of publications (and the writer *should;* s/he's paying for them). *The Encyclopedia of Governmental Advisory Organizations,* published quarterly, lists addresses and descriptions of federal agencies and other units that serve "in an advisory, consultative or investigative capacity." *The U.S. Government Organization Manual* also lists the different information agencies willing to supply materials to inquiring writers. The *Congressional Quarterly's Washington Information Directory* provides the names, numbers and capsule descriptions for information sources— governmental and private; arranged by subject. And *The Almanac of American Politics 1976* is an invaluable run-down on "the senators, the representatives, the governors—their records, states and districts."

Once you have determined that there is an agency in your field of inquiry (and there are some precious ones: note the Dialer and Answering Devices Advisory Committee), a request for information can lead to background brochures, phone interviews, and a willingness to answer any specific queries you may have by mail.

Who Knows What

When general sources have been exhausted, one needs a list of books to seek in the library card catalog. An excellent source for a fast bibliography is the *Subject Guide to Books in Print*, published annually. Look under your topic and related fields. You might also sample the *Bibliographic Index*, which lists those books and articles with bibliographies. Now check to see which titles are among the library's holdings. Chances are that unless you are working in a major library, you will not find every title. Some will be out on loan; for others, you will be out of luck. If an unavailable book seems crucial to your research, ask if the library has an inter-library loan service. Otherwise, check a bookstore or your state library.

When you find a book on your subject, see if other books on the shelf nearby contain related information as well. Books often contain bibliographies in their back pages, and here you may find out-of-print titles (therefore not in the *Subject Guide to Books in Print*) that are still to be found on library shelves.

Even the best book, though, is bound to be old news. Its information must be updated with articles from newspapers and periodicals. The best American newspaper index is the biweekly *New York Times Index*. In addition to indexing the *Times*, which is known for in-depth coverage of day-to-day events, the *Index* can be used for local newspapers as well. If a story of national importance appeared in the *Times* on a given day, chances are that a local paper may have run a feature or a localized story concurrently on the same event. A number of libraries also have indexes to the *Wall Street Journal, Christian Science Monitor, National Observer, Washington Post, Los Angeles Times, Chicago Tribune* and the *New Orleans Times-Picayune*. A few even have indexes to *The Times of London* and *Le Monde*. Your library may also have files of clippings from local newspapers.

The Readers' Guide to Periodical Literature is the standard index to articles appearing in some 130 general interest magazines. More scholarly publications are covered in the *Social Sciences Index* and the *Humanities Index* (until July 1974, these two were combined). Other guides include the *Public Affairs Information Service, Business Periodicals Index, Applied Science and Technology Index, Drama Index,* and *Music Index* (the last two will cover showbiz well).

Anyone doing research on a famous figure should check the *Biography Index*, which summarizes the work of several other indexes under the subject's name. *Current Biography* contains biographical summaries (and short bibliographies) on people in the news. If the subject is a local figure, ask if the library keeps clipping files on such celebrities. Many do.

And now, time for the *Who's Who* trap. *Who's Who* is a social register for British and Commonwealth high society; very few Americans have made it (Bernard De Voto, you're not among them). *Who's Who in America,* however, is a whole 'nuther cat. Founded by an English noble late last century, *Who's Who in America* is just barely exclusive. It and the others of the series *(Who's Who in Finance and Industry, in the World, in the East/South/West/Midwest, of American Women, of Medical Specialists)* provide quick summaries on just about every notable. But *Who's Who* they are not.

Who Knows—and What, among Authorities, Experts, and the Specially Informed is an index to some 12,000 potential interviewees in 35,000 areas of knowledge.

Other timely sources include *Editorial Research Reports,* a weekly publication that supplies background briefings for newspaper editorial writers on current controversies; *Editorials on File,* which reprints key newspaper editorials; and *Facts on File,* which contains a weekly synopsis of world events. For background information on particular countries, the annual Fodor and Fielding travel guides are excellent.

"Don't overlook the juvenile department of your library as a source of information," suggests Kirk Polking. "Children's books on factual subjects often give the writer an easy-to-read, brief picture of an idea he is researching." Marilyn Durham, author of the bestselling western, *The Man Who Loved Cat Dancing,* did much of her preliminary research in this manner—and did not travel west of the Mississippi until after the book was published.

Care and Feeding of Librarians

Increasingly, libraries have on tape the oral memoirs of prominent figures. Historian Arthur Mann found that the lively anecdotes recorded at Columbia University (where some 2,700 individuals are on tape) were invaluable for his biography of former New York mayor Fiorello La Guardia. The tapes "gave me a sense of contemporaneity with the past that I might not otherwise have," said Mann afterward. Libraries also feature special collections of manuscripts and documents donated by people in the public eye.

If you still have difficulty in the library, ask a librarian to assist you. Most librarians are too busy to be spoon-feeders, but they are always willing to help someone who is serious about research. It's a good idea to mention that you are a writer preparing for an interview, too. Librarians are likely to push harder if they know their work will be used for something more than a mild curiosity. Don't forget to send tearsheets—and candy, and discreet and loving bribes—to helpful librarians.

PR and information offices are usually most cooperative when writers request material. Make your requests as specific as possible, and ask for photographs. If you have a go-ahead from an editor, mention it. "Once you've received the information or materials you want, don't hesitate to ask for more," suggests a PR veteran. "Any good public relations agency that gives a hoot about its professional reputation would rather you'd ask more questions than put out something that isn't clear, that might be misinterpreted, or that simply isn't true." Again: send tearsheets to the helpful PR department. It'll help again.

Ain't Necessarily So

With all of this research behind you, an interview should be like a visit with someone you've known for years, no? No. Don't be surprised if your subject is not exactly what your research has led you to believe. Oriana Fallaci found Henry Kissinger to be much more introverted than she expected, while South Vietnamese President Nguyen Van Thieu was more outgoing than she was prepared for. On the contrary, director Alfred Hitchcock was *too* much like the material Fallaci had read beforehand, to the point of suffocation. "In the same way as we assume that intellectuals are necessarily intelligent, and movie stars necessarily beautiful, and priests necessarily saintly, so I had assumed that Alfred Hitchcock was the wittiest man in the world," recalls Fallaci. "He isn't. The full extent of his humor is covered by five or six jokes, two or three macabre tricks, seven or eight lines that he has been repeating for years with the monotony of a phonograph record that's stuck. Every time he opened a subject, in that sonorous voice of his, I foresaw how he would conclude; I had already read it."

Be warned, too, that library research is only as infallible as the facts in the stacks. It's the writer's job to check his facts for accuracy.

"Libraries and newspaper morgues are crammed with information, but much of it ain't necessarily so," said the late Robert J. Levin. "And if the subject happens to be a celebrity, especially from the entertainment world, *most* of it ain't necessarily so." Levin, the author of numerous profiles, explained: "It's partly their own fault. Celebrities or their publicity people either encourage or actually create the nonsense on the principle that 'you can say anything about me that you want, so long as you spell my name correctly.' In addition, other false facts on file include malicious gossip, popular myths, and honest lies (try to find out a movie queen's actual birth date!)."

Back to School

One method of checking facts is to interview *around* the subject beforehand. Friends and relatives of the subject are excellent sources, and can be great door openers as well. Flora Rheta Schreiber once did an article about Sargent Shriver, former head of the Peace Corps. When they met, the first thing the writer said was, "I bring you greetings from two of your old teachers at Canterbury." "Sargent Shriver looked at me in consternation and delight," the bestselling author of *Sybil* recalls. "I had been at his old preparatory school recently; he had not. I had delved into his past by talking to his teachers and this filled him with nostalgia. Before I knew it, he was asking me questions about his old school and we were talking like human beings. The formal interview had been abolished before it began. The result was that by the time I left I not only had personal and human material for my article, but I also found myself involved in a book about Shriver."

Alex Haley likewise researches the early years of his subjects. He goes to the subject's hometown, meets and talks with people who knew the celebrity before the age of 15. "People are somehow immensely flattered to know that back home where they were in fourth, fifth, sixth grades, people have little anecdotes about them," says Haley. "That means more to famous people than the latest headlines about them." Haley told author John Behrens: "I found time and again with the people I was interviewing, who were famous, heavily interviewed people, that their attitude almost automatically is, 'Okay, buster, what are you going to ask me that fifty people haven't already asked?'.... And then I would drop something like, 'You know, I was in contact with so-and-so who was with you in fourth grade,' or 'Your fourth-grade teacher mentioned you had a great passion for lemonade.' Something as ridiculous as that. And it immediately does a couple of things. It raises a little bit of interest. . . . 'How much does this person know about back there?' And it also serves to start moving that person into a kind of nostalgic point of mind, *before* they were famous, *before* they were controversial, before they were whatever they are. And it's disarming. And a person will start talking and reminiscing."

Stalking the Bashful Billionaire

Consider how Albert B. Gerber went about researching his unauthorized biography of Howard Hughes. The author found that after he had gone through *Readers' Guide,* the *New York Times Index,* and had assembled what he could find in newspapers, magazines and government reports, he "hardly had enough material to write an article, let alone a book." Hughes was one of the most elusive personalities in twentieth-century America. Obviously, Gerber needed interviews.

He struck out completely when he tried to set up interviews with Hughes, his former wife Jean Peters, and people close to the reclusive billionaire. He was about to abandon the project when he took another approach: back to little people, and to the early years. "I would see what I could do with the hundreds of people who had briefer contacts with Hughes," recalls Gerber. Thus he went after the actors who has starred in Hughes's pictures, the barber who had cut his hair, old school teachers, distant relatives and the like. This research meant "ferreting out names and addresses, writing to people, sorting replies and encouraging anyone who cooperated to furnish not only information but also more names and addresses." Thus, a pyramid effect was established through personal contacts: one potential interviewee led to others, and to others, and so on.

In addition, Gerber selected certain categories — among them, lawyers involved in cases against Hughes, and actors, actresses and directors who had worked with him during his Hollywood years. For these he checked addresses in trade publications — such as the Martindale-Hubbell directory for lawyers in the United States. He obtained entertainment addresses from the Academy of Motion Picture Arts and Sciences in Hollywood. Other prominent people were researched through regional *Who's Who* editions, and the outcome was "a phenomenal success," according to Gerber. "Many people asked me not to mention their names," he adds. "Others, like Ben Lyon, star of *Hell's Angels* (Hughes's greatest picture), gave me reams of anecdotes with no limitations. A distant cousin called and related tales of life in Texas. Lawyers sent me transcripts of cases involving Hughes." When *Bashful Billionaire* was published, it sold a million copies in hardcover and a Dell paperback edition.

A celebrity's early years are vital to understanding his stature and moods. "One's own feelings about oneself — the barometer — don't change because of external changes," reflected actor Dustin Hoffman to interviewer Tim Cahill in *Rolling Stone*. "If you become successful, become a star, it doesn't matter. I've been a star for about six years. But my feelings about myself and my work are based on the first 30 years. The feelings I had when I couldn't get a job, the way people treated me then. People that meet me since that summit can't understand that." An interviewer should.

The Prisoner of Facts

When interviewing friends of the cooperating interviewee, it's a good idea to tell the subject beforehand. "After the first session, I ask the subject's permission to talk to his wife," wrote Richard Gehman. "Then I inquire about his relatives; sometimes I go to see them, sometimes I write them letters. Relatives of famous people are mysteriously eager to write letters about them; it must give them a vicarious feeling of fame." Occasionally a subject would even suggest that Gehman talk to his enemies. He did.

For a cover story on actor Jack Nicholson, *Time* magazine correspondent Leo Janos asked the actor at the outset for "a list of people in your life who may not be obvious to me — leave out close friends, former wife and girl friends." Nicholson reeled off more than 40 names, and Janos was off. A few days later, when the writer was at Nicholson's home, three separate phones began to ring. "My friends are reporting in from all over the place that they're being interviewed," said the actor. "It's like undergoing an FBI full-field check for a top-secret job."

In addition to serving as a check on facts, preliminary sidebar interviews can supply the writer with background information and tiny brush-strokes that add truth to an article. While researching a piece for *New York* magazine on the firing of special prosecutor Archibald Cox by President Nixon, Aaron Latham interviewed former attorney general Elliot Richardson's staff and found that a key scene in the Watergate drama occurred at Washington's Jean-Pierre restaurant. It was here that Richardson and several of his aides lunched after one of the most crucial press conferences in Richardson's career − he had just gone before the cameras to defend his handling of the investigation of Spiro Agnew, who, the day before, had resigned the Vice-Presidency. "When the waiter appeared," wrote Latham, "the attorney general ordered quiche, mussels, salad, white wine, Brie and espresso." How did he know what Richardson ate that day? "In separate interviews, I asked Richardson's two aides what he had ordered," said Latham. "They recalled his meal in great detail. Then I asked what they had eaten. Neither could remember." Moral: "This is what it is like to be the aide of a 'great man.'"

In just that way, the journalist is an aide to great events − a man who may forget his room key, but who remembers the most painstaking details of feasts and skirmishes. Yet his memory − and his charm, and contacts, and rich writing style − are for naught if he is not, above all, a researcher. "Assuming that all authors have a flair for a well-honed phrase," columnist Jim Bishop once ruminated, "the difference between the winners and the losers is research; the digging of facts."

3. Face to Face

*You start a question, and it's like starting
a stone. You sit quietly on the top of a hill;
and away the stone goes, starting others.*

— *Robert Louis Stevenson*

Some interviewers come away with a flurry of good quotes; others
barely get the story. Why? It's all in your rapport with your subject,
face to face.

"The object is to get the interviewee relaxed, to make him really
talk instead of just answer questions," John Gunther once remarked.
The interviewer should try to build an atomosphere of mutual trust
and respect, or risk ruptured communication. "Forming a rapport
is a prerequisite for anything other than the most superficial work,"
says psychiatrist John Rich.

Rapport can be instant or it can be impossible. Larry DuBois, for
instance, interviewed Jack Anderson for *Playboy* in a weekend; but
Roman Polanski took a whole summer — "because I had to convince
him to trust me." DuBois worked on the interview with Hugh Hefner
that appeared in *Playboy*'s twentieth-anniversary issue for nearly a
year, off and on, living in Hefner's Chicago mansion to do a good,
in-depth job.

How do you go about it? Everything matters. Even unspoken
communication can influence the replies one gets during an interview.

When meeting someone for the first time, it's usually best to be
a little formal at the outset. Never be familiar. A cautious interviewer
will not even sit down until he has been asked. Other taboos include
gum chewing, smoking (without asking permission), and handling
things in the subject's office or home. In short, don't take liberties

or make assumptions that a guest would not be expected to make in your own home. "Good manners are valuable," says Red Barber, the veteran of thousands of sports interviews. "It is an asset when a manager is glad to see you come into his dugout — he moves over and invites you to sit beside him; he is ready to be interviewed."

"It is only the young writer portrayed on the silver screen who achieves success by entering his interviewee's office chewing gum or smoking and who sits slumped in his chair, hat, if any, on the back of his head, while he takes a few notes on any scraps of paper he has at hand," adds Helen Patterson. "The successful writer is extremely careful to see that his personal appearance is attractive and that his manner is gracious and considerate toward office boys and secretaries as well as toward the interviewee." Even though a celebrity may be known to millions by his first name, when meeting him for the first time it should be "Mr. Presley." Once rapport has been established, you might ask, "May I call you Elvis?" When he says "yes," you have moved that much closer in establishing a good working relationship. (If you think he's likely to reply "no," however, best to stay with Mr. and let him make the first move toward informality.) And if the interviewee has a professional degree, get the title right from the outset.

One interview technique developed for student reporters by the University of Oregon school of journalism is to address the subject by name in practically every sentence. "Do not do much talking yourself in the first part of the interview," the Oregon guidebook suggests. "Your main purpose is to encourage your subject to talk freely and interestingly while you are sizing him up and sizing up the matter under discussion. Little expressions of interest, approval, or curiosity are all you ought to permit yourself in this part of the interview. Yours is a THINKING role, not a talking role, in the first part of the interview."

What to Wear

The first impression that an interviewer makes on his subject is probably his physical appearance: clothing, accessories, and — if the interviewer is female — make-up. "Clothing should be 'average,' " suggests one researcher who feels that the interviewer's physical appearance should be as low-key and neutral as possible. "It should be neither too fashionable nor too plain. The same applies to the accessories of women interviewers." The important thing to remember is not to compete directly with the subject. Women who wear absolutely no make-up or nail polish, however, risk creating an impression "of coldness, even of masculinity. These impressions, whether right or wrong, are to be avoided. The interviewer may feel that he is being asked to mask his 'personality' by suppressing indications of where he belongs in the social matrix. He is being asked to do exactly this, but he should remember that it is part of doing his job well."

Some writers alter their clothing for the occasion. While researching *The Business Healers* (a book on management consultants), Hal Higdon wore a plain tie, high-rise socks, and a vest: "the costume of the consultant," says the author. "I modified my uniform considerably sometime later while writing an article about the play *Hair*." The interviewer, then, is a man for all seasons — and fashions.

The interviewer, too, has winning confidence — although some beginning interviewers may doubt theirs. Maurice Zolotow was once struck by the fact that many writers-to-be were reluctant to interview people. "Not the Secretary of State or a head of government," he reflected, "but somebody like the outstanding barber in town. I realized a great many people are afraid of interviewing." Which is understandable. An interviewer can be likened to someone who attends a dinner party, and sits next to a stranger. He must keep the conversation going, without monopolizing it. The beginning interviewer, who is perhaps more comfortable with books than conversation, may feel that the social craft of interviewing is well beyond him. It isn't. It only requires an uncommon blend of common abilities — to overcome nervousness, draw the other person out, and be a good listener.

Still, a grain of stage fright is natural when meeting new people. "Try the actor's trick," suggests author Hayes Jacobs. "Before entering the room where you must meet someone, stand tall and take several very deep breaths. Some of the tension, and nervousness, will vanish. When you go in, smile, and don't be in a rush to 'get down to business.' Engage in some chit-chat — even if it's about the weather."

Follow That Lead

If the *subject* seems self-conscious or on guard at the outset, there are a number of devices a writer can use to put the person at ease. Hal Higdon, for example, begins by talking steadily for several minutes, regardless of how much the subject may know about him or his project. "I call this my song and dance," Higdon says. "This permits the person being interviewed to observe me, examine the color of my tie, and decide whether or not he likes me." "Until the celebrity, or anyone for that matter, feels comfortable with you," says Barbara Walters, "it's not likely that he will feel like disclosing anything more intimate than his hat size."

At the outset, the interviewer is like a good horse: he follows the subject's lead. When I arrived at Gay Talese's apartment for an interview, Talese was on the phone. I immediately began a conversation on telephone answering services, and the importance of the phone in research. When I arrived at Rex Reed's apartment for an interview, Reed was opening his morning mail, complaining about the ridiculous invitations he often received. The conversation began right there: "What sort of wild invitations have you turned down lately?" The point is this: be flexible, and be ready for anything at the outset. Chances are good that the subject will be in the midst of some activity when you arrive; few people are simply sitting around waiting to be interviewed. Take the subject's mind off the interview by talking about unrelated matters which may interest him. For all but the busiest subjects, small talk is a smooth icebreaker.

One journalist tells of a memorable chat with Queen Elizabeth at a cocktail party that began when she asked how the Queen's clothes had weathered the previous day's visit to an iron mine. Barbara Walters got through to the usually aloof Barbra Streisand by asking how she chose a nursery school for her son Jason. And with Mamie Eisenhower, Walters' topic was a favorite grandchild. If your research shows that the subject has a favorite author, you might consider bringing a book as a small gift (no gift should be large enough to resemble payola). Todd Everett uses an old theatrical technique to establish rapport. He goes into an interview with both a tape recorder and a notepad. "Gee, I've got all these questions I want to ask you, but that's a silly interview," he says. "Let's just forget these questions and chat." He then tosses the notebook aside and turns on the recorder. "During the course of our chat, of course, I ask all the questions which were in the notebook," he adds. "It's like the politician throwing away his prepared speech. It gets your audience's attention, and it conveys a sense of trust. It works."

Sociologist E. S. Bogardus has published a paper suggesting that different types of persons are moved to conversation by different devices. Subjects who are traditionally on the defensive — such as lawyers or police officers — are likely to talk freely only when drawn away from their daily environment. Other subjects can be reached through a sense of rapport, or through an interest in truth for the sake of science. "To urge the interviewee to be frank, or to overurge him, is inhibiting," cautions Bogardus. "It is better for the interviewer to create the atmosphere rather than to urge frankness."

The self-centered interviewee will often open up when the interviewer appeals to his ego. Gail Sheehy found that her apprehension over interviewing David the Pimp for her study of Big Apple prostitution (*Hustling*) was unfounded — the man was an egomaniac. "Packing the most inconspicuous notebook I could find, I bused across town feverishly trying to invent an identity that wouldn't inhibit a pimp," wrote Sheehy. "I decided to do what I have always done before and since: tell the truth. 'A writer! Listen to me, sit down, you have the honor of interviewing the second greatest pimp in New York —' and David was off on a two-hour roller coaster of self-revelation which gave me an insight into pimps: ego generally gets the better side of caution. I couldn't get David to *stop* talking for the next eight months."

Kinship

Role playing is common among interviewers. "I majored in theatre in college," recalls Sally Quinn. "I studied the Stanislavski method, and then I quickly forgot it, because I thought it was ridiculous. But I recently started thinking about how, in a sense, you can almost use that method when you're interviewing somebody. You can put yourself into that person's place and try to feel what he's feeling, what she's feeling; try to think what the things are that really get to them. They can sense that empathy, and they'll open up to you, and this just never fails." One interviewer studying ex-Communists in the United States said that he sometimes found himself playing therapist for people who really wanted to open up. "All reporting is, after all, role playing," says Richard Reeves. "Tell them everything, the most personal details about yourself and your life. As human beings, they respond in kind, only their answers appear in print. That is a perfectly valid print technique and if the details of my life were interesting enough, I'd try it."

Marlon Brando's "most famous and unhappiest encounter with a journalist," according to biographer Bob Thomas, occurred under similar circumstances. Writer Truman Capote was sent to the movie set of *Sayonara* in Kyoto, Japan to profile the actor for *The New Yorker.* Brando was remarkably candid, even telling Capote about his mother's alcoholism: "... I didn't care any more. She was there. In a room. Holding on to me. And I let her fall. Because I couldn't take it any more — watch her breaking apart, like a piece of porcelain. I stepped right over her. I walked right out. I was indifferent. Since then, I've been indifferent." Brando was understandably disturbed when he saw the piece, and his friends were astounded that he had let it happen. "Well, the little bastard spent half the night telling me all his problems," explained the actor. "I figured the least I could do was tell him a few of mine." Observed a studio press agent: "An old trick."

Maurice Zolotow opens up to subjects, too. "If I have any technique, it is that I just forget about technique," he says. "I simply try to talk with my subject as though he were somebody I have always enjoyed talking with. Sometimes I talk a lot myself — about things that interest me, my own life, my own problems. But when the other person is speaking, I listen."

Don't be afraid to make mistakes — those too can create rapport. "I'm pretty terrible with a portable tape recorder," confesses Studs Terkel. "And sometimes the person, particularly if it's a noncelebrated person — an old lady in a housing project — will see my tape recorder isn't working. She'll say: 'Hey, it's not working!' And I will say: 'No, I goofed.' Well, you see, my own vulnerability makes her feel more kinship."

Kinship. Now there's the magic word for reaching an interviewee. "You want him to accept you as a friend," says one veteran magazine writer, "or at least as a substitute doctor/psychologist to whom he can unload his problems. Thus in one sense an interviewer provides a form of therapy for the person he interviews. The person gets to unbottle many of the thoughts that have been occupying his mind for months, or maybe years." Adds Rex Reed: "My success as an interviewer really has been pretty much based on the fact that my subjects have treated the interview like an hour of analysis except they haven't had to pay me. They have saved themselves $65 and they have unburdened themselves of a lot of things." How? "I just kind of follow people around and they tell me about their lives and I tell them about my life and suddenly a story forms in my head."

Establishing rapport is honorable; faking it is . . . well, risky. In Hunter Thompson's *Hell's Angels,* the author tells of the time a reporter tried to get an interview with gang leader Sonny Barger in a bar by being one of the boys:

> He came into the El Adobe and immediately asked to buy some marijuana. Then, before they could decide whether he was a poison toad or a narco agent, he pulled out some grass of his own and offered it around. This didn't work either, although it might have broken the ice if he'd rolled a joint for himself. Then he offered to buy a round of beers, talking constantly in bop jargon. The Angels tolerated him for a while, but after several beers he began asking questions about Hitler and gang rapes and sodomy. Finally Sonny told him he had 30 seconds to get his ass out of sight and if he showed up again they would work on his head with a chain.

Risks of Idolatry

Sometimes it's best to drop all of the little introductory tricks and get down to business. Veteran AP writer Saul Pett came away from an interview with labor leader James Hoffa wishing he had been more direct. Pett thought he would soften the hostility he sensed by using a trivial personal question to break the ice. "First a crucial question," he began. "My wife wants to know why you always wear white socks." Replied Hoffa, icily: "Because my feet sweat less in them." "It was an unusual interview," Pett reflected afterward. "In tone, it ran the gamut from frigidity to mere coldness."

Timidity can be as crippling to an interview as cuteness. "Although the timid, awkward cub may get what he wants by creating pity," says Curtis MacDougall, "it is the person who gives the impression of self-confidence, self-assurance, and self-respect whose success is enduring. It is in the presence of such persons that others feel most at ease." Some subjects—if they suspect the interviewer is obsequious—will become verbal steamrollers. Jim Wooten of *The New York Times* was once interviewing George Wallace when the governor began talking about "niggers." "Governor, you don't have to say 'nigger,' " said Wooten firmly. "You don't have to impress me."

Some interviewers go on the job as fans, which is—to say the least—unprofessional. Such writers either come away from the interview glassy-eyed (and unreliable), or bitter at the discovery that their gods often have feet of interviewing clay. The written result is usually either a valentine or hate mail. It could hardly be the truth. Best to strive for some middle ground—going on an interview neither to praise nor to condemn César Chavez. Even veteran writers have found that flattery is risky. A. J. Liebling was interviewing General John J. Pershing for a *New Yorker* profile, and the old man wouldn't loosen up. So the writer tried a little praise. "When they started to cut down the Army after the Armistice in 1918, General," he said, "you were against it, weren't you, because you foresaw this new European crisis?" Pershing, looking at Liebling in angry disgust, replied, "Who the hell could have foreseen this?" So much for flattery.

As a rule, it's best to treat the subject as someone worthy of respect, but not idolatry. If praise seems to be due, aim it at the deed, not the doer. "Gee, I think you're wonderful" sounds oafish, especially when coming from a stranger. "I really enjoyed your last book," however, shows an interest in the man's work, not in the man per se—which is often more convincing. At any rate, the interviewer's interest in the man should be professional, not personal. "Rarely does a person you interview become your friend," observes Barbara Walters.

But John Underwood, a senior writer at *Sports Illustrated,* is of the friendship persuasion. Well, almost. "The secret of getting to anyone is to achieve some kind of empathy," says Underwood, "to understand what has contributed to his particular character." Underwood starts by reading everything he can. "Then my preference is to get to know him almost as a friend. You may lose objectivity, but it's worthwhile in the long run; if you don't pierce that crust, you'll never find anything out. And I think it is important to get them where they live, literally. It helps to see how they interact with their families and friends. You may not use a lot of it, but you learn so much."

Underwood, who has done *SI* cover stories on many giants of sport, draws an interesting distinction between being a friend and being a fan. "Remember that if you tend to be awed by athletes," says Underwood, "you never allow yourself to see a man's inner sanctum, and that will, in itself, distort the picture. The thing about sports heroes is that they are just a cut away from the friend you play golf with. There's a whole lot of difference between Einstein and the guy who makes A's in his college chemistry class, but the professional athlete and the kid who wins letters in college are only a shade apart."

Still, friendships based upon interviews can backfire. "My biggest problem in writing about celebrities," says Rex Reed, "is that because I was once an actor I have an empathy for their pain which often leads them to tell me more than they realize. Print a few of their candid remarks and suddenly you've got a reputation for being a bastard." When Reed interviewed actress Natalie Wood, she treated him "like her long-lost college boyfriend," recalls Reed, but "she hasn't spoken to me since I wrote a funny description of how she sat on the floor of a New Orleans hotel room eating eggs Benedict off the coffee table, opening a bottle of Dom Perignon with her teeth, and doing Russian imitations in her nightgown. Now she tells everyone I made her sound like a gun moll." When Reed interviewed actress Sandy Dennis, once again it was true love. According to the writer, Dennis was "one of the kookiest girls I ever met, but when I printed that she had dirty feet and ate cold sauerkraut out of a Mason jar and served ginger ale in a champagne glass full of cat hairs, she nearly went into a coma." So it goes.

Mm-Hmm

One risk of fandom is failing to ask the Obvious Question. In the much-discussed 1967 National Football League championship game, for example, the Green Bay Packers were three points behind the Dallas Cowboys with 20 seconds remaining in the game. The Packers had two downs to go. The question was time. Should they go for the field goal that would tie the game? Or try for a touchdown, and, that failing, rush in with someone to try for a field goal? The question was: would there be time for two plays? As any football fan will tell you, quarterback Bart Starr took the ball over a Jerry Kramer block for a touchdown. Green Bay went wild.

Afterward, CBS had Tom Brookshier in the clubhouse, and Frank Gifford was plugged in from the booth "Neither of them thought to ask Starr if he thought he had enough time for two plays," observed Leonard Shecter. "Neither asked coach Vince Lombardi if *he* thought they had enough time for two plays. They just oohed and ahhed and made me want to, in the immortal words of Dorothy Parker, fwo up." Eventually, according to Shecter, the truth came out: "Starr and Lombardi were certain they *had* time for two plays. This made them only slightly lesser heroes than TV would have it. But they told the truth. TV didn't." Because CBS hired fans to do an interviewer's job.

Editors are aware of the intimate nature of many interviews, and try to avoid assignments to writers that result in fine friendships but poor copy. "I like to remain at one remove from the subject so that I can remain unseduced," says Murray Fisher, who edited *Playboy*'s interviews for 12 years before retreating to the post of contributing editor. "By the very nature of celebrities, they exude a charisma that is intoxicating if not irresistible. It's easy to become swayed into friendship, into becoming protective and soft on them—which can ruin an interview. Too much rapport of the wrong kind. Occasionally I've had to step in when the interviewer lost his objectivity. I'm interested in conveying a sense of what a person is really like, deep down inside, for good or ill, warts and all. The essence. I consider it a responsibility to be tough."

Listen Up

Definitely, tough does not mean talkative. "The worst thing an interviewer can do is talk a lot himself," observed A. J. Liebling. "Just listen to reporters in a barroom. You can tell the ones who go out and impress their powerful personalities on their subject and then come back and make up what they think he would have said if he had had a chance to say anything." Again, it comes down to acting like a professional. "Never forget who the star of the interview is," advises Charles Samuels. Psychologist Charles Anderson once conducted a study of employment interviews, measuring the amount of time that the interviewer and the potential employee talked. Anderson's results showed that the more the interviewer talked, the more likely the applicant was to get the job. For the writer on an interview, the conclusion is clear: let the subject talk. The more he talks, the more likely you will be "hired" or trusted—and thereby come away with better material for your story. "The observation may be elementary, but it is important," says author John Hohenberg. "No talking reporter ever held a decent interview."

Don't interrupt when the subject is talking; and on most occasions, it is probably best to show neither signs of approval or disapproval, regardless of what the subject says. Neutral expressions such as "uh-huh," "Yes, I see," or a simple nod of the head are usually sufficient to prod the subject along. One researcher has even found that an interviewer who says "mm-hmm" got longer responses—up to twice as long as the replies given to interviewers who gave no "mm-hmms." So: mmm's the word.

Hearing is believing, as far as the conscientious interviewer is concerned. Problems occur when an interviewer doesn't listen to what the subject is saying, *closely.* "The problem of getting people to talk really isn't a problem at all," says Maurice Zolotow. "But to do it you must listen carefully and not be thinking of what you plan to say next. If you are listening and really interested and excited, you will get a good interview." Should you miss a point or three, rephrase what you think the subject has said, and ask him if you have understood him correctly.

The good interviewer listens carefully—but not passively. "You can't have even a reasonably decent conversation, much less an 'extraordinary' one, with someone who is just a listener," says Rust Hills in a review of *Supertalk,* a book of Q&A's by Digby Diehl. Hills also says a "real conversation" has an element of surprise; and he suggests that the interviewer upset his subject from time to time with—horrors!—thoughts of his own.

Should the interviewer argue with the subject? "In general, if a person is superior, he will enjoy being talked up to or argued with," says John Gunther. "The job of an interviewer is to get information, not to show himself off. Just the same, there is no better way to get a spark off some dignitary than to disagree with him, if you are sure of your own ground." But Rust Hills says it is nearly impossible to provoke veteran subjects with debate. Looking at Digby Diehl's conversation with Hugh Hefner, Hills observes that "Hefner says more or less exactly the same things to Diehl that he said to me when

I interviewed him once, and I was arguing with him every step of the way." Ah, the unflappable subject.

Love, Booze and the Interviewer

Perhaps more dangerous—or futile—than arguing with a subject is seeming overly curious about someone else—as though the subject were second fiddle. Barbara Walters tells of interviewing director Mike Nichols at a time when everyone was talking about Richard Burton and Elizabeth Taylor in his first film, *Who's Afraid of Virginia Woolf?* "Mr. Nichols, I'm not interested in hearing about Elizabeth Taylor or Richard Burton," she told the director. "I want to know about you." Instant empathy. Phrasing is important. When Walters was interviewing the mother of Martin Luther King, Jr., she wanted to avoid asking "What's your famous son really like?" So she asked, "What qualities did you most want to instill in your children?" This resulted in a good relationship for the interview, and in many revealing anecdotes about Mrs. King's famous son.

Occasionally, an interview will really take a turn for the worse. If the subject is in a bad mood, it's best to pretend not to notice it. If he is in a mood for amor, however, look out. When Marie Torre was "too young to know how to cope with the breed," she was assigned an interview with an opera star "who turned out to be more interested in making love than talk." At one point he told her that he was not especially fond of opera. "Then what do you like?" the writer asked. Answer: "Bee-yoo-ti-ful young women!" Says Torre: "After trying to stave off his advances for the better part of the interview, I departed with nothing to write about—not for a family newspaper, anyway!"

If flirtation comes during interviews, can booze be far behind? John Gruen got drunk during an interview with actress Bette Davis. "But it was my first encounter with a lady whose personality and stardom had dazzled me for half my lifetime," explained the writer. "Miss Davis seemed unperturbed at my rapid swilling of her generous drinks and seemed unconcerned over my slurred questions. That I managed to get what I got was a tribute to my sense of survival." Pat Putnam, an editor at *Sports Illustrated,* is an interviewer in the *in vino veritas* tradition, maneuvering subjects into the nearest pub for conversation. "But I have a rule," he adds. "If they take a drink, everything is off the record. I'll call the next morning and ask them if it's OK to quote them, and 90 percent of the time they say that it is."

Mike Wallace tried to use booze to loosen the tongue of G. Gordon Liddy after arrangements had been made for an interview by CBS. During dinner with Liddy and a CBS producer, it became apparent that the subject "would not talk substantively about the whole Watergate break-in at all," recalls Wallace. "So we were a little concerned as to what, indeed, we might get out of him. . . . We sat there and proceeded to try to get him a little bit loaded. . . . We figured we were smart as hell; but he was smarter than we—he didn't drink a damn thing, and so we finally began the film and filmed about an hour (of which we played 15 minutes) and went our separate ways—I back to CBS and he to Federal prison in Danbury, Connecticut." There's mud in your eye.

The Eyes Haven't It

"To look is not always to see," goes an old axiom. Eye contact can be important for rapport, but it may be overrated, too. William Glover, the AP drama critic, calls eyes "your best conversational guides"; but when an actress showed up for an interview with dark glasses on, he was unnerved.

Marrianne LaFrance and Clara Mayo, two Boston University psychologists, once analyzed films for eye contact and direction of gaze. A white subject, they determined, tends to look away from the person he is talking *to* and to look toward someone he is listening to. Blacks tend to do the opposite. Thus, if a white interviewer glances momentarily at a black subject, he may think he has lost his subject's attention because the interviewee is looking off into the distance. "Why don't you look at me when I'm speaking to you?" is an inappropriate attitude here. On the other hand, a black interviewer asking questions of a white subject may encounter such eye contact that there is a feeling of scrutiny and critical inspection.

Psychologists have also determined that females engage the eyes of their subjects more often than do males. One study found "male interviewers obtain fewer responses than female and fewest of all from males, while female interviewers obtain their highest responses from men, except for young women talking to young men." Yes.

Femininity on the Job

Indeed, the interviewer's sex can make a difference. It can add pizazz or suspicion to the interview—depending on the subject's biases, and the interviewer's charms. Some subjects feel more at ease with a member of the same sex. "I know that there are certain types of people who just don't take women seriously at all," says Nora Ephron. "I think that policemen, detectives, athletes, all of your basic locker-room-boy professions are very difficult to get in contact with. They have never talked with a woman before so why are they going to start now!" Ephron finds businessmen "a *little* easier but not *much*" for interviews, and says that "politicians are also rough."

But sex cuts both ways. Billie Jean King, after being interviewed by women for this first time, told a writer: "I looked at them and started choking because I wasn't used to talking to women. But they gave me a better write-up. They understood what I was referring to in those quotes, they didn't take them out of context."

Many women writers find in practice, however, that they have to "act like a lady, look like a girl, think like a man, and work like a dog." Oriana Fallaci believes that being female is an advantage to an interviewer "as long as you do not use your sex or behave like a girl," she adds with pouts and giggles to illustrate her point. Fallaci asks tough, uncompromising questions, and has a reputation for being hard-nosed with some of the world's best-known—and male—leaders.

"Men, as a rule, have a hard time taking a young woman seriously," says Marianne Means, the syndicated columnist. "They want to pat you on the knee, but not give you serious information." Adds Nora Ephron: "Interview subjects do tend to underrate women interviewers, and it seems to me the best approach to this is not to be helpless and feminine but to work terribly hard at the beginning to prove yourself, to show them that you *know* what you are talking about—that you've read up and that you are not there cold."

Some women milk their femininity for all it's worth, however. "I never try to pretend or impress the executive that I know all about his subject," says Mildred Tyson. "As a woman I find this pays off well. When I tell the executive that I won't understand the technical answer I know he must provide for my question, but that I will just take it down word for word as he explains it, I find the executive becomes very cooperative in his explanation and usually then tells me far more than I expected." If the helpless waif bit doesn't work, a reverse approach may be worth a try. "One British reporter that I know has developed a special style in dealing with diplomats, assuming a posture of knowing all sorts of secrets to the extent that the ego of the diplomats often drives them to demonstrate that they know even more than the reporter and to share all sorts of inside information," says Louis B. Fleming. "The fact that this particular reporter is a woman may have something to do with it, of course." Perhaps.

A woman interviewer is an interviewer first. Consider Nina Totenberg, who covered the Justice Department for *The National Observer*. She acquired such a reputation for hard-nosed reporting that J. Edgar Hoover once tried to have her fired, and Jack Anderson labeled her "that brassy blond reporter" after a celebrated exchange she had with then-Attorney General John Mitchell. "Mr. Attorney General," she asked, "is it true that the President said, 'Fuck the American Bar Association'?" Mitchell paused. "Please," he said, "there are ladies present."

Kid Stuff

A special kind of rapport is necessary for interviewing children. For one thing, the interviewer should never talk down to his young subject. "If a fairy came in the door and offered you three wishes," an interviewer once made the mistake of asking a precocious nine-year-old, "what would you say?" "A fairy?" was the reply. "I'd ask him if he thought I was queer."

For tips on talking *with* (and not *to*) the young, one of the best guides available is child psychiatrist John Rich's *Interviewing Children and Adolescents*. Books by the late Dr. Haim Ginott, available in paperback, are also excellent. "The key to successful communication is having a common ground with the child," says Rich. "Some interviewers interpret this as meaning that they should be childish and should pretend to have interests and an outlook they do not have. This is ruinous—children are quick to spot such a phony approach. It is not so much interests and preferences that are important, as an attitude to life." Rich goes on to point out that if a child says he loves chocolate, and the interviewer says he personally prefers olives, they are "still on common ground because the interviewer can get as enthusiastic about olives as the child can about chocolate—we can have interesting conversations with children even though our likes and dislikes may be different." The child may not recognize the common ground at once; it is often the interviewer's job to point it out.

Children are often an untapped source for information that a writer may seek about the youngster's parents. "It is often possible to question a child indirectly about his parents and gain information that he will not give in answer to direct questions," adds Rich. "You can ask children how they intend to bring up their own children when they have them. It is then usually easy to discover from their replies whether they approve of their own upbringing or whether they think they are going to make a better job of it than their parents did." In this approach, cautions the psychologist, it is important to make the child feel there are no "right" or "wrong" answers, "but that you are asking for the child's opinion and that he has every right to one."

One gaffe made by adults, according to Rich, is starting a conversation by asking how the child is doing at school. "They would not think of opening a conversation with a stranger at a cocktail party by asking, 'Are you successful in your job?' " he reflects. "Most children do not *want* to talk about school, but do want to talk about their leisure activities and hobbies. The interview should therefore begin with these rather than with school topics." Questions for young children with limited vocabularies and powers of understanding should be as concrete as possible. "What are your hobbies?" may be answered, "I don't have any." But "What do you do when you're not at school?" may encourage discussion. Don't use big words for little people.

Trauma Situations

Above all, the interviewer should strive to make the subject feel he can be himself. That is the aim of rapport: to engender honesty in the subject, not phoniness in the writer.

Joseph P. Blank's trademark as a *Reader's Digest* writer is the compelling article on those who have endured a catastrophe. Vital, of course, is rapport with ordinary people who have gone through extraordinary situations. "It is absolutely essential that the principals in a story feel that they can trust you, that you genuinely care about them, that you will not hurt them," says Blank. "If the chemistry between the subject and myself is right, we simply become friends, sometimes very close friends, within quite a short period. On occasions, communicating becomes so close that the person I am talking to forgets that I am on assignment." One night when Blank was interviewing a couple about a traumatic experience, the wife excused herself for a moment. While she was out of the room, the husband leaned forward to the writer and confided, "I don't want my wife to hear about this, but you should know. ..."

"He went on," says Blank, "having completely lost awareness that I was taking down his words for an article that might be seen by some 50 million people." Now *that's* rapport.

Woodstein's Nighttime Fishing

Perhaps the ultimate example of establishing rapport with unwilling subjects in recent memory occurred when reporters Bob Woodward and Carl Bernstein of the *Washington Post* were investigating what a Presidential press secretary described as "a third-rate burglary attempt" at the Watergate hotel. Initially they encountered tremendous resistance from people afraid to talk. The reporters had been calling on people associated with the Committee to Re-Elect the President at their homes in the evening, after their first-edition deadline at 7:45 p.m. When Bernstein knocked on his first door, the occupant was trembling, literally. "Please leave me alone," the reporter was told. "I know you're only trying to do your job, but you don't realize the pressure we're under." Another near-subject said, "I want to help," then burst into tears, adding, "God, it's so awful." Bernstein was shown to the door.

"The nighttime visits were fishing expeditions," the reporters recall in their book *All the President's Men*. "And the trick was just getting inside where the conversation could be pursued, consciences could be appealed to." They decided on a "less than straightforward" approach. Woodward told subjects that he was a registered Republican; Bernstein said he had antipathy toward both parties; and the duo served up something along this line: "A friend at the committee told us that you were disturbed by some of the things you saw going on there, that you would be a good person to talk to ... that you were absolutely straight and honest and didn't know quite what to do; we understand the problem—you believe in the President and don't want to do anything that would seem disloyal." With empathy like that, how often could they fail? Often.

When a subject asked who at the committee had given her or his name, the interviewers explained that they must protect confidential sources—assuring the subject that s/he would be likewise shielded. Once inside, they never used notebooks. And the information began to flow in. One time Bernstein knocked on the door of the home of a woman who worked for Maurice Stans, and whom he was told "knows a lot." "Oh, my God," she said, "you're from the *Washington Post*. You'll have to go, I'm sorry." On a table in the background, Bernstein noticed a pack of cigarettes. After holding his ground momentarily, he asked for one. "I'll get it," he said, moving toward the table and getting ten feet into the house. Once there, he bluffed, saying there were many people like her who wanted to tell the truth. Then he asked if he could sit down to finish the smoke.

"Yes, but then you'll have to go," came the reply. "I really have nothing to say." The subject was drinking coffee, and before long Bernstein was sipping coffee, too—slowly. Soon the bookkeeper was telling Bernstein that he and Woodward had "really struck close to home" with some of their early published stories. "Sometimes I don't know whether to laugh or cry," she reflected. "But in some way, something is rotten in Denmark and I'm part of it." In the end, Bernstein was even able to take notes in front of her, assuring the bookkeeper that she was not going to say anything he did not already know, and that nothing would go into the paper that could not be verified elsewhere.

And so it was that through a key interview Carl Bernstein learned of the nature and the political uses of the cash slush fund in Maurice Stans' safe. This in turn led the reporters to Hugh Sloan, the man who handed out the money, and from there the story mushroomed into national headlines and the downfall of a President. All because of some astute footwork, and an inordinate ability to create rapport with a subject, willing or not. All things are possible to a reporter with rapport.

4. Popping the Questions

REPORTER
Glad to be back, Mr. Kane?
KANE
I'm always glad to get back, young man.
I'm an American. (Sharply) Anything else?
Come young man — when I was a reporter
we asked them faster than that.

—*Citizen Kane* shooting script
Orson Welles,
Herman J. Mankiewicz

Oriana Fallaci — small, nimble in mind, vulnerable — was like a rabbit stalking a toothy fox.

Fallaci: But, Dr. Kissinger . . . how do you explain the fact that you have become almost more famous and popular than a President? Have you any theories?

The Adversary: Yes, but I won't tell you what they are. . . . Why should I, while I'm still in the middle of my job? Instead, you tell me yours. I'm sure you, too, have some theory on the reasons for my popularity.

Fallaci: I'm not sure, Dr. Kissinger. I'm looking for a theory in this interview. But I haven't found one yet. I expect the root of all lies in success. What I mean is, like a chess player, you've made two or three clever moves. China, first of all. People admire a chess player who makes away with his opponent's king.

The Adversary: Yes, China was an important element in the mechanics of my success. And yet, that isn't the main point. The main point. . . . Well, why not? I'll tell you. What do I care after all? The main point stems from the fact that I've always acted alone.

Americans admire that enormously. Americans admire the cowboy leading the caravan alone astride his horse, the cowboy entering a village or city alone on his horse. Without even a pistol, maybe, because he doesn't go in for shooting. He acts, that's all; aiming at the right spot at the right time. A Wild West tale, if you like.

The tale spread quickly — and not everybody liked it.

"It was high noon in the old West Wing," said one aide about the White House reaction, according to *Kissinger,* by Bernard and Marvin Kalb. "At least a half a dozen people who matter here in the White House hit the ceiling when they read that story. They called it the biggest ego trip anyone has ever taken."

Another aide said the interview was regarded as just "a blunder — Henry talking to a pretty girl; the whole thing had gone to his head."

And Henry may have been holding his head in embarrassment, too, like the cowboy who shot off his big toe. "I couldn't have said those things," he would later sigh about the tape-recorded interview. "It's impossible."

Nothing is impossible for the interviewer who knows how to lure his game into the open with an irresistible question. Voltaire says, "Judge a man by his questions rather than by his answers." Certainly the interviewee will judge accordingly — and the depth and drama of his answers will depend heavily on how much he thinks his interviewer knows and will understand.

The Wrong Questions

Interviewing is the modest, immediate science of gaining trust, then gaining information. Both ends must be balanced if the interview is to be balanced and incisive. Yet they are often fumbled in the anxious heat of an interview. The interviewer will either yearn too desperately for his subject's trust, and evoke flatulence, or he will restrain his sympathies, demand data — and get like in return.

Much depends on popping the right questions. It is the only way to persuade the specialist (your subject) to accept and feed the ignoramus (you).

"It is impractical to know something about everything," says Robert Wells of the *Milwaukee Journal,* "although that would be the ideal preparation for your career. But if you know enough to ask the right questions about as many topics as possible, you're doing pretty well."

"Mr. Wells puts it mildly," retorts Neale Copple in *Depth Reporting*. "If the reporter knows the right questions to ask, he has an unbeatable edge on the competition."

When he asks the *wrong* questions — the snide, the vacuous, the tasteless — he is in for an edgy interview. Take those hungry television newsmen, who seem compelled to match the stomach-churning impact of a Minicam shot with a stomach-churning quote. Nora Ephron tells of working side by side with TV reporters, and watching "in dismay as the cameras moved in and the television reporter cornered the politician ('How do you feel about the vote, Senator?') or cornered the man on the stretcher being carried out of the burning building ('How do you feel about the fact that your legs were just blown off, sir?'). ..."

How Do You Feel?

In his fine collection of TV writings, *Living-Room War,* Michael J. Arlen elaborates on the proliferation and uselessness of the "how do you feel" school of broadcast interviewing:

> I mean, the 'how-do-you-feel' stuff would be okay if it led anywhere, if it were something people could respond to ... but in a professional interview what it really amounts to is a sort of marking time while the reporter thinks up some real questions, or maybe while he hopes that this one time the Personage will actually include a bit of genuine information in his inevitably mechanical reply, which the reporter can then happily pursue.

Arlen maintains, and rightly I think, that "How do you feel?" is either ridiculous — "Well, Archduke, how does it *feel* to have been shot three times in the thigh and shoulder?" — or unanswerable except for occasional mumbles and vapidity:

> Or, to put it another way, if time is running short, and you have cornered the man who has just thrown the convention over to Oscar W. Underwood as a result of having brought up 117 votes from the State of New Jersey during teatime, "How do you feel?" or "What's your reaction?" might be fairly far down toward the bottom of a list of the 37 most useful questions you

might ask him at that point. In these circumstances what in hell is anybody going to say except "Well, Buzz, I feel real good."

Arlen envisions the ultimate in "how do you feel" journalism:

> Sometimes . . . I have this picture of the last great interview: The polar icecaps are melting. The San Andreas Fault has swallowed up half of California. . . . The cities of the plain are leveled. We switch from Walter Cronkite in End-of-the-World Central to Buzz Joplin, who is standing on a piece of rock south of the Galápagos with the last man on earth, the water rising now just above their chins. Joplin strains himself up on tiptoe, lifts his microphone out of the water, and, with a last desperate gallant effort — the culmination of all his years as a TV newsman — places it in front of the survivor's mouth. "How do you feel, sir?" he asks. "I mean, being the last man on earth and so forth. Would you give us your personal reaction?" The last survivor adopts that helpless vacant look, the water already beginning to trickle into his mouth. "Well, Buzz," he says, gazing wildly into the middle distance, "I feel real good."

Well, I Feel Put Upon

Often the thin question is the offspring of thin research. "I don't mind doing *interviews,*" rock star Ian Anderson told Colman Andrews. "But I don't like answering questions such as 'How'd you get the name Jethro Tull?' or 'How many of you are there in the group, and which one of you plays the flute?' In a country like Japan or New Zealand or Australia, where we've just been on tour, people ask these questions because they're genuinely curious, and they don't have access to a tremendous amount of information. But I shouldn't have to answer those questions here. Jethro Tull has been around five or six years. We answered those questions the first, second and third time we toured here. All the facts about us are available in this country, because there are lots of press handouts here — which were done at *my* request to make life easier for me. So I shouldn't have to waste time answering those kinds of questions."

Ask a dumb question, and you may get a dumb answer. "Tell me, Miss Perrine, what do you look for in a man?" someone asked Valerie Perrine, who had been bombarded with intimate inquiries after starring in *Lenny.*

"Oh . . . about ten inches," she replied.

Worst of all, the careless interviewer may draw the weary, all-too-obliging subject. "Some of the media ask questions that are not really questions," says baseball superstealer Lou Brock. "They're requests for confirmation of opinions they have going in. They've already written the answers in their minds and what they want from me is reassurance. I'll give it to them to keep everybody happy, if it doesn't go against my conscience."

Know What You Want to Know

The thoughtful interviewer works in an open, critical spirit. He does not judge his subject; he waits for his subject to judge himself. An interview often depends less on questions than on one's spirit of questioning. Fragmentary research and clumsy, sore-eyed questioning will convince the subject that his interviewer is uninterested. And he'll clam up. The good interviewer is deeply interested, of course — but he is also disinterested. He is a conduit for his readers.

And he fashions the interview in the interests of his readers. If he is writing for the *Cincinnati Post,* he may ask his subject about the future for open education in Hamilton County. If he is writing for *Harper's,* he may want to know about open education's hopes nationwide.

Above all, the interviewer knows exactly what he wants to get from his interview. He is like a chess player; he does not move a piece — or ask a question — without a purpose, a plan.

"When you start asking questions," says Dr. George Gallup, the famed pollster, "the other person immediately wonders, 'Why does he want to know?' Unless your purpose is clear, he may be reluctant to talk, or he may seize the opportunity to tell you all about his problems."

Arranging Your Questions

How many questions should the interviewer prepare? That can vary dramatically — from a lone question to flesh out a minor statistic in a business story (usually done by phone) to an array of hundreds of questions scattered over days or weeks for a *Playboy* interview. Generally, the more questions the writer prepares, the more thorough his interview and story will be.

Some believe the professional interviewer should memorize his questions, like a CIA agent who memorizes his instructions, then puts them to the torch. But it seems more sensible to keep handy a list of essential questions, lest one forget. It's incurably human, and embarrassing, to come away from an interview with an opera singer with some terrific, unexpected material about her childhood — but nothing about her current production.

Don't strip mine in an interview — dig deep. The temptation to cover *everything* yields only a blurry interview studded with intriguing, but isolated, tidbits. Devise your angle, and build your interview around it.

Check with your editor; he may have an angle in mind. Omer Henry tells of one editor who had heard of a firm that was using a new wage-incentive plan for its mechanics. "He wanted to know how the plan worked. Knowing exactly what this editor wanted, I was able to draft a set of questions, the answers to which gave me the facts I needed to write and sell the article."

Meticulously arranging your questions can be deranging. "The list of questions and the logical sequence invariably disappear very quickly," notes Edward Linn. "If they don't, you're in trouble." Even so, a good interview is sensibly structured. It begins with easy, rather mechanical questions; shifts to knottier, more thoughful questions; moves back out with mechanical questions (favorite writers, future projects) and closes with a query that offers a ring of finality (one effective question: how would you like to be remembered?). If the interview has logical structure — a sense of beginning, middle and end — it will have emotional structure as well. The interview as a whole will have an impact that exceeds the sum of its parts.

The interview outline need not be dictatorial, or detailed, or even committed to paper. It can be a single, tacit purpose. In fact, the simpler it is, the better. It is only a device to give the interviewer confidence, and his questions, momentum. It gives the interviewer the reins of the interview.

Know Your Funnels

The interview outline may take two shapes: one, like a funnel, and the other, like an inverted funnel.

The *funnel-shaped interview* opens with generalities — "What are the benefits of nuclear warfare, Mr. President?" — then pins down the generalizations — "When and where has it produced those spectacular sunsets that you mention?" It appeals to the thoughtful, creative interviewee, because it allows him some say in the direction of the interview. Freelancer Edward Linn opens each topic with a broad question "so that the subject can take it in any direction he wants. If you make each question too specific, too direct, too narrow, you run the risk, I think, of ending up with an article that reflects your own preconceptions; an article that you have written in large measure before you leave home. If the guy I'm interviewing takes that opening question and goes off in a direction that never occurred to me, I figure I'm way ahead; I'm finding out what interests *him* most, rather than what interests me."

The wide-open question not only gives the interviewee room to breathe; it gives the interviewer room to grapple. Alex Haley says he's interested in abstract questions because "I value being able to go to the subject almost ignorant of him. Then, I have a feeling I represent more nearly Mr. Average Reader who doesn't know much about this person. I want to meet him, form an impression of him — which I hope will be fair, honest and accurate — and try to communicate this to the reader. I have never known anybody beforehand."

Open an interview with a question as broad as the Dakota hills, though, and your subject may cut you off at the pass. Hal Higdon once started an interview with, "Why don't you tell me a little bit about what you've done?"

"If you don't know," retorted the subject, "what are you doing here?"

Adds Higdon: "It took me about ten minutes before I recovered and steered the interview back onto safe ground."

Sherlock Holmes would have been fond of the *inverted-funnel interview;* it opens with hard, fast, specific questions, then ascends to more general ground. It's effective for interviewing that frankest and most baffling subject — the child. He may be stymied by a wide, world-weary question like, "Are you ambitious?" unless the ground is broken by specific questions like "Do you try to make straight A's in school?"

"A child may not be able to say, 'I dislike the authoritarian personality,' " says one veteran child interviewer, "but, if asked which teachers he likes and which he dislikes, he will be able to say."

The inverted-funnel technique makes getting answers from a former IRS agent as easy as taking candy from a baby, as Max Gunther found one wintry day in New York.

"When I walked into that interview, I wanted that ex-agent to tell me everything interesting that had ever happened to him in his tax-collecting job," recalls Gunther. "But how could I get him started? I *could* have asked a vague, general question: 'Has anything exciting ever happened to you in your IRS job?' But I didn't. It was too broad."

Instead, Gunther asked the revenooer to itemize: "When you were auditing people's tax returns, did anybody ever try to bribe you?"

"That question wound him up — in fact, very nearly overwound him," recalls Gunther. They talked for four hours. "I barely asked another question the whole time, and I came out of the interview with a wealth of fascinating material about the inner workings of IRS. My broad question — Did anything exciting ever happen? — had been fully answered without my asking it."

When shrewdly handled, the to-the-quick question can convince the subject that the interviewer speaks his lingo. A. J. Liebling, a legendary and acerbic journalist, said that one of his best preparations was for a profile of jockey Eddie Arcaro. Liebling brought some horse sense to the interview: "The *first question* I asked was, 'How many holes longer do you keep your left stirrup than your right?' That started him talking easily and after an hour, during which I had put in about 12 words, he said, 'I can see you've been around riders a lot.' "

How do you know whether to bet on a funnel or an inverted-funnel interview? Generally, if your subject is at home with words and ideas, lead him out with an open, general question. If he is ill at ease, make him comfortable with a question about the concrete, the easily explained.

The interviewer can establish rapport with open questions, then strengthen it with closed ones. The open question is like an essay question on a test: it gives the subject his head. "What do you think of Women's Liberation?" does not suggest a "yes" or "no" answer. It suggests an opinion; and the flattered subject would be hard put to withhold his.

The open question produces generalities, though, which are not enough to carry the story. In nonfiction, generalities whet the reader's appetite; he must be sated with anecdotes, details, hearty facts. So the interviewer must follow up an open question with closed questions — "Could you give me an example of that?" "What to you mean by . . .?"

Getting Anecdotes

Insist on anecdotes, although the subject may seem more comfortable spinning generalities. If he says, "I owe my 40 years of marriage to absolute understanding and compatibility," ask him, "What do you mean by understanding and compatibility? Can you give me some examples?"

Follow-up questions do more than secure specifics — they brace rapport. They indicate that you are genuinely curious about the subject's life and charred times. With sufficient rapport, the writer can even get away with a hard-bitten closed question. An interviewer asked George Frazier, the late and stylish columnist for the *Boston Globe*, "Which comes first — friendship or work?"

"That's phrasing it a little harshly," replied Frazier. He paused. "I make no bones about it. I'm a lonely man. The column precludes friendships."

A quote like that resurrects Frazier more acutely than a half-page of recitations in *Who's Who in America* ever could. "Your purpose in conducting an interview is partly to get facts," says Max Gunther, "but you also want color; you want anecdotes; you want quotes; you want material that will give readers an impression of the interviewee's personality."

Gunther gains color by structuring his interview loosely. He asks a few questions to get the interview rolling then sits back and allows the subject to tell his own story, at his own pace. Meanwhile, Gunther looks around. "If everything goes well, the starter questions wind him up like a clock, and I quietly fall back from the status of questioning to that of listener. If he omits some area of subject matter that I want to hear about, or if he explains something inadequately, I resist the temptation to interrupt him. I wait until he winds down, then wind him up again by asking the questions he has left unanswered."

One key word will incite anecdotes: when. "When did you realize you would need open-heart surgery?" Like a slow pan in a movie, "when" takes the subject to a scene, a setting, and thence to a story. The reporter's four other W's, of course, are also solicitors. "Where were you when you heard John F. Kennedy had been shot?" "Who told you your house was on fire?" "What are some of the most unusual questions children ask about sex?" "Why did you run away from home on Christmas Eve?"

"One way of obtaining anecdotes is to recite an anecdote you have already collected on the subject at hand," suggests Hal Higdon. "Often the person you're interviewing will respond to this challenge by trying to top you with a still better example." It may be unwise, however, for *you* to attempt to top your subject's anecdote.

The writer should never lose sight of The Definitive Anecdote, which he instinctively knows will give his article a rousing beginning or a thoughtful ending. "Quite often, in the course of interviews about a subject, the writer will stumble upon the single telling anecdote that either sums up the character or illumines one facet of it compellingly," wrote Richard Gehman. It may occur to him as soon as the research has begun, or during a follow-up phone call after the research has effectively ended. No matter. "If that anecdote 'feels' right," said Gehman, "he ought to write it at once and put it aside for later use."

Dumb Is Smart

To elicit eye-opening anecdotes — or eye-opening anything, for that matter — the interviewer does not have to impress his subject, to put on a natty and knowledgeable front. In fact, he may well learn that playing dumb is not dumb. "Stupidity is a reporter's greatest asset," said Cornelius Ryan. "Don't be afraid to say, 'I don't understand.' You'll be amazed at the help people are willing to give, once they know you are being honest with them."

And you may pay later if you feign understanding. "For fear the news source will think they are dumb or especially thick-headed, many beginning reporters fail to ask enough questions, even though they don't clearly understand what has been told them," says John P. Jones. "In such cases they may learn by bitter experience that the dumbest thing they can do is return to their office with unanswered questions in their minds."

When a subject rambles or is unclear in his answers, draw him out by putting the onus on yourself: "I'm sorry, but I don't understand"; "That's not quite clear to me. Could you give me an example?" If he still fumbles, move on to another topic, and try the original question later, from a different direction. Don't make the subject feel he is unable to get his point across, no matter how hard he tries.

Toward the end of the interview, if you still need an explanation of a certain point, volunteer a summary of what you think your subject has said, and ask him to correct you.

Openers Can Be Closers

Innocuous, even trivial questions at the outset can put the subject (and interviewer) at ease. "A human being likes to stick his toe into water that isn't cold," says Red Barber. "I always start with a pleasantry."

On the other hand, people who are busy, and who are likely to be interrupted by business during an interview, often prefer that the initial question get right to the point.

Regardless: nobody likes a smart-aleck — not even a professional smart-aleck. A *Rolling Stone* writer showed up for an interview with Don Imus, whose radio show is called *Imus in the Morning,* with dirty Levi's and a risky opener.

"Imus in the morning," he said, "I want you to meet Sidney in the flesh."

"It was downhill from there," recalls Imus.

The premeditated quip betrays a wily, merciless enemy of any exchange: the interviewer who is out to steal the show. He hangs out in multitudes at 1600 Pennsylvania Avenue, according to Dr. Joyce Brothers, who says this about Presidential press conferences:

Far too many of these questions are thought up on the way to the conference not for the purpose of getting information but in order to put the President on the spot or the reporter himself in the spotlight.

Even before he asks a question, body language betrays the newsman more interested in impressing the television audience than in pressing for information. He beams when the President calls him by name. He smiles broadly, squares his shoulders and adjusts his tie. These are the body signals of someone about to make a speech. And that is often what he does, under the guise of asking a question.

Dr. Brothers adds that at a televised press conference, questions weigh in at 50 words apiece, and are rarely related to the previous query. "When there are no cameras around, questions average 14 words and tend to develop one subject until probed in depth."

Less Is More

Which is not to say that hot camera lights alone spawn the filibuster question. It breeds wherever the interviewer gropes aloud, or is determined to hold the floor, and is mindless of the Law of Diminishing Returns: the longer the question, the shorter the reply.

And there is a point of no return. When one reporter persisted in asking George C. Marshall involved questions, Marshall said, "Would you mind repeating what you have just tried to say?" If you *must* ask a complicated question, and the subject seems puzzled, never ask, "Did you understand that?" Instead, ask "Did I make myself clear?" You don't want to seem condescending.

Keep your questions short, even if unsweet. If your question requires background, give it to your subject as concisely as possible, then keep your question short and separate from that pack of facts. "Busing means that thousands of white students will be attending predominantly black schools. (Pause.) How will you recruit those students?"

Don't short-circuit your interviewee: ask him one question at a time. I once asked Gay Talese a long-winded, two-part question in the midst of a discussion of celebrity interviews. "Sinatra is known as a man who is not very cooperative with journalists," I began, "and you say in your introduction to *Fame and Obscurity* that DiMaggio started to cooperate with you on the profile you wrote, then had a reversal. When this happens — when you run into someone like Sinatra who is insulated from journalists, or when you run into a reluctant subject like DiMaggio — how do you get in there close enough to do the story anyway?" Ouch.

"Let's take the Sinatra one first," began Talese — and, of course, the discussion of DiMaggio was bypassed. A two-part question is often like a baseball pitcher wasting a pitch: a discriminating batter just won't go for it.

Leading Them On

As the pitcher must peel off each pitch with studied skill, the interviewer must pick his words with care. The power of suggestion is too easy to trigger by a blunt or loaded phrase. Pollsters do not ask "How old are you?" — which invites a Jack Benny fib — but "What year were you born?" or "What is your date of birth?" Name-dropping may also color a reply. In 1940, when Charles Lindbergh was unpopular in America, the American Institute of Public Opinion asked subjects, "Lindbergh says that if Germany wins the war in Europe the United States should try to have friendly trade and diplomatic relations with Germany. Do you agree or disagree?" Forty-six percent agreed. The same question with "It has been suggested" replacing "Lindbergh says" garnered 57 percent agreement.

It is best to plan the wording of key questions with care. Few interviewers leave the wording to the stir of the moment; under battlefield conditions, the interviewer's prejudices may be irrepressible. If you are doing a story on a possible strike at the local pet food factory, you will have to interview some of the employees who might abandon their duties — and the Alpo generation — if union demands are unmet. You will want an untainted cross-section of opinion, because ultimately the decision to strike or not to strike will depend on the members' vote. A simple, carefully planned question like "Would you go on strike if a call is issued?" should do the trick. But a Johnny-on-the-spot interviewer with a secret sympathy may blurt, "As a member of the union, you would be obligated to go on strike if a call were issued, wouldn't you?" — which stops just short of answering itself.

That is, of course, a leading question, i.e., one that suggests the answer in tone, inflection or phrasing. The leading question may be more statement than question: "You don't care a fig about Roger Ackroyd, do you?" "Dr. Livingstone, I presume?" An interviewer who likes to lead when he asks may do so by merely using the definite article "the" rather than the indefinite "a": "Did you see *the* body?" instead of "Did you see a body?" is provocative.

Exactly what the leading question provokes may depend on the rapport the interviewer has established. A subject tiring of the interview may blurt something he does not mean; and an edgy subject may say something he means all too well. In a terse, talk-to-my-agent interview with Warren Beatty, Rex Reed began a question, "Well, then, would you say —"

"*No!*" Beatty cut in. "I wouldn't say. I only say what *I* say."

Alfred Kinsey, the D.A. of sexual research, was a proponent of leading questions, preferably served up in rapid-fire fashion. "The interviewer should not make it easy for a subject to deny his participation in any form of sexual activity," he wrote. "We always begin by asking when they first engaged in such activity."

When they are not gracefully abandoned, however, leading questions can deteriorate from bulldogging to badgering, and produce nonanswers. Consider this exchange between Theodore Irwin and *Playboy*'s Hugh Hefner, in *Cosmopolitan* magazine:

> *Irwin:* At what age do you believe a woman becomes undesirable to men?
> *Hefner:* There's no such age.
> *Irwin:* At what time? At what stage in her life?
> *Hefner:* It simply doesn't exist. In other words, it depends on the woman and it depends on the man.

Yet leading questions can also lead to lively, pointed quotes. Here's Hefner again in a robust bout with Mike Wallace:

> *Wallace: Chicago* magazine quoted you to the effect that sex will always be a primary ingredient of the magazine. Isn't that what you're really selling — kind of a high-class dirty book?
> *Hefner:* No, I don't think so at all. There's an important distinction here. Sex always will be an important part of the book, because sex is probably the single thing that men are most interested in . . . we think that's a healthy way to be. But I would estimate that no more than five percent of any issue of *Playboy* is concerned with sex, and we seem to be devoting an entire half-hour program to it here tonight. . . .
> *Wallace:* What's wrong with the muscular men's magazines?
> *Hefner:* Nothing at all. I think —
> *Wallace:* What's wrong with outdoor sports? With hunting and fishing and he-man adventure?
> *Hefner:* Not a thing. But I felt there was a good-sized male audience that was a little more interested in urban living — in the nice things about an apartment, hi-fi — wine, women and

song. And these are the things that *Playboy* concerns itself with.

The leading question requires a subject with a sense of spirit and fight — and an interviewer with a sense of timing. When injected into a touch-and-go exchange, it may disrupt rapport. But in secure surroundings, it may spark a surprisingly honest answer. The difference, perhaps, is in whether the subject sees his interviewer as close-minded or simply unpersuaded. The success of the leading question — and the success of much of interviewing — is a matter of trust, of rapport.

Off on a Tangent

Although the interviewer is in charge of the interview, there are times when he should follow his subject's lead. Following a tangent, for instance, is often more productive than trying to rein the subject back in. NBC's Red Barber once asked superslugger Willie Mays if he spent much time in the batting cage taking practice.

"I asked him this as the first question," recalls Barber, "just to start things smoothly. All players, even pitchers, love to hit. They won't give their mothers a swing in batting practice.

"I counted on Mays smiling and allowing as how he certainly did, and that this would break the ice and get us going. Instead, he replied to the effect that he hit well, so he didn't fool around the batting cage much, but spent his time working on what he didn't do 'good.'

"Well, we went on from there, for suddenly he had put his finger on one reason he is a star — he works on what, as he put it, 'I don't do good.' Let me say that I don't know today what Willie doesn't do very well, but that remark opened up a fine interview." Follow that tangent.

Follow-ups

Following up on a tidbit the subject dangles before you can also yield fine quotes. In a *Playboy* interview, Howard Cosell referred to Curt Gowdy as "the best play-by-play announcer in the business," then added, "Don't ask me who I think is the best color man in the business."

"Howard, who do think is the best color man in the business?" asked the interviewer.

"Thank you for not asking me," said Cosell. "I really believe *I'm* the best, for I have sought to bring to the American people a sense of the athlete as a human being and not as a piece of cereal-box mythology. My relationship with the men who play the game — *all* games — is probably unparalleled in this country, and I bring information about them to the public."

One of the most potent follow-up questions is a nonquestion: the Sympathetic Noise. "You feel very strongly about that, don't you?" "Sounds like you had a tough time of it, cleaning barrooms." On its face, the Sympathetic Noise may seem to do little but stall the subject until the interviewer can think up a *real* question. Actually, it takes account of the fact that subjects, like human beings at large, are cautious soul-barers; they are reluctant to confess until they have proof positive that their interviewer is sympathetic. (Then they are all too willing.) The Sympathetic Noise — which is often simply reinforcement, or a gentle rephrasing of what the subject has just said — can unlatch a torrent of anecdotes and naked quotes.

William J. Lederer (coauthor of *The Ugly American*) recalls the time he told his interviewer, Frank Ensign, of "some little thing I had done."

Ensign lifted his eyes with surprise. "Honest?" he said enthusiastically. "Did you do that? Gee, that's wonderful."

Says Lederer: "I thought, here's a guy who understands my problems. I shot off my mouth for two hours, telling him things I never planned to tell him."

Sure-fire Openers

You can also persuade a reluctant interviewee to change his plans by feeding him a Day-in-the-Life question. "Whenever I sense that the interview has hit an unresponsive snag and I am stuck with an inarticulate interviewee," says Mort Weisinger, "I resort to a gambit which has worked wonders. I simply say, 'Mr. Jones, could you describe to me what you do on a typical day in your life, from the moment you get up until going to sleep at night?' Brother, does this question move mountains!"

Even small talk can move mountains. A tired, almost trivial question can pry open the soul of a politician, for instance, if it hits home. "Ask him how he handles the risk of disappointment when campaigning for office," advises Barbara Walters. "We've all wanted something desperately, but only the daring or the tough try for it so publicly. Ask him about the pressure on his family to be model people because all eyes are on them. Ask him if he was a leader when he was a small boy. Ask him what taught him the most about succeeding in life. Ask him if politicians with opposite views ever become close friends. Ask if he feels an obligation to be trim, neat, and barbered at all times. Ask him if he can manage the time to have a hobby. Ask if he has a hero."

Sounds from Silence

Don't interrupt your subject, unless his house is burning or you are running out of time. Barbara Walters, who is not too shy to cut into a subject's ramblings if time is short, introduced Mercedes McCambridge on the *Today* show as a fine actress who once had been an alcoholic. "Not *was* an alcoholic," said McCambridge. "*Is* an alcoholic." She then delivered a moving monologue on her battle with the bottle, consuming the entire time slot. At the conclusion, Walters spoke for the first time since the introduction: "Thank you, Miss McCambridge."

Silence is golden as an interviewing technique. "The single most interesting thing that you can do in television, I find, is to ask a good question and then let the answer hang there for two or three or four seconds as though you're expecting more," says Mike Wallace. "You know what? They get a little embarrassed and give you more."

Silence by omission can elicit information perhaps impervious to the most pointed query. Kap Monohan, a drama critic for the *Pittsburgh Press,* once heard a rumor that Clara Bow — the "It" girl of films — was going to retire at the height of her popularity to marry and raise a family. When the head of Bow's studio came within Monohan's range, the writer boned up on his man and requested an interview.

"How are Patti and Connie?" Monohan asked as they shook hands. The man's face lit up at the mention of his granddaughters.

Then Monohan ticked off the names of the stars the man had discovered — purposely omitting one.

"You forgot Clara Bow," the studio head said. "You've heard about her retiring, I guess?"

"Oh, yes, but that's a lot of hooey — press agent stuff." Monohan tried to change the subject, but his subject was insistent.

"If you think she's not quitting, you're crazy," he finally said. "She is."

By the end of the interview, Monohan had a world exclusive on Clara Bow — without asking a single question about her.

Taking Stock Questions

Finally on follow-up: pursue the details, but don't run them into the ground. "If you make a man stop to explain everything," wrote A. J. Liebling, "he will soon quit on you, like a horse that you alternately spur and curb."

Some subjects, of course, curb themselves at the drop of a pretext. You: "How do you spell your last name:" He: "Talk to my lawyer." This is the Difficult Subject. He is stingy in stories and spirit. He requires special handling.

Often the Difficult Subject requires no more than an open-minded interviewer. "Interviewers are like actors," Warren Beatty, notorious as an impregnable subject, told Lawrence Grobel. "An interviewer can ask you a cliché question, but you can tell what he's either capable of hearing or what he's really searching for by his inflections. You can almost tell physically what someone is going to intend to do to you by his face, his body type or his body language. And most interviewers have their story written when they show up, and they want you to do something to prove they're right or to fill it in for them."

Celebrities are often drained by the persistent, yapping pack of stock questions. "It's always the same old stuff," laments Ava Gardner. " 'Tell us about the dancing on the table tops. Tell us about the bullfighters. Tell us about Sinatra.' God, haven't any of them got any imagination at all?"

Maybe not. But they do have teem spirit. Billie Jean King: "Before the Riggs thing I had 300 people who wanted exclusive interviews. And each of them wanted at least a few hours. So a few hours times 300 was ten years as far as I was concerned. That's the trouble. And when you interview all the time, people keep asking you about your feelings. How did it feel to do this? How did it feel to do that? I want to get away from it. I want to get out of myself."

Moral: Know thy subject — and know her/his predicament. Avoid prime-time interviewing — the first days after an Event, when the subject is waylaid by cameras and clamor, when he will dispose of interviews like Colonel Sanders shoveling out chicken parts. Avoid questions that leap too easily to mind; they have lept to too many minds before.

Concentrate on the celebrity not as a celebrity, but as a human being. That is a novel angle, for the celebrity as well as the reader. And it produces. *Boston Globe* columnist Bud Collins tells of the cold, morose night at a deserted Toronto race track in 1961 when he and George Frazier combed the barns for Floyd Patterson. The heavy-weight champion was hiding out before his bout with Tom McNeely.

"Floyd was as talkative as Mona Lisa," recalls Collins. "But George, wincing at the strains of Mantovani from Patterson's record player, got the champion talking. About music. About jazz when he spotted a Charlie Parker album. . . . George, who had known Parker and began to tell stories about 'Bird,' got the album on. 'Repetition' was playing. Floyd dug the strings behind Parker's sax. He talked. We both got good stories."

Whimsy works, as Barbara Walters found when she interviewed Sir Laurence Olivier. She had recently taped an interview with Lord Lambton — a member of Parliament who had been caught in bed with two women — when she went to see Olivier. "I knew Sir Laurence was a shy man, hard to interview," recalls Walters in her excellent *How to Talk With Practically Anybody About Practically Anything.* "So when I met him I said, 'Sir Laurence, I'm afraid I didn't have time to write my questions, so I'm going to ask you all the questions I asked Lord Lambton.' He burst out laughing, and everything went fine after that. We spent the day together. He talked about his childhood, his insecurity. And he finally read a Milton poem. It was a love poem, and I looked at his wife and there were tears rolling down her face.

" 'Are you crying?' I asked, and she said, 'I always do this when he reads.' "

Sure-fire, Guaranteed Questions (Maybe)

Walters once revealed to the *New York Times* her five "foolproof" questions for the over-interviewed:

1. If you were recuperating in a hospital, who would you want

in the bed next to you, excluding relatives?
2. What was your first job?
3. When was the last time you cried?
4. Who was the first person you ever loved?
5. What has given you the most pleasure in the last year?

Walters says that question three is "an especially good one for comedians. They're hard to interview because you're always the straight man."

When the *Times* asked Walters how she would answer her foolproof questions, though, she demurred, "Uh, well ... I don't think I want to. It would take too long to think of some good answers." (Which may confirm that the most difficult interviewees are often interviewers.)

Walters' foolproof question #1, and many similar icebreaker questions, are hypothetical. And the interviewer skates at his own risk.

Walters recalls the time she asked Prince Philip of Great Britain if, in the event England elected a president, he would have enjoyed being a politician. Philip replied, without warmth, that this was a hypothetical question, which he normally didn't answer.

"I was crushed," says Walters, "but I learned a valuable lesson about talking to people in very high places: avoid the hypothetical question, of the sort that usually begins 'What if ...' and then departs into some fanciful situation that never happened and never will. That type of question can be asked of creative people, for whom imaginary situations are intriguing, but practical, crisp people dismiss it as a waste of time."

When the subject is inventive and in the mood, however, hypothetical questions are fecund. Kenneth Tynan asked Richard Burton, "If you had your life to live over again, would you change anything?" — a question that is as worn out as vaudeville. But Burton's reply was fresh and revealing: "I'd like to be born the son of a duke with 90,000 pounds a year, on an enormous estate. . . . And I'd like to have the most enormous library, and I'd like to think that I could read those books forever and forever, and die unlamented, unknown, unsung, unhonored — and *packed* with information."

Tynan's *Playboy* interview ended, in fact, with a string of hypothetical questions:

Tynan: You meet a man at the end of the world, and he asks you three questions which you have to answer spontaneously and immediately. The first is: Who are you?

Burton: Richard, son of Richard — for I am both my father and my son.

Tynan: The second question is: Apart from that, who are you?

Burton: Difficult, devious and perverse.

Tynan: And the third is: Apart from *that,* who are you?

Burton: A mass of contradictions. As Walt Whitman said, "Do I contradict myself? Very well, I contradict myself. I am large, and I contain multitudes."

There are multitudes of hypothetical questions, most of them of the office party strain. Some that may work in the rare, playful interview are:

What three books (records, movies, Presidents) would you take with you if you were stranded on an island?

If you were fired from your present job, what sort of work would you undertake?

If you could live any time in history, what age would you choose?

If you could be anyone you wanted to be today, whom would you be, and what would you do?

If someone gave you a million dollars, how would you spend it?

If your house were afire, what would you grab on the way out?

Such questions may not set an interview on fire — particularly with a Difficult Subject — but they should elicit an irreverent, penetrating detail which will enliven your article. Of course, you can gather such sparks with more direct and realistic questions. Mrs. Dorothy Schiff, publisher and editor-in-chief of the *New York Post,* once suggested these human interest questions:

What person influenced you most in life? What book, if any?

What do you do for relaxation?

What was your greatest opportunity?

What do you believe about people — can they be changed for better or for worse?

Indeed, a question about beliefs can be an intriguing icebreaker. "One thing I have found out is that almost any person will talk freely — such is human frailty — if you ask him the measure of his own accomplishment," said John Gunther. "One effective question is to ask a man what he believes in most; I have collected an interesting anthology of answers to this."

Above all: ask. Pursue the blind alleys; voice your human — as well as professional — curiosities. Ask intriguing, innumerable questions, with enthusiasm and only civil restraint. In the end, interviewing is less a technique than an instinct. An interview is simply a lively and thoughtful conversation. The more life and thought you invest in your questions, the more answers you'll get.

5. Getting Tough

*Brian, they say you're a pug, a patsy, a
dirty fighter, that you have no class, that
you're just in there for the ride and fast
pay day and that you have no chance against
Ali. Now what do you say to that?*

—*Howard Cosell
to boxer Brian London*

Getting tough in an interview means never having to say you're
sorry that you didn't get the story. The importance of being sternest
can be overemphasized, however. Most interviews are conversations,
not inquisitions, and rarely call for hard questions. Even when an
interviewer must be tough, he needn't be cruel. "Do a little needling
on interviews," Humphrey Bogart once advised a beginning Hollywood writer (notice that word — *little*). "The best technique is to
make tiny pricks in the subject's ego and let him expel hot air slowly.
Don't go plunging toward a main artery. That only provokes their
hostility. That's neither gentlemanly nor bright."

"A reputation for asking tough questions is a reputation I like to
have," says Dan Rather, CBS's iron newsman. "A reputation for being
an antagonist is one I avoid. I don't court that at all."

The interviewer, then, is not the loyal opposition — he's the skeptical
observer. His purpose is not to provoke the famous into furies, but
to dig behind the story for its meaning. If he fails to ask tough questions
when he must, then he is risking the fate of many smalltown journalists
who serve as news clerks rather than newsmen.

He might think that a reputation as a Man of Steel might scare
subjects away — like a stick suddenly thrust into a stagnant pool
of fish. Actually, a tough reputation might reel some subjects in.

Tough Guys Finish First

"I have found that if you have a reputation for being a tough interviewer, for doing people in, that can be an advantage," says Richard Reeves, "because many public figures are bored with the reporters they deal with all the time. And they always think that they can take you. Which is one of the reasons they talk to people you think they wouldn't talk to. They enjoy the challenge." Perhaps.

"People are always asking me why I don't give more interviews," says actress Ava Gardner. "The answer is simple; I'm tired of all the lies that have been written about me. The last time I trusted an interviewer, Rex Reed, he crucified me." "Did she say I misquoted her?" Reed asks. "No. She merely said I crucified her, which in my opinion, I did not. I have no defense or explanation to make. The Ava Gardner piece stands on its own. Every word of it is true and it was written in as flattering a way as it is possible to write something when the subject will not let you ask questions, take notes or give any semblance of a dignified interview. Also, she was completely drunk."

Writers known as tough interviewers usually get ahead. Rex Reed's early reputation was as the "hatchet man" or the "enfant terrible" of show business writers, mostly because of his incisive interviews for the Sunday *New York Times* and *Esquire* magazine. Barbara Walters has become the best-known woman journalist on TV chiefly because of her tough approach to interviewing — "asking the question your mother said never to ask," as *Newsweek* put it. After Walters asked Mamie Eisenhower if she was aware of the longstanding rumor that she was a dipsomaniac, friends asked the interviewer, "How could you have asked?" Says Walters: "I find very often people like to confront rumors. It depends on how much they trust you. And you have to have a line between what is tasteful and what isn't." (In the case of Mamie Eisenhower, it turned out the former First Lady had an inner-ear infection that made her appear woozy on occasion.)

But generally, television interviewing seems more like gentlemanly exercise than hand-to-hand combat. "One of the things that happens when you're in front of a TV [camera] is that the person is always aware that the set is there," says Sally Quinn. "After I left CBS I did an interview for the *Washington Post* with Alice Roosevelt Longworth, and she really told me a lot of things. She talked to me about her lesbian experiences when she was a young girl and discussed various parts of the male body. She was very open, and Hughes Rudd, who was my co-anchor on CBS, called me the morning the piece ran. He said, 'Jesus Christ, why didn't you have a camera in there?' and 'We should have had that on CBS' and 'That's the kind of stuff you should have been doing.' And I said, 'Hughes, she never would have said those things to me in front of a camera, are you kidding?' That's one of the big differences."

Tough Becomes Hostile

Whether it appears on the tube or in the tabloids, the more probing an interview, the more likely it is that an interviewer will have to get tough. "The Q&A interview is one of the oldest ideas in the world," says Murray Fisher. "The point is, how three-dimensional, how wide-ranging, how in-depth do you go? Our *Playboy* interviews are long personality interviews for the most part. We are trying to find out what makes people tick — what makes them do what they do, what makes them the way they are. We devote the space necessary to reveal someone as totally as possible, and our approach is very probing, very psychoanalytical, tough and persevering." Fisher says that over the years *Playboy* interviewers have gotten better at zeroing in on a subject "through searching and sometimes relentless interrogation — to the point where the subjects reveal themselves." He calls this kind of interviewing an "exhaustively psychoanalytic technique," explaining: "If you've ever been in analysis, the doctor often lets you fill whatever vacuum he creates by his own silence. He will be a passive repository, a blank slate. Sometimes he will pose leading questions to elicit a defensive response, and in this way peel off the onion skins of your facade, your self-image. When you've run out of onion skins, you're left sometimes with a pulsating nerve, or at least a glimpse of the truth about someone. Then you can *begin* to get at really substantive matters."

Some interviewers make the mistake of striking directly for the pulsating nerve. Ask Sally Quinn, who has been on both sides of the "tough" interview — notably during the period she served as co-host for the *CBS Morning News*. "I was being interviewed and I had gotten a lot of bad publicity and the people who came to interview me, having read the things about me, decided they didn't like me before they ever met me," Quinn remarked during an A. J. Liebling Counter Convention panel discussion. "And so they would come on very hostile, I mean really vicious. It was like, you're guilty until proven innocent. They'd sort of attack me with the first question — what makes you think you're so hot, sweetheart? My reaction was to close up immediately. They weren't going to get anything out of me at all and none of those interviews ever came out giving the reader any idea of what I was like because I was very terse and not at all open."

Love-Hate Relationships

Some writers get tough with a subject they *like*. It's an overcompensation, perhaps; a declaration of journalistic independence. To know him is to be tough on him. In a 1972 press conference, for example, George McGovern accused local Republicans of bribing Spanish-American voters to stay away from the polls in Chicago. Reporter Jim Naughton, of the *New York Times,* had voted for McGovern for President by absentee ballot a few days earlier, and was a True Believer; yet he raised his hand and said, "Senator, you've made a fairly serious charge about Republican involvement in this nefarious activity, but you haven't given any details and you haven't told us where details can be obtained. As a student of history, how do you distinguish what you are doing from what Joseph McCarthy used to do?"

There were groans and glances as McGovern stumbled for a reply. Afterward, McGovern's press secretary Dick Dougherty expressed chagrin at the question. At the time, Naughton thought the McCarthy question was a fair one. Later, though, he wondered about its tough tone. "In looking back on it," he told Tim Crouse, "I wonder whether I would have been as cutting, as direct and as vicious in my question if I had not voted for McGovern a couple of days before. I think I may have been tougher on McGovern after that."

Forget your ballot; forget your preconceptions. An interviewer should only get tough when he thinks he can get *somewhere* — or get an answer that the subject wasn't prepared to give. "Obviously a key goal of an interview, whether it's on television or in newspapers, magazines or books, is to get the interviewee to say something that he or she is not prepared to say," says Nat Hentoff, "and sometimes to say something that he or she may not really have thought about, or thought out clearly and that would be terribly revealing if it finally comes out. Those are memorable moments in interviews that work. I'm always fascinated by how journalists do this."

No Comment

What makes an interviewer tough? Situations. Most writers get tough when a subject refuses to answer questions. Office rules for a Connecticut newspaper, for instance, say: "We are to tell the public WHY no statement of [the interviewee's] appears. We are to state that he refused to talk; that he was in New York for the weekend; he refused to come to the telephone; the reporter rang his doorbell but the house was dark and there was no response to the bell. Loose reporting is poor reporting. The specific statement is what makes good work."

Thus, if a subject refuses to give a specific statement, the interviewer is under pressure to obtain one — and he gets tough. When a subject refuses to answer a question, veteran feature writer Jim Carty uses persistence. "I insist, explaining that my editor will send me back with a repeat of the question," he says. "I point out the gap can be more damaging since it can lead to rumor or speculation. If the person still declines to answer, I attempt to find the answer from his friends or other associates. Sometimes I come back to the person with another interview. This doesn't always obtain desired results, but it produces more answers than simply 'no comments.' "

Whenever Lowell Limpus of the *New York News* ran into a kindly but persistent "No comment," he tried to prod the subject into losing his temper, "resorting even to direct insult as a last desperate measure. If that doesn't work, I'm licked."

With tough subjects, getting tough means getting ready to be put down. Sander Vanocur interviewed Rita Hayworth at 50, and wondered if an aging sex goddess, who once had it, and who now found it hard to get work in Hollywood, didn't regret not having it any more. "Do you miss the attention?" Vanocur asked. "No, because I didn't like it when I had it," replied Rita.

Vanocur: "How is a sex goddess manufactured?"

"That's impossible to tell unless you have several hours."

"I have."

Rita, testily: "Well, I haven't."

Truth, Lies, Consequences

Sometimes interviewees you would suppose to be hostile are helpful instead. William Manchester divides subjects into Friendlies and Unfriendlies — using espionage terminology. "With the Unfriendlies," he says, "you get unexpected cooperation, partly because people are compulsive talkers, or because they think they can straighten you out, and mostly because if they realize that you've done your research you are going ahead anyhow. And so they think they may be able to help you, and very often they can, though in ways that are not evident to them." He adds: "Sometimes, you get a very hostile person, and this can be a real workout ... and it is important to retain the professionalism of the interview. You don't quarrel. You don't introduce color words. You ask questions that are as objective and detached as possible. I'm not one of those who believe that you can lie your way to the truth. You present yourself as exactly what you are, and you play it dead straight."

Still, one method of getting information from a tough subject is to imply that you know more about the situation than you actually do. A *Wall Street Journal* reporter, for instance, once tried to get a difficult source to admit he had invested in a particular project. His research for the interview included an unconfirmed report that the subject had invested $77,000. "How did you happen to invest $77,000 in the XYZ project?" he asked the subject. "The figure happened to be accurate," said the *Journal's* managing editor afterward, "and the man being interviewed assumed the reporter knew a good deal more than he did about the investment. Consequently, he offered an explanation as to why he had made the investment. If the reporter had simply asked, 'Did you invest in the XYZ project?' the chances are overwhelming that the man would have denied making the investment."

When Jessica Mitford was doing research on her article "Let Us Now Appraise Famous Writers School," she found that "the Famous ones" were "understandably reticent" on the delicate question of money. "That's a private matter," Bennett Cerf told her. Yet when she asked Phyllis McGinley about a report that each member of the Guiding Faculty received an annual stipend of $4400, the housewife poet replied: "Oh? — Well, I may have a price on my soul, but it's not *that* low; we get a lot more than that!" And Mitford got a good

interview for her article. Posture is all. "Often a person can be induced
to give facts by questions which make him believe the reporter has
wrong information which he'll use if not corrected," says Curtis
MacDougall. "From fear of having a wrong impression broadcast,
he may open up and tell the truth."

Pals and Paranoids

Some veteran interviewees open up wide, reasoning to themselves,
"He won't quote me — he's too much like me." Well, now. "I find
I love to interview liberal Democrats," says political reporter Richard
Reeves. "They always deny it in public, but they believe what Pat
Buchanan said: that we reporters are all one of them. So, the liberal
Democrats will often give you an extraordinary amount because they
think you are going to protect them — as women subjects now give
women interviewers more information because they think they will
be protected. Maybe they are sometimes; but they aren't all the time.
And politicians often think because they perceive your political
position to be close to theirs that they can tell you things and you'll
protect them; well, tough bananas, baby."

Yet getting tough does not mean getting mean. When C. Robert
Jennings, whose "first and lastingest love" is the theatre, was sent
by *Playboy* to interview playwright Tennessee Williams, he found
"a highly private and complex human being with his poetic if not
his personal madness under control." Jennings also came to know
that Williams held with André Gide's warning: "Do not understand
me too quickly." The interviewer met the playwright backstage after
the final performance of Williams' *Small Craft Warnings*. At first,
after an introduction by Williams' manager Bill Barnes, Jennings was
greeted warmly; but then Jennings, thinking that Williams was
somewhat uneasy, began talking about the play (in which the author
had acted). "I asked him if he was a ham," recalls Jennings. He looked
at me with malevolence and flashed: 'And who are *you?*' Then to
Barnes: 'Who *is* this?' Bristling, I countered: 'I'm the guy who just
crossed a continent to see you, with your OK. We just met.' 'Mmm,'
he muttered and wandered uncertainly away."

At their first lunch, Williams was 45 minutes late and made no
apology. "Knowing that he drinks mostly wine, I asked if he'd like
a cold dry white," recalls Jennings. Without looking up from the menu,

Williams snapped, "I think that all depends on what we're eating, don't you?" By Jennings' third day in New York, the interviewer was about to split, when somehow he engaged the playwright's confidence. "Though still paranoid, he suddenly dropped his guard and became warm, open, courtly, hospitable, funny — and piteously vulnerable," says Jennings. "He never spoke off the record. For Williams, having virtually stripped himself naked in his work, no longer has anything to hide. He is an open wound." Jennings spent the next six days interviewing Williams after the playwright invited him to fly to New Orleans with him. The resulting interview, with intimacies on Williams' homosexuality, was one of the toughest in *Playboy* history. Murray Fisher approved.

Courtesy counts — even when you're toughening up. Music writer Todd Everett prides himself in that he has never "blown" an interview — though he does occasionally get "antagonistic" with a subject. How so? "I think there's a difference between coming in on somebody and saying, 'Where do you get off being a superstar? What qualifies you to be one?' and saying 'You've done so well in the past. How did you screw up the last album?',", says Everett. "There's a whole lot of difference. That's the sort of approach I use. It usually is sincere and civil, without being insulting or pandering. They are, as I am, just people doing a job."

Easy on the Neo

The tough interviewer owes especial consideration to the neophyte interviewee. "The writer must remember that the interviewee may be frightened," says Helen Patterson, "because many people hold writers, even beginners, in great reverence, if not awe." On the other hand, the interviewee with little experience may be suspicious. "The novice about to be interviewed for the first time," says veteran reporter Henry F. Pringle, "assumes that all reporters are ghouls waiting for the emergence of the family skeleton." Regardless, people unaccustomed to being interviewed deserve consideration by the writer, and ground rules should be explained. "After all, you are very experienced in what you're doing, and they're totally inexperienced," says Richard Reeves. "Because of that, you owe them a lot more than you owe a public figure."

Sally Quinn agrees. The writer once spent three days with a

Washington, D.C. policeman for a story. "He had never been interviewed before and he was scared to death," recalls Quinn. "He didn't know how to deal with me and I decided the best way to do it would be to set the ground rules first. . . . I explained to him about off the record and not for attribution and all of that, and I made him explain it back to me so he would understand what I meant. And then I said, OK, now you're on your own. I think that's only fair. With public figures, though, it's too bad if they don't know the rules by now. Then it's their problem, I think."

No Bridge Too Far

Often a gun-shy subject will agree to an interview only if limits are placed on what is to be discussed. With such subjects, you do not get tough; you get subtle. Henry Ford had not done a national interview for 18 years when he agreed to an interview with Barbara Walters — saying he would talk only about the rebuilding of downtown Detroit, a favorite Ford project. "I agreed on that basis, but I knew that if that was all he was going to talk about I would have no interview when it was over," says Walters. Consequently, the interviewer prepared 30 questions; and once the rebuilding project was out of the way, she began, "Mr. Ford, we're talking about a business proposition which is also a social undertaking, which brings up the whole matter of the social responsibilities." With this word-bridge, Walters recalls going on for 90 minutes interviewing "about the problems of the auto industry, what he thought of Ralph Nader and, finally, at the end, the sensitive personal questions."

Barbara Walters is an expert at using the word-bridge to cross from routine ground to an off-limits area. When President Nixon told her he wanted to talk about his wife on her birthday, Walters said yes — but later confided to a reporter, "I couldn't talk about her for 40 minutes. So I had to figure out how I would go from that to Vietnam to marijuana and some other things. After a while, as we sat there on the couch, I said, 'We've talked about your family, Mr. President, now let's talk about the problems besetting the American family." And Nixon did.

Easing into the toughies is a demanding — and foxy — technique. Jessica Mitford uses what she calls the "kind-to-cruel" approach. "You simply let your subject take all the time he wants to tell you his story," she explains. "And then, when he'e not really expecting it, you slip in your real questions." In the research for her Famous Writers School exposé, for example, her visit to the School's Connecticut headquarters "all began pleasantly enough, but by the end of the day the school executives were on the ropes." The chief reason for this is the extensive preparation that Mitford pours into an interview:

> In this case it was things like how many salesmen did they have and who were their published graduates. They gave me their school quarterlies, which contained students' work and success stories. I noticed that their advertising sometimes repeated student testimonials, and sometimes they were from people who'd been in the course years before. So I called a few of those people. Also I went to their flossy-glossy Madison Avenue ad agency, and got all their financial reports, which were public because they were traded on the stock market. So, by the time I had an interview with Bennett Cerf, I knew more about the actual operation of the school than he did, although he was head of the faculty.

"When painful areas have to be approached, one might use the analogy of trying to find a passage in a ship through a rocky channel," says psychiatrist John Rich. "Some of the rocks are evident and can be avoided. The submerged ones can be foreseen by taking soundings and changing course when the water suddenly becomes shallow. By making a series of approaches from different directions, it is possible to map out the shallow areas and predict with reasonable accuracy where the dangerous rocks below the surface are. An interviewer uses the same sort of technique when he approaches each submerged problem from a different direction and in that way delineates the whole sensitive area."

The Bishop and the Recorder

Rich's analogy would be appreciated by veteran interviewer Alex Haley, who asks tough questions when the subject has been put at ease. "You soften him, while you prepare for the tough ones," Haley told John Behrens. "I may put the tough questions to him in a different setting. We go for rides or go to lunch ... sometimes I go with [my subjects] when they make speeches or that sort of thing. We exchange stories. . . . This helps keep the interview on a personal level." Another Haley suggestion for working with a difficult subject is to "interview by day and study what has been said by night. Listen to the tape and you learn what to explore the next day and you know more about the type of question which evokes more response from the person. You can get a subject — a famous person or hard-to-interview subject — to the point where you can play on them like a harp. You know what evoked what from them. Lull them, make them a little mad, back away — really, it is like conducting an orchestra. The approach is not determined by me, it's determined by the person. It is what you infer from your meetings with this person. You let them set the pattern."

For sensitive topics, Haley likes to "catch people in soft moments." He adds a dramatic flourish for the occasion: "Dispense with whatever you're using to record the interview visibly before you go on. If you are writing notes, put down the pad and pencil so that the person can see it. Try to approach it in a relaxed way. He may tell you he doesn't want to talk about it. I have had that happen. Later, you may find that they may bring it up themselves and tell you more than you expected. It depends on how you feel them out."

"Sometimes it is helpful, when you have just been refused a piece of information, to shift at once to something else, going right on as if you had received what you wanted," says Hayes Jacobs. "Later, you return to the critical topic. In a new context, and after having had more time to think about it, your subject may yield to your request."

One of the toughest questions that Haley ever had to ask arose during his interview with Bishop James Pike for *Playboy* — which took place shortly after the subject's son had committed suicide. "We were sitting by the pool at his home in Santa Barbara when I kind of moved into the area of talking about his son," recalls Haley. "I could tell that Bishop Pike wasn't his usual flowing self when we started on it. I began to back away — it wasn't what he said but a kind of psychic thing. I could feel he was tightening up." Suddenly there was an interruption: Haley had to change the tape on the recorder. The interruption reduced the strain for both men.

"Now we should say something here about Jim, Jr.," Haley said to Bishop Pike as the fresh tape began. "The machine is on, so you just go ahead." Then the interviewer excused himself and went to his car, ostensibly for cigarettes, leaving the recorder on. "I started to run back when I saw him, from a distance, bent over the mike," recalls Haley. "He looked like he was communing with it — and suddenly I realized that if you leave a person with a question and a recorder, after he is used to the machine and used to you, you'll get from him something he perhaps wouldn't say to you or even to himself. I played back that section later and I was so moved by the way he went into that answer. He was feeling into himself. It was the kind of thing that came from his being — not his intellect."

Tough Techniques

Tough questions are often as difficult to ask as to answer. When Barbara Walters asked Senator Tom Eagleton, who already had tears in his eyes, what he told his son about resigning the Vice Presidential nomination, she later reflected: "I don't think I'm a tough interviewer. I think I'm gentle. Tough interviewers don't get people to come on their shows — not more than once anyway." Then: "The Eagleton question was a sensitive one, yes. But I prefaced it with some cushioning words. The 'people-are-saying' line that means 'This isn't Barbara Walters who is attacking you, Senator.' "

How do you ask an embarrassing question? Allen Barton's classic guide for asking "Did you kill your wife?" may be of some assistance:

The Casual Approach: "Do you happen to have murdered your wife?"

The Everybody Approach: "As you know, many people have been killing their wives these days. Do you happen to have killed yours?"

The "Other People" Approach: (a) "Do you know any people who have murdered their wives?" (b) "How about yourself?"

The Kinsey Technique: Stare firmly into respondent's eyes and ask in simple, clear-cut language such as that to which the respondent is accustomed, and with an air of assuming that everyone has done everything, "Did you ever kill your wife?"

Some real suggestions for asking tough questions:

1. *Blame someone else for the question.* Indicate that other people have what might be considered a frowned-upon opinion, and serve up the question as though it were an opportunity for the subject to answer his critics. When Barbara Walters was interviewing the Shah of Iran, she used this approach. "Your Majesty," she began,

"there are people who say you are a dictator, a benevolent dictator perhaps, but a dictator all the same. I know you have heard these criticisms. This is your opportunity to answer them."

"Yes, I have heard them," the Shah replied — and Walters pursued her tough line of questioning. "They're always aware of what's being said about them," Walters later recalled in *TV Guide.* "And they usually welcome a chance to answer."

When Barbara Walters interviewed Richard Nixon, she used the occasion for a similar polite but provocative line of questioning — "There has been a lot of talk, Mr. President," began one question, "about your image and the fact that the American public — forgive me, Mr. President — sees you as a rather stuffy man. . . ."

2. *Imply that the question is a playful one.* "I'd like to play the devil's advocate for a moment" is a neutral introduction for a tough question that often works.

3. *Preface the question with some praise.* "The movie seems certain to win several Academy awards, Mr. Beatty — and your own performance has been highly praised by nearly all the critics. Except, perhaps, John Simon, who says. . . ."

4. *Use separate, apparently disconnected questions.* The two-part approach means asking a subject "At what age do you think a girl should be able to start dating?" and later asking, "When did your parents allow you to date?" The answer to the first question may be "Fourteen," while the reply to the second is "Sixteen." The subject may see no conflict in these replies, yet may deny that there is a conflict between her parents and herself if the question were put to her directly.

Sometimes, however, a side-door approach using disconnected questioning may turn out to have been unnecessary. When Todd Everett was interviewing singer Anne Murray, he wanted to get into a discussion of her avid lesbian following, but did not know how to approach her on it. "I'm sure she was aware of her fans," said the writer, "but beyond that there was a question as to whether or not she's a lesbian. If she was, or even if she wasn't, I thought she would be sensitive about that question. I didn't want to appear anti-gay. I'm not. But I didn't want to say anything to be construed that way — for fear of offending her either way. So I thought back to the last time I had seen her perform live, and how every woman in the audience looked like her. They might have been shorter, they might have been taller, they might have had a different hair color — but there was just something about them that was very cohesive. It looked like a roomful of Anne Murrays.

"It was sort of scary, and I asked her if she ever noticed it — if she had the slightest idea what I was talking about. She said, 'Yeah, I have a lot of lesbian fans.' I don't know how that connects, but then we talked about it. She went on to say that she is not a lesbian, and that at first her following kind of scared her, but she had talked with Helen Reddy and Peggy Lee, for instance, both of whom had similar followings, and neither of whom is lesbian — and that she had conditioned herself out of that old attitude and now she welcomed all her fans. In the end, she was glad to talk about it, but it took quite a while to get the proper approach to the topic because Anne Murray is a celebrity, but she keeps her private life very, very private."

5. *Use jargon when it is available for sensitive topics.* Kinsey and his colleagues found that numerous euphemisms are used in discussing sex-related topics. "Have you ever had venereal disease?" might get a "no" reply, but "Have you ever had bad blood?" might get a "yes."

Maurice Lezneff, a sociologist, found that a good way to build rapport at the beginning of interviews with homosexuals was to ask the subject for help in compiling a list of terms used by homosexuals. The topic, therefore, was language — an almost clinical approach to a sensitive topic, homosexuality. In addition to learning the vocabulary he needed to know, the interviewer was able to begin the interview without any of the awkwardness that can result when a stranger asks about one's sexual preferences.

6. *Your best bet: ask the question in a matter-of-fact manner, no matter how sensitive the area.* Until 1970 the brilliant playwright Tennessee Williams never talked openly about his homosexuality. Then he was asked matter-of-factly by television host David Frost if he were a homosexual. "I was very embarrassed," reflected Williams afterward. "I said, 'I cover the waterfront.' [Frost] called a station break, mercifully, and I said, 'I should think you *would*.' And the audience gave me an ovation." Still, despite the subject's embarrassment, Frost's straightforward delivery produced the candid reply — which led to subsequent discussions by Williams on the topic in *Esquire* and *Playboy* magazines.

Asking questions about one's love life is working a High Risk area — particularly if you pussyfoot into it. When Herb Sargent and some people from the *Tonight Show* called upon Broadway star Tallulah Bankhead to see if she would be on the show, they all chatted about friends of the actress who might be guests on the program. When Bankhead mentioned a famous theatrical personality, one of the show's writers interrupted: "Miss Bankhead, uh, Tallulah, do you mind if I ask a question? Uh, since you know him and all, I wonder ... listen. Is it true he really, uh, really, uh, is a homosexual?"

"I don't know, dahling," Tallulah shot back. "He has never grabbed my cock."

Perhaps the writer should have used a straightforward line of questioning — instead of all the insipid "uhs" and leering verbal tics.

"Never beat around the bush, and never use euphemisms," says veteran British television interviewer Bryan Magee in his book *The Television Interviewer.* "Do not say: 'How long ago was it when you first discovered that some of your natural impulses were not altogether the same as those of other people?' when what you mean is: 'How old were you when you realized you were homosexual?' " Magee goes on to say:

> The fear that there is something rude about saying what you mean is ill-grounded. On television I have interviewed psychopaths, prostitutes and their clients, lesbians, cripples, the mothers of thalidomide babies, even married couples about their sex lives, and interviewed them all with simple and direct frankness, yet not one such person has ever taken offense, nor has any viewer or critic complained.

Magee says that questions which may be controversial in content should not be made to seem controversial in nature. "You should never make it possible for the interviewee to take issue with the question, least of all as an alternative to answering it." Thus, homosexuality should not be referred to as a "problem," because the subject may not consider it as such. Nor should the interviewer ask, "But isn't homosexuality morally wrong?" — for this implies that the questioner thinks it is. "Do you think homosexuality is morally wrong?" is more neutral. "The interviewee is likely to be sensitive to the difference between the two questions, and to give you a much freer answer to the second than he would to the first," adds Magee. More than anything, the subject needs the feeling that he is talking to someone who is sympathetic, who understands intensely personal feelings.

Ask Away

Don't be *too* sympathetic, at the risk of seeming obsequious. If the interviewer merely nods and accepts anything, the subject soon feels, understandably, that he need only gloss over his stand on a topic, oblivious to differing points of view: he has a captive audience. If you find yourself in disagreement with your subject, a good rule to observe is to speak only after you have clearly restated your subject's ideas to the subject's satisfaction. This leads to give-and-take rather than to argument. Remember: an editor is interested in good quotes. Strive for communication, not debater's points. Avoid hard words and harsh feelings.

If the subject tosses back a question — "I don't know; what do *you* think about it?" — do not leap for the bait. You lose control and become the interviewee rather than the interrogator. When a subject is evasive and gives answers like "yes and no," or "occasionally," or "in some cases," try to pin him down. Ask under which conditions he would say yes, and under which he would say no. Strive for concrete answers. When you get a definite answer, however, be cautious in using a high-pressure follow-up like "Is that what you *really* think?" Such a rejoinder should be used only when nothing else will get the desired information, or when the reply is so incredible that there is genuine disbelief. And be alert for answers that contradict previous answers in the interview.

How far do you push a subject? "Asking questions is the reporter's first line of fire in seeking information," says Willard R. Smith, former head of the *Milwaukee Journal* news bureau. "The reporter who asks, asks, asks, soon shows no hesitancy in asking embarrassing questions — questions that may be embarrassing to the person interviewed but not to the reporter asking them. Often they are the key which unlocks and releases stories which otherwise might be withheld from publication or public knowledge." One recalls the evening when Edward R. Murrow, on *Person-to-Person,* asked a question of Krishna Menon, the Indian delegate at the United Nations, who became annoyed and said, "That is an improper question for you to ask me." To which the interviewer replied: "Perhaps it is an improper question for you to answer."

In the post-Watergate era, a new breed of tough interviewers has emerged. "The country, it seems, has had it with its politicians, with the inoperative inbeciles in the White House and the equivocating eunuchs in Congress," observes Richard Reeves in *New York* magazine. "The politician I would most not want to be is Ted Kennedy. If reporters are now going to write the way they themselves talk — and that seems to be starting to happen — then they are going to write some very unpleasant things about Teddy. A lot of influential people in press and politics consider Kennedy an over-age adolescent and are more than a little frightened about what kind of President he would be." When Kennedy appeared on CBS's *Face the Nation,* for instance, reporter Marty Nolan of the *Boston Globe* asked him for the first time why anyone should trust a man who had to meet secretly for seven days with speechwriters and political advisers before he could tell the world what he remembered happening at Chapaquiddick. Wrote David Broder of the *Washington Post:* "What the viewers saw was the unedifying spectacle of one man being defensive about an automobile accident." Adds Reeves: "There is a new tone creeping into the middle of American political journalism, and [in future campaigns] you may just find out all you ever wanted to know and were afraid to ask about politicians."

Sometimes an interviewer can go too far, and threaten rapport with a question. Even the usually unflappable Barbara Walters once fell apart on the air when she told actor Oscar Werner, after he had appeared in *Ship of Fools,* that she had heard he was very difficult. "How do you know?" he replied. "We have never had an affair." Recalled Walters afterward: "I flushed, began to stammer and couldn't get the next question out. Our producer said he wanted to walk on camera and throw a pail of cold water over me." Get tough at your own risk.

How do you know when and where to stop? You don't. Be mindful, though, of particularly sensitive categories — income, sex, family relationships, and education — and prepare your game plan accordingly.

A Tough Finish

Most interviewers agree that sensitive, tough questions should be placed toward the end of the interview. It's the same psychology you might employ when asking someone you don't know for a date. Only the reckless would approach a stranger and ask, "Would you like to go to the movies tonight?" Chances are the interviewer would get no response at all, except perhaps a dirty look and a kick in the shins. If there is more wooing before serving up the Big Question, however, happier results should ensue.

Jimmy Cannon, the great sportswriter, said "you can always tell a new reporter on the baseball beat." In fact, he called them "chipmunks" because they were always jabbering away in the pressbox. "The chipmunks refuse to follow the techniques of the interview," he complained. "They go up and challenge guys with rude questions. They think they're very big if they walk up to an athlete and insult him with a question. They risk the chance of ending interviews in the first few minutes.

"The trick of interviewing is to start with the easy questions," advised Cannon. "I usually start with a little small talk. You warm up slowly. Then you drop the bomb, and if the guy doesn't answer, the interview will be almost completed. I save the tough questions for last because I don't want an empty notebook."

Joseph Trento, who was once chief investigative reporter for columnist Jack Anderson, suggests that in a tough interview, one should open with easy questions, then "bear down on the tough ones and keep hitting harder and harder until, say, the last two questions." Then the interviewer should "ease up ... become friendly ... leave the subject with a good taste and try to get an invitation to come back for more if you need it." He adds: "Most of the time these last two questions change the tone and make you seem more like a devil's advocate than the devil Spiro Agnew has made you in the eyes of many influential Washingtonians."

If a question is important, apply some pressure for an answer — but remember that *excessive* pressure can destroy your interview early. Therefore, if it is a key question, hold it for late in the interview and ask it as forcefully as you can, even if it risks rapport. Rapport, after all, is a means — not an end. You are there to get answers, not to create a good impression.

Let It Be

Remember: if a question burns to be answered, ask it. Don't hang back. An interview is generally between consenting adults; if a subject has a mind not to answer, he'll let you know. Then you must decide whether the question is important enough to pursue; and, if it is, how to pursue it.

Those are the mechanics of tough interviewing, and they are far easier to come by than the spirit — the willingness to gamble rapport and friendship for one (perhaps unprintable) answer.

Of course, the rule is simple: truth comes before etiquette. And the subject is likely to better respect the truthful interviewer than the polite one — no matter how that feeling is masqueraded.

Sometimes it's best to walk away from an interview that is obviously in shambles. When baseball star Reggie Jackson gave sportswriter Wells Twombly a series of non-answers, the writer walked away, saying "I'm as good a writer as you are a home-run hitter. If you want me to write about you, you'll have to call me." Jackson called him back and got serious.

What was the outcome of the Ava Gardner-Rex Reed snit? Reed recalls the time he was at Terence Young's villa in the south of France. Young, in addition to being the director on several of Ava's films, was one of the actress's best friends. "I just wanted to tell you how much I loved the piece on Ava," Young told Reed. "It is the best thing that has ever been written about her."

"I don't think Ava will agree with you," replied Reed. "I have heard she was very upset."

"That's not true at all," said Young. "I mentioned it to her and she said, 'That sonuvabitch knows more about me than I do.' You have to remember you are dealing with a total paranoid schizophrenic and you captured her truthfully and with great delicacy. To write a hatchet job on Ava Gardner is the easiest thing in the world to do, but you handled her with perception."

` "If stars get mad after they see what I have written about them," says Rex Reed, "they usually forgive and forget in time for the next interview."

For the interviewer, too, getting tough means just that: forgiving, forgetting, and preparing for the next interview.

6. Off the Record

I am persuaded that, with rare exceptions, what must be said off the record had best not be said at all.

—John Kenneth Galbraith

Bennett Cerf was on home turf — in his posh office at Random House in New York — and he was being charmingly candid with Jessica Mitford, who was in pursuit of Famous Writers.

"I know *nothing* about the business and selling and I care *less*," said Cerf of the Famous Writers School, a correspondence school for writers. Cerf was on the board of directors. "I've nothing to do with how the school is run. I can't put that too strongly to you. But it's been run extremely cleanly."

Mitford asked the Random House chief how many books by Famous Writers alumni his house had published.

"Oh, come on, you must be pulling my leg," said Cerf. "No person of any sophistication, whose book we'd publish, would have to take a mail-order course to learn how to write."

No, mail-order selling was for the unwashed, the simple pigeons. "The crux of it is a very hard sales pitch, an appeal to the gullible," said Cerf. "Of course, once somebody has signed a contract with Famous Writers, he can't get out of it. But that's true with every business in the country."

Cerf looked at Mitford. She was writing. His coziness vanished.

"For God's sakes, don't quote me on the 'gullible' business," he said. "You'll have all mail-order houses in the country down on my neck!"

"Then would you like to paraphrase it?" said Mitford firmly.

"Well ... you could say in general I don't like the hard sell, yet it's the basis of all American business."

"Sorry," Mitford said sternly, "I don't call that a paraphrase. I shall have to use both of them. Anyway, why do you lend your name to this hard-sell proposition?"

Cerf grinned. "Frankly, if you must know, I'm an awful ham — I love to see my name in the papers!"

The Brier Patch

Not everyone is delighted to see his name in the papers — particularly when it is attached to a volatile quote. One loves truth, but not when it explodes in one's face. So the interviewee demands — and the interviewer sometimes grants — a pliable facemask: the off-the-record disclaimer.

Now some interviewers are impatient when a subject drops his voice like a spy in church and says: "Uh, this is off the record, but. . . ."

"Sorry," they cut in briskly. "Nothing off the record." Going off the record, they believe, allows the subject to gallump through the brier patch of rumor and self-promotion. "We are in the business of publishing, not being handholders to sources that need the ego trip of putting on a reporter," one writer told Jim R. Morris for *Journalism Quarterly.*

But other interviewers — less puritanical, and more sensible — hold their tongues when the subject wanders off the record. "Why not?" asks one newspaper reporter. "If he's not willing to say it on the record, you won't get it anyway, and it can't compromise anything you have. It could flavor the other information you obtain."

And off-the-record talks may be essential for investigative reporters. Says one: "In the type of interviews with which I am generally concerned, I can't play the game 'You either talk on the record or we don't talk.' Many times it is no big deal to wangle the off the record around to on."

Imperfectly Clear

Many times, too, the "off the record" tag does not mean what it would seem; so interviewer and subject should agree — preferably at the outset — on the ground rules for using off-the-record material.

"If an interviewee says he will talk only 'off the record' or 'for background only and not for quotation,' this means to me that he is not to be quoted," says Al Balk. "Direct quotations are not to be used at all. If he will talk 'not for attribution,' this means to me that he can be quoted, but not by name — he is 'a spokesman for' or a 'representative of' or 'a close observer of the scene.' "

The interviewer who will not budge off the record must make himself particularly clear. "I explain at the beginning that nothing is off the record," says Jim Carty, who has written over 500 articles for over 100 magazines. "If a person doesn't wish to say something he should refrain from commenting — otherwise he may become confused later about what was permitted and what was excluded. This frankness often gets the interview off on a good start."

Calling the Shots

But wordsmanship is all. If the interviewer sonorously presents a Rube Goldberg maze of what he will consider off the record, on the record, and in the grooves, the subject may become bewildered, then paranoid. Think positive. In a study of questions used by reporters, Yandell C. Cline found that "Do you mind if I quote you?" was less productive than a more assertive remark such as "That's fine, I'll quote you on that."

Sometimes it's best not to even initiate the matter of off the record. "Asking a person if something is off the record, I've found, usually guarantees that it will be," says one reporter. The power of suggestion is irresistible for many.

Generally, the problem of off-the-record remarks is best handled with businesslike frankness when dealing with veteran interviewees. Once it is dragged from the closet, the subject will relax more during the interview, and chafe less at the printed result. Well . . . usually.

Maury Levy double-faulted when he interviewed Billie Jean King shortly after she racked up Bobby Riggs. Ironically, it had been love at first serve. Levy, a writer/editor for *Philadelphia* magazine, showed up for the interview wearing a rugby shirt, faded jeans and blue suede Adidas. King, who had been questioned to death by scores of bodies in tailored suits, dug him immediately.

"I told her I didn't even want to hear about Bobby Riggs anymore," Levy wrote in *Philadelphia*. "She was happy about that. She perked up in her chair and the two of us sat there with our legs folded under like a couple of Buddhas and talked about everything but tennis. It was very nice."

Levy showed King the off/on switch of the recorder next to her, and stated the rules of play: to put a remark off the record, she only had to shut off the recorder. At times, she did just that, or asked Levy to; and none of the delicate material was used.

But King was not entirely delicate in the recorded interview. Early on, she dropped a "to-hell-with" something. She stopped, putting her hand to her mouth and her eyes to the recorder; then she shrugged, and continued talking. During the two-hour interview, she used "shit" a few times, and "fuck" once. "Neither of us gave those words a second thought," recalled Levy. "We were both about the same age and had grown up as members of a pretty uninhibited generation, a generation where a woman, in the true sense of liberation, was not considered a foul-mouthed tramp for using that kind of language."

By the end of the interview, King and Levy were friends. But three weeks later, when *Philadelphia* came out with King on the cover and Levy's stunning profile inside, the friendship was over. At a press conference, wrote Levy in a follow-up piece, "Larry King gave me a very disgusted look. And Billie Jean greeted me with an ice-cold stare that would have scared Bobby Riggs right off the court."

"Billie Jean and I really think you're a super writer," husband Larry told Levy eventually. "We think that was the best piece anyone's done on her. Except for those 16 (four-letter) words. That ruined the whole thing. That's just not Billie Jean. That's just not her image."

Levy explained that Billie Jean had the option to shut off the recorder when she was concerned about her image, but the tennis star's husband said she had assumed Levy would "clean up her act." Levy: "I told her since she didn't say they were off the record, I assumed they were on the record."

"That's just not her image," Larry King repeated. "I've never seen her so mad in her life. . . . She says you've betrayed her. You've betrayed her friendship. She had a special relationship with you and she opened up a lot more than she ever did and you betrayed the whole thing."

Levy shucked etiquette. He told Larry King of the favorable response the piece had drawn, of the people who thought "it really made Billie Jean look like a real and believable person, not some carefully packaged and protected version of Goody Two-Shoes."

Larry King looked at the writer, shook his head, and asked: "What's wrong with Goody Two-Shoes?"

A Solitary Craft

Waste no tears for the subject who moves swiftly — even if belatedly — to defend his image; he's quite capable of fending for himself. But when a guileless subject allows the interviewer to glimpse the private, unmade rooms in his life, the interviewer becomes more than an interviewer; he becomes a confidant and, one hopes, a compassionate and discreet one. That's a difficult role for the steely journalist who wants nothing off the record; as William Manchester notes, it is all too easy for that journalist to be unfair to subjects unaccustomed to interviews. "They forget it's an interview, and they let all sorts of personal detail spill out," explains Manchester. "Then, I think, it becomes an invasion of privacy, and this is something that one must be careful of. One can easily invade privacy."

Sometimes a subject is so taken with the lure of his voice that he unwittingly reveals family affairs. In one interview, a TV actor told Debbie Sherwood that his 16-year-old daughter had been "deflowered" at the age of 13. "I'd rather she'd have waited a little longer," the actor said offhandedly. "But since she didn't, I just put her on the Pill."

The quote was an insight — but it was also an intrusion into a young girl's private life. On reflection, Sherwood decided that the story of the deflowering was for the daughter to reveal, not the father. "Perhaps if I had been able to contact the girl and get the story straight from her, I could have used it to advantage," Sherwood later wrote in *Writer's Digest.* "But as she was in Europe and I was under pressure to meet a deadline, I simply didn't use it at all."

The journalist, then, must know when to relent to conscience; yet he must also know when — out of conscience — to be relentless, even toward friends. "I don't like having people mad at me," says Sherwood. "I don't like having people I have known for years refuse my phone calls and look the other way if we meet at a party. And yet, I am a writer. Writing is my business, and my joy." It is also a consumption, intolerant of buddy-buddy compromise; the honest journalist may well be a solitary man. Sherwood recalls that Henry Luce once advised a *Time*man, "No journalist can expect to have a friend outside the profession."

Newsworthy Friends

Probably he cannot expect to keep a friend if he dissects him dispassionately and publicly. "If you have a friend who is newsworthy, but who uses crude language, is in group therapy, and has been married six times, it would be difficult for you to present him properly without mentioning at least one or two of these things," says Sherwood. "And if you did mention them, he would not be likely to thank you for it."

Rex Reed says he never writes about his personal friends. That is sensible, but not always possible. If your childhood friend is elected President of the United States, you cannot rush out to interview the loser.

No, the journalist probably must interview his friends eventually — and fearfully. Yet even the tenderest of friends can be managed, if the interviewer will make his intentions clear and his manner businesslike. When Debbie Sherwood was researching an article on announcers, she pointedly arranged interviews with acquaintances, even though she could have easily based the piece on stories she knew from informal chats. "Those anecdotes were told to a friend, not a writer," she says. "Perhaps because some of the announcers knew me personally, they were (to their later regret) more relaxed and chatty during our interview than they would have been had I been a stranger. But the point is, the information was obtained in a business, rather than a personal, way. Therefore, I could reasonably assume that anything said was grist for the mill."

It is not always possible, however, to divine what the *subject* will consider grist for the mill. When Earl Wilson reported that Frank Sinatra threw Ava Gardner out of his Palm Springs house, the actress didn't object. "But after I revealed that, during an interview with her, she had walked around barefoot and had said she was a sharecropper's daughter turned millionaire," says Wilson, "she sent word she wouldn't see me anymore." Ya takes your chances.

Interviewees Anonymous

But you needn't put up with ludicrous requests for off-the-record status. Harry Truman, when he was President, gave a televised speech before the Women's Press Club that was billed as "off the record." Absurd. And intolerable. What is said at a public meeting is, by definition, on the record; one cannot share a secret with 200 listeners.

Generally, the interviewer can easily dispense with a simple, cranky claim to off-the-record rights. But he cannot deal so briskly with more complex claims: the claim of a cop whose information is vital to a story, but who cannot release his name without penalty; the claim of a disgruntled employee who talks freely, too freely, but who wants total anonymity. The interviewer becomes a journalist, juggling his options, deciding between the public interest and private fears, between his need for lively copy and his need for documentation.

When a subject — a doctor disturbed about the AMA, a policeman revealing corruption in the force — requests anonymity, the interviewer has two options:

• He may quote the subject directly, and attribute to "a reliable source."

• He may paraphrase his remarks, but without attribution — thus assuming the onus for their accuracy.

To be sure, the Anonymity Gambit produces. "If the people you're interviewing can remain anonymous," says Jess Stearn, "they're happy to unload." The problem is whether they'll unload all over the interviewer. William Rivers explains why guarantees of anonymity can be disastrous: "First, a writer may offer anonymity of one sort or another too freely and thus hide sources who should be identified. The writer may even discover that he has granted anonymity to so many sources that his article reads as though he had made it all up. Second, the conventions that allow anonymity tempt the source to grind his axe as he likes, unobserved. At bottom, anonymous interviews circulate information for which no one takes public responsibility. The writer may wake up to discover that he held a cloak behind which a source was manipulating facts and fashioning his own version of truth. The worst of it is that these interview conventions may serve or destroy the ultimate aim, which is to play fair with the reader. This is a dilemma."

And what is the solution? As always, the reader's interest must come first. If anonymity inspires the source to make charges that he is unwilling to document, then naturally the interviewer must request attribution — which is a kind of documentation, although the thinnest kind. But if anonymity assures accurate, revealing information that can not be had any other way, then it is well worth its price.

Concealing Sources

When it is legit, unattributed information can lend an article the intimacy of truth. Freelancer Franklynn Peterson was making no headway in his investigation of buying adoptable babies. After phone calls to several states, "I found a bevy of pleasant and talkative adoption officials, but they could provide me with only suspicions and statistics." One official, however, provided the name and phone number of a New York City detective whose specialty was adoption irregularities.

"I shouldn't talk to you," the detective told Peterson. He then talked for more than a half hour, "practically writing the story for me, with facts, figures, dates, anecdotes, the works!" recalls the writer. "These 'lucky breaks' aren't luck at all, however — an exposé writer creates them by plodding blindly down so many different avenues that at least one is bound to pay off."

To protect his sources, Peterson withheld the names and even locations of the agencies he had contacted. "They'll be ready to talk with me another day, as a result," Peterson says. "But at the same time, I carefully pinned down virtually every fact and incident with a loosely defined source. The reader might not be able to trace the specific source, but the essential flavor of authenticity is retained. A good editor is willing to conceal sources which must be concealed, but he rightfully retains an option to check himself with the sources before publishing your piece."

Sometimes a source won't even settle for anonymity. Instead, he asks the interviewer to keep the material to himself. If the material is personal and painful, it's probably best to acquiesce. For instance, Gay Talese — whose nonfiction can be as intimate as a Frenchman's memoirs — knows when to keep a secret. When he interviewed George Plimpton for an *Esquire* profile, he learned of a trouble that had occurred in Plimpton's prep school days. Plimpton asked him to keep if off the record. "And I did," says Talese. "I never dealt with that subject because it was very painful to him, and to his father, as I recall."

Lewis A. Harlow would consign off-the-record material not only to the mind, but to the incinerator. "By all means, when you edit the interview, destroy those passages," he says. "Your integrity must never be questioned."

A subtler and chancier form of destruction is to allow the subject to approve his quotes. The interviewer is lucky if the subject does not "improve" them as well; for a man's quotes are as incisive an index to his thinking as a mirror is to his slovenliness. Few can resist the temptation to take a blue pencil to the mirror and touch up the image, highlighting a cheekbone and covering over a liver spot.

There'll Be Some Changes

If the interviewer must submit copy to the subject, he should stress that he is checking for accuracy, and that only the editor may perform surgery on the manuscript. Else the interviewer may find himself in a pickle reminiscent of Marie Torre's audience with Arthur Godfrey. Torre was a writer for the *New York World-Telegram & Sun* who in 1954 approached Godfrey — then showbiz's biggest celebrity, self-quarantined from reporters — for a series of "as-told-to" articles for her paper. After months of negotiations with CBS vice presidents and Godfrey's press agent — "it might have been easier to arrange an appointment with the White House tenant," Torre later recalled — the writer was ushered into her quarry's office. She told Godfrey that since the article was to carry his byline, he would have the right of approval.

"Heck, I'm not a writer," said Godfrey. "You're a writer. You put your byline on it." But he kept the right of approval.

"So desirous, so eager were we to have a Godfrey series that we were willing to let him pass on it," Torre said, "even though this is not good newspaper practice and hardly ever done."

The first session was two and a half hours, and included quotes "which would have resulted in page-one stories around the country," said Torre. Godfrey confided that his ambition was to quit broadcasting and become a U.S. senator. He opened up on the Julius La Rosa Affair — La Rosa was a singer Godfrey had dismissed on the air for a so-called loss of "humility" — and "when the facts were known," said Torre, "sympathy was with Godfrey." A second meeting, suggested by Godfrey, was "equally fruitful."

One week later, Torre shipped three articles from the five-part series to Godfrey's office for approval. Within hours, a press agent called. He turned the phone over to a CBS vice prez.

"We have just seen the articles," he said, "and I'm afraid there's been a misunderstanding. Arthur does not want anything written about becoming a senator. Nor does he want to be quoted on Julius La Rosa."

"But the quotes are Mr. Godfrey's," said Torre. "He saw me taking notes on everything he said. If he did not want to see the quotes in print, what did he think I was going to do with them?"

"I can understand your confusion. But you see, when Arthur likes a person — and he liked you very much — he will talk to that person as a friend. Anyway, we've made some changes. I don't think you'll be too unhappy."

Marie Torre *was* unhappy. In fact, "I was positively shattered." All three articles had been reduced to excerpts, with a smattering of meaningless quotes.

"I picked up the pieces and deposited them on the desk of my managing editor," said Torre. "We brooded over the shame of it all. Another newspaper might have run the series even without Godfrey's OK, but we had given our word and it wasn't in our genes to go back on it." The newspaper killed the series.

Make Your Own Breaks

Far better than kowtowing to the subject is to make an end run around him, and to confirm his off-the-record material through another source. "Nine times out of ten," says one writer, "the story can be 'broken' through another source." Like winning a poker showdown, breaking a story only takes ingenuity, ingenuous bluffing, and luck. Here's how one veteran interviewer played his cards:

> I was interviewing our mayor once on a feature story. There had been interest at the time on who he was going to name as his public safety director. He said he would tell me, but it must be off the record.
>
> "Wait," I said, "I don't want you to tell me." I said that actually I had done a lot of research (which I hadn't), and that in my judgment, only two men were qualified.
>
> I said I was planning to write a "speculative type" story in

which I was going to discuss three leading contenders. He asked me which three men I was mentioning. I gave three names. Then I said that since I had given him my three names, it would only be fair for him to tell me on the record whether one was the correct one — that I did *not* want him to reveal the man but only to save me the embarrassment of writing a story and not including the right man in the speculation.

He said that in fact his choice was in my list, and that the man had been offered the job and was considering it.

I asked if he planned a meeting with the man soon. The mayor said yes. One of the three men was out of the state and would be for some time. I eliminated him. The second man had drawn a sort of amused look from the mayor when I mentioned his name, so I eliminated him.

I went almost immediately to a telephone after leaving the mayor's office, called the only remaining possibility, and got him to admit he had been offered the job.

Archie Bunker, Reliable Source

Often, however, the value of an off-the-record quote depends not on its substance, but on its style, its sound and fury. The interviewer then can rarely confirm the quote through another source, unless there was a third party to the interview. But he can — if he has the wile and lacks the scruples — use the quote in a sneak play.

Bill Davidson, a veteran freelancer for *TV Guide,* is a master of the technique. Consider the time he tried to interview controversial Carroll O'Connor — alias Archie Bunker — on behind-the-scene seethings at Tandem Productions. "Since Carroll O'Connor would not allow himself to be quoted on the subject of Tandem," wrote Davidson, "the following must be attributed to 'a source close to the investigation.'

"Says the SCTTI: 'Maybe Carroll isn't a hundred percent right, but he and the others have had to fight Tandem for money, for dressing rooms, even for a place to sit down during rehearsals. . . .'"

An off-the-record matter can also be revealed by describing the circumstances that led to the *on*-the-record statement. When Sada Thompson, the fine Broadway actress, made her debut as an *All in the Family* regular with much advance fanfare, Carroll O'Connor was in a foul mood — and Bill Davidson was on hand to take note: "In the studio, O'Connor ignored Miss Thompson completely and spent the afternoon conversing with no one but Rob Reiner." But apparently, O'Connor's snub did not stint Thompson's acting. "In the taping, I thought Miss Thompson was superb," wrote Davidson, "possibly overpowering O'Connor with her performance."

But that Sunday morning, according to Davidson, Norman Lear phoned the writer at his home and reported that Thompson was out of the series and would be replaced by Betty Garrett.

"Did Archie have anything to do with that decision?" Davidson asked.

"Do you want me to tell you the *real* story — off the record?" Lear said.

"No."

"*On* the record, Sada wants to get back to her children, who are in school in New York."

"Strangely," Davidson wrote, "Miss Thompson doesn't have any school-age children."

The off-the-record zinger can be revealed even by camouflage — although the ethics of *that* are debatable. When Neil Hickey was a judge for the Miss World contest (and doing a piece for *TV Guide* on same), he espied the king and his court. "Right up there on the bare stage — natty in a box-backed coat and flared trousers — was Dick Clark and 50 of the niftiest cutey-pies I had ever beheld, rehearsing the tableaux that would dazzle TV viewers when ABC broadcast all the excitement as a 90-minute TV program," wrote Hickey. "I cornered Clark and asked him how he felt about beauty pageants in general." Here's how Hickey handled the language problem:

"What do I think about beauty pageants?" Clark said. "I think they're ***********. And besides, *******************."

Startled, I said: "But you're the master of ceremonies."

"**********," Clark explained. And he added, "****** ********." He walked back toward center stage to resume rehearsing. Over his shoulder, he said, "Of course, everything I've said is off the record."

"Of course," I said.

Cerf and the Serfs

Off-the-record is often thought to be a unilateral decision by a source, but it need not be. Some writers, if they are hot on a story, will simply inform the subject that off-the-record won't protect him. "When a source declares that what he's about to say is off the record," says one reporter polled on the subject, "I try to assess as quickly as possible whether it's worth it and tell the source that I agree or don't agree."

As we have seen, Jessica Mitford didn't agree — and did quote. "You use your judgment in these things," Mitford told me after her Famous Writers School article appeared. "If you are talking with someone of top sophistication, like Bennett Cerf, who is perfectly aware that he is being interviewed for publication, and he tries to get sort of cozy with you by saying things like, 'This is off the cuff, but confidentially between you and me ...' — it seems to me that one can say to him: 'Well, I think I will quote you on that because this is obviously your *real* point of view. I'm not interested in making some sort of deal based on the fact that we are two sophisticates looking down on these poor little people who have signed up for the School.' That's my feeling."

Wouldn't such an open feeling lead to closed doors? "Well, I don't know," says the veteran muckraker. "The point is that in my experience, if you ask people directly about something they are connected with, they will usually give you a truthful and direct answer."

But it may be off the record. And then it becomes — as so many curve balls in interviewing — a judgment call: whether to abide by the gentleman's agreement, and suppress a bit of the truth; or to quote the man, and lose the source.

The call is rarely clear-cut or convenient; but it is made easier when the writer remembers *his* umpire — the reader. If the reader is entitled to see the quote, and to glimpse the man who said it; if the quote and the man bear on *his* affairs, on the measure of security he may expect from the police, on the measure of safety he may expect from the airlines: then the source's loudest protests should not detour the interviewer from quoting without restraint.

That may cost the interviewer a few sources, and more than a few friends — but most important, it will help give the reader his money's worth.

"I used to have to take Tums all the time," says Rex Reed, "because I would get an upset stomach if someone didn't like me because of something I wrote. But now I kind of trust to people's intelligence. Writing is a job, and I treat it as a job."

7. Notes on Notetaking

*See the pencil mark on that finger? That's
really a good size callus, and it's from taking
notes with a pencil all day. It's the occupa-
tional deformation.*

— *Martin Mayer*

The three most dreaded words for a journalist — next to "Interview
Greta Garbo" — are "I've been misquoted." He is thrown into shame
and confusion, like an actor who has blown his lines; if he cannot
trust his own ears, who *can* he trust? Moreover, a major misquote
can render his interview story worthless, if not downright epochal.
"Misquoting the President can boom or depress the stock market,"
Merriman Smith once reflected. Now generally, the Republic with-
stands the erosion of a misquote — but a journalist may not. So he
protects himself by either tape recording the interview or taking notes.
Usually, he takes notes. Heaven knows why.

You would think that, with a reporter's passion for precision and
a writer's passion for words, the journalist would sooner part with
his byline than with his recorder, which can capture every lunge,
every lull in a man's struggle for words. Notes can sketch the man's
message, but message, sir, is nothing without its nuances — its
inflections of voice and vocabulary — and the recorder captures those
with whole fidelity. And that is its weakness.

For a tape must be transcribed, and a transcription must be boiled
down and ironed out for publication, and in the process, the tape's
fidelity become tedious and exasperating. You will play a barely
audible passage, rewind, play it again, rewind, play it again, pummel
the typewriter, and wish to God that you had, after all, resorted to

notetaking — a hasty and inventive enterprise that, through sheer panic, boils down and irons out a man's remarks almost as he remarks them. With a tape recorder, you listen to his congestion of words several, innumerable times; with notes, you listen once, and pray.

And it really comes to this: some prefer the stick shift to the automatic, the pencil and pad to the typewriter, the unwieldy sheaf of notes to the tape recorder. We were not all born to the Age of Electronics and Ease.

It All Comes Back

Actually — if you are dead set against ease and crutches — you can do without pencil and pad, too, and rely on the vexatious memory. While researching *In Cold Blood*, Truman Capote found people tensing up whenever he began taking notes, so he used his trained memory to retain the events and conversations of a day — then took elaborate notes in his Kansas motel room at night.

"If you write down or tape what people say, it makes them feel inhibited and self-conscious," observed Capote after *In Cold Blood* began to amass attention. "It makes them say what they think you *expect* them to say." How did Capote train himself to be a portable tape recorder? "It wasn't as hard as it might sound. What I'd do was have a friend talk or read for a set length of time, tape what he was saying, and meanwhile listen to him as intently as I could. Then I'd go write down what he had said as I remembered it, and later compare what I had with the tape. . . . Finally, when I got to be about 97 percent accurate, I felt ready to take on this book."

Daniel Lang, a writer for *The New Yorker*, told some fellow writers that he took notes during interviews, but never referred to them while writing the story afterward, except for very precise information — an exact quote or a date or figure. "After I'm finished writing the first draft, I go back and check the notes." Freelancer Richard Gehman tried this on his next piece. "I was astonished to find that I remembered nearly everything I had put down while taking notes," Gehman enthused afterward. In addition to boosting one's powers of recall, this system streamlines that endless poring over notes, and is good training for the day when a writer may not be allowed to take notes at all.

In fact, some reporting texts suggest that writers take notes in, at best, minimal fashion. "The best kind of interview is that which proceeds in a natural, friendly, informal way," writes Curtis MacDougall in his standard text, *Interpretative Reporting*. "It is wise to take as few notes as possible during an interview of this kind. Often it is disastrous to take a single note. If the reporter can get his subject to forget that he is speaking for publication, he will obtain much more than if the person is constantly reminded that the interviewer is taking down verbatim what he is saying."

MacDougall says the reporter might note spellings, figures and addresses, but in asking for such data he must be careful "that he does not suggest to the interviewee that he had better start designating which of his remarks were for publication and which not.

"The reporter must train his memory to recall, an hour or so afterward, all the important remarks of the interviewee," adds Mac-Dougall. "He should make immediate mental note of any startling statement which he will want to use verbatim, and should keep turning it over in his mind during the rest of the interview." The reporter should jot down his notes at his first opportunity after the interview. "If he has an hour or so before he must write his story, he will be surprised to find that, bit by bit, virtually the entire interview will come back to him."

Doing a Capote on Schweitzer

Certainly an interviewer should have — or be willing to train — a good memory. A reporter once described NBC's correspondent Cassie Mackin as having "developed a waitresslike memory which juggled profiles like orders." At a political convention "she knew the names and salient features of about 300 county chairman, delegates, and campaign staffers, and she knew the first questions to ask each of them if an interview should materialize." Even the toughest of subjects is likely to be softened by an interviewer who remembers his face in a crowd, and would-be interviewers with shabby memories would do well to read *The Memory Book*, by Jerry Lucas and Harry Lorayne, to improve their skills.

Often it is impossible for an interviewer to take notes, even if the subject *is* willing. Woodrow Wilson was once interviewed by a reporter while he drove in an open car from Trenton to Sea Girt, New Jersey. "I have interviewed men on trains, ships, in the air, and under the ground," the writer recalled afterward. "Yet I doubt if any similar work was done under the handicaps that marked that first talk with Mr. Wilson. The car jolted; constituents shouted greetings to him from the roadside. All the while I had to keep up a running fire of questions and remember what was being said. We touched every possible subject from tariff and good government to the personal guilt of corporations. It was impossible to take many notes. I had to remember what I heard."

Thus, a trained interviewer must sometimes depend mostly on memory, even if he has pencil and pad in hand. Remember that. And occasionally, resistance by the subject is thorough. "I don't want to be on tape" may be followed by "Why are you taking so many notes?" In such cases, memory is all.

The shortest *Playboy* interview ever run was with Albert Schweitzer — five columns. Schweitzer refused to give the magazine ample time for its customary probing. In addition, he insisted that no notes be taken, and no recordings be made. "So the interviewer had to do a Truman Capote," says Murray Fisher, "which means memorizing what Schweitzer was saying as he said it, then stopping him every 15 or 20 minutes and running around a corner to copy it down."

Wielding Pencil and Pad

Many interviewers, in order to appear natural, forego "unnatural" props such as pencil and pad — and so disarm the wary subject. "I deliberately show up without a pencil and things like that to convince my subject that I can make mistakes," says Rex Reed. "That way they know you're human and respond in kind." Playwright Robert Anderson, who was profiled by Reed, says the writer "has an uncanny ear. He picks things up. And he doesn't carry a notebook around at all, doesn't take things down, yet in terms of other people ... he picks up things and you can see and feel the people."

Some subjects are frightened at the sight of a notebook. "Some kinds of people are rendered nervous by any kind of notetaking," says Max Gunther, who has dealt with policemen and underworld types. "They talk more fluently when the reporter simply slouches in a chair or stands around with his hands in his pockets as in a casual conversation between friends."

Easing your notebook out of your back pocket can be an art in itself. "The reporter should carefully measure the time to reach for pencil and paper," adds Paul Sheehan, author of *Reportorial Writing*. "To the wary or timid, this action could bring increased uneasiness, for it will remind him that what he says will go into print. If the subject is obviously uneasy about the interview and is likely to be frightened by the sight of a notebook, the interviewer should hold back, get a conversation going, and introduce the notebook at some uplifting statement (not during a blast at some political enemy or an ex-wife), and use a statement like, 'I want to make sure I get that name right,' or 'That's good. I want to be sure I get that just right.' " And write away.

Despite the arguments by some journalists that no notes are good notes, several studies have shown that reliance on memory during an interview is risky. Lapses occur. "The psychological margin for human error is too great," observed B. H. Liebes in *Collegiate Journalist.* "In one study the interviewer wrote down the responses as they were made, then a taped recording was used to check the accuracy and completeness of the interviewer. The record showed that even under optimum laboratory conditions the interviewer was guilty of omission and distortions."

Distortions? Well, consider the interviewer who reported his subject's references to the distinguished philosopher Jeremy Bentham as "Jeremiah Benjamin." Or the Columbus, Ohio reporter who called Robert M. LaFollette — who ran for President in 1924 — "Lafayette." (The interviewer's story soon appeared on the newspaper bulletin board under the graffito "Lafayette, we are here!") When names, dates, addresses and specific information is distorted, one can only assume that more abstract notions are likewise unreliable, and that the subject has every right to holler "I was misquoted!" afterward.

Detail Work

Another important reason for taking notes is that the interviewer is there not only to note what is said, but *how* it is being said. A good interview, oddly enough, is like a good lie: rich in the tiny details that give it the inestimable ring of truth. Texture. Little things mean a lot for the observant interviewer jotting it all down, especially in a personality interview. Gestures, physical appearance, verbal inflections — things that make a subject an individual. Color. The "feel" of the interview. Does the subject pace a lot? Smoke cigarillos? Play with his glasses?

When striving for color and mood in an interview, consider little details that add up to the dominant impression a subject leaves with you. It may be his appearance — from clothing and posture to watery eyes and a protruding Adam's apple. It may be his house, car, office. It may be orderliness or disarray. How does the subject react to interruptions? Is his memo pad personalized? Is his office decor modern or traditional, light or dark, neat or sloppy? Are there pictures or paintings in the room? Look at his hands. Do they reveal mannerisms or a manicure? Are they stuffed like peppers into his pockets most of the time? Are they wrinkled or smooth-skinned?

For a profile of actor Michael Caine, Gloria Steinem caught the actor "polishing off a lunch of gin and veal cutlets." Then, in extraordinary detail, she lends depth of observation with a few succinct strokes:

> His suit was expensive and well-tailored, but his shoes were in need of repair. His pale blue shirt (of which he owns 50, all alike) was an elegant match for his eyes, but the collar was button-down because "these damned little bone things get lost at the laundry." He owns 20 pairs of glasses (probably a reaction to the time when his one pair was held together with adhesive tape), but the ones he had on were covered with thumb prints. The overall effect of his 6-foot-2 frame was patrician, but his hair needed combing and his tie was askew. As he lit up a Gitane to go with coffee, there was no flash of gold cigarette case or lighter; just book matches and a squashed paper pack. All in all he seemed in little danger of becoming that classic New York-London success who can't face the day without Schlumberger cuff links.

Detail work such as this usually comes from careful notetaking. While the first rule of interviewing is to capture what a subject has to say, the second is to capture his spirit; the writer who gathers color in his notes can be agile, and he is more likely to be true to his subject. "The head of a government is not likely to reveal in an interview anything he would not say in a public speech," says Anne O'Hare McCormick. "But he does reveal himself — and this is of the utmost importance to the interpretation of the action in which his character, his vanities and ambition, his personal reactions are decisive factors."

On the Sly

Many writers find it necessary to take notes surreptitiously. "There are people who dry up at the sight of a pencil," said John Gunther, who was often assisted by his wife in secretive notetaking. "Moreover, we always do a lot of newsgathering at parties — lunches, dinners, whatnot — and it really is impossible to take notes during a formal dinner party." At a party in Tokyo, Gunther once found himself in the midst of a fascinating conversation. He excused himself, went to the men's room, and jotted it down on the back of an envelope.

When talking with experienced subjects who did not wish to be interviewed, Lowell M. Limpus never permitted them to see him take a single note. "My own pet gag is to stroll in carrying a copy of the community's most conservative newspaper, carelessly folded so that a big department store ad with lots of white space is on the underside," the reporter told author Stewart Harral. "I have a small pencil already palmed. If possible, I seat myself across the desk from the interviewee, drop the paper down on one knee (below the level of the desk so he can't see it), slip out my pencil and start taking notes on the white paper as soon as he begins talking."

Milton Golin, a medical writer, uses a similar technique, for which the writer should be single-minded and double-jointed. "I've used a number of methods for taking notes . . . so as not to be too noticeable. One is to attach a lead pencil point to the ring on my right hand and to scribble either on my cuff (laundry bills are not too high because this doesn't happen too often) or on the inside of a matchbook cover. There is also the method of leaning over as you are seated with your left hand holding a small note pad underneath the upper part of your right leg and your right arm stretching over the other side of your right leg so what you are doing is keeping notes underneath your right knee and out of view." There was a time when you could get on *The Ed Sullivan Show* with this kind of act.

Instruments and Impedimenta

The old school of notetaking prescribes a soft black pencil and a wad of yellow copy paper folded pocket-size. Like the late-show reporter with a press card in his hatband, these tools are arcane. Today an interviewer is likely to show up with a camera and a tape recorder. If he takes notes, he's likely to use a pocket-sized, spiral-bound notebook, with a felt-tip pen for greater permanence. The felt-tip (unlike the time-honored #2) is unbreakable, and (unlike the ballpoint pen) defies gravity if one has to write on a sloped surface.

Defying gravity, by the way, is a commendable risk; defying the laws of chance is not. Look what happened to Robert Bird of the late *New York Herald Tribune.* "I found myself one night, after working like a dog to get the interview, in a dimly-lit library of an old-fashioned mansion off Fifth Avenue talking with Einstein about the atom bomb," wrote Bird. "He had just written a blast against use of the bomb in the *Atlantic.* What he said about the bomb is not nearly as memorable to me as the fact I had one lousy pencil which broke about at the outset of the interview. Einstein had a fountain pen stuck in the V-neck of his sweater and I asked to borrow it. With a shattering look, he took it out, unscrewed the cap slowly and reluctantly gave it to me. I started to scratch away with the pen, but he asked me to excuse him, took the pen away from me, screwed the cap on, put it back in his sweater-V and said he would get me a pencil." Einstein returned with a pencil in five minutes, but by now reporter Bird was taking notes from an offended genius. "I had the impression he disliked reporters anyway, and I must have made it worse for all reporters who followed." Moral: bring along back-up supplies for notetaking, no matter what you decide to use.

Contortions and Cuneiform

More practical notes for the beginning notetaker:

• *Consider learning shorthand, if you don't know a little already.* In England, it is unusual for a journalist *not* to know shorthand. "Many journalists think that American reporting suffers because reporters don't use shorthand," says Mitchell Charnley. "The validity of this view is hard to deny; the more precise and complete the reporter's notes, the more accurate and meaningful the story based on the notes." Shorthand also gives the notetaker convenience and flexibility — assets one doesn't always have, even with a tape recorder. Tom Wolfe uses Gregg shorthand: "I can't do without it for extensive quotes."

Mildred Tyson, whose subjects are often business executives, recommends shorthand (and a shorthand notebook) for two reasons. First, it is a timesaver. Second, the notebook "has a psychological effect" on the business executive. "It is a business tool he uses," says Tyson. "He automatically assumes a 'dictating mood' and is more relaxed."

"If there's anything that distracts the subject, it is his saying something and then watching the writer go through contortions getting it down in longhand," says Frank P. Thomas, who uses shorthand. "That dead spot can hurt the flow of your interview. Usually I'm through putting it down just seconds after he says it. This, I find, surprises and pleases a busy man and gives him the feeling that he is dealing with a professional, which in turn makes him more willing to talk." Nor does using shorthand turn an interviewer into a stenographer. Thomas: "I don't by any means take down every word. . . . I take key words and phrases down in shorthand, just as many of my colleagues do in their contrived shorthand using letters of the alphabet. However, I have come to sense when a man is going to make a key statement. When that happens, I take down every word."

• *Consider homemade shorthand, if you don't know the real stuff.* Various handbooks on speed writing are available in any good bookstore. Many writers improvise bastardized shorthand forms of their own. Proper names become initials, after one full spelling. With becomes w/; without become w/o. Key words are reduced to letters. For a piece on engineering, engineer become E in an interviewer's notes. An article on nursing — N for nurse; Ng for nursing. Use the vowel-less shorthand of TV weathermen: Ptly Cldy tdy, wrmr tmrw. And so forth. Vowels are optional in many words: excellent becomes xlnt, fr xmpl.

A skillful interviewer's shorthand is often so compact that an onlooker would be puzzled if he were to look through the notes comprising the background for a published interview. Here, for example, are some notes made by Merriman Smith after a press conference with Franklin D. Roosevelt in 1944:

tnk be gud tng sy smtg re ILO NA 20 Apl — 34 cntrs — vry impt mtg bcs undbtly whn we cme to devise UNs org, ILO will be ind but afltd cum new org of UNs.

They rough out this way:

> I think it would be a good thing to say something today about the meeting of the International Labor Organization in Philadelphia on the twentieth of April. Thirty-four countries will be represented. It will be a very important meeting because when we come to devise the United Nations Organization, the I.L.O. will be independent, but affiliated with the new organization of the United Nations.

The importance of translating such notes as soon afterward as possible cannot be overstressed. Cold notes become cryptic, even meaningless, if time has passed them by. Robert Benchley once went through some notes several days after an interview and found they resembled cuneiform. After several efforts at translation, he gave up — and wrote a light piece on how he found it impossible to read his own notes.

There are many homemade methods an interviewer can use to increase notetaking speed. He can take notes while attending meetings, listening to radio speeches, or attending night classes — even though a story is not likely to result. Concentrate on both speed and accuracy — with occasional verbatim quotes for important material. Look upon each notetaking situation as an opportunity for sharpening a key tool for an interviewer. Test your notes for accuracy by comparing them with the reliable memory (or notes) of someone else, or with a tape recording.

Another method is to play records of popular songs, and try to transcribe the lyrics as they are sung. After a few hectic efforts, you will find that abbreviations and short forms quickly become part of your notetaking style. Or else.

• *Edit your notes as you jot them down.* It is more important to get a few good complete quotes than to have a paraphrase of everything. "If the speaker is talking rapidly and starts to say something very important while you are still trying to get down a previous statement," advise Phil Ault and William Emery in their journalism text, "jump ahead in your notes to the more vital comment. Then concentrate until you have that down in firm, usable manner."

While a public figure, experienced in interviewing, may talk slowly and distinctly so that an interviewer may take notes, less experienced subjects will not. And it's awkward to ask the subject to stop or slow down so that you can catch up with your notetaking. "If you fall behind," says Max Gunther, "the reason probably is that you are trying to take down the source's words too fully." Gunther believes that only "a tenth of the average talker's total word output is really meaningful," and that the interviewer soon learns "to recognize what is meat and what is mere fat." Gunther: "Nobody ever talks fast enough or meatily enough to get ahead of a practiced reporter."

One way to capture the good quotes, while editing out small talk, is to ask innocuous questions while jotting down key responses you are likely to use later. "If I fall behind," says Martin Mayer, "I direct the conversation into a backwater which does not greatly interest me while writing down what does. My memory for speech is deadly at any range up to about five minutes, excellent for individual sentences and for the gist of a statement up to about an hour after the end of the conversation, if for any reason it is impossible for me to make my notes while chatting."

To single out good material, some interviewers use a "slash" system — a simple slash of the pen in the margin alongside a particularly revealing quote, with double or triple slashes for further emphasis. "One slash to call attention to something I may need later, a double slash if it's likely to figure in the lead, a triple slash if it really seems hot," says Arthur Everett of the AP. For a story with a fast-closing deadline, such editing is helpful when the interviewer sits down with a flurry of notes and barely enough time for a fast draft. Slashes show where the action is.

Verbatim quotes should be marked while taking notes, too. Put a check mark or the letter Q or some symbol in front of exact quotes. Otherwise, when going over your notes afterward you will be uncertain of the statements to be paraphrased and those to be quoted for effect — especially if the interview is lengthy.

Another editing tip: use a new page in your notebook each time the subject starts talking about a new topic. Later, when you sit down to organize your notes and write the story, pages can be torn out and shuffled according to subject matter — which is considerably easier than trying to pry quotes out of notes touching on some 20 topics crammed side by side onto eight pages. And never take notes on both sides of the same sheet of paper, for the same reason.

Bagging a Bon Mot

You would think that the more notes the interviewer took, the more accurate his reconstruction would be — but t'ain't necessarily so. In an experiment conducted by F. E. Abel at Stanford University, two matched groups of students listened to a seven-minute taped interview regarding an offshore oil leak. One group took extensive notes; the other group took none whatsoever. Each had 40 minutes in which to write a story after listening to the interview. It was found that the group taking no notes omitted some 26 percent of the "units of meaning" from their stories (as compared with 21 percent in the other group), but they also made only about one-third as many errors as did the notetakers. Thus, notetaking should not be so profuse as to interfere with the simple act of listening attentively — the interviewer's first function.

But do take notes. While some newspaper veterans consider a notebook the sign of an amateur, any writer doing extensive research for a magazine piece had better bring along a pen and pad. This is especially important if the subject wants to get across a point that is complicated. Many subjects *like* to see an interviewer jotting down notes, and are wary of the writer who hardly appears to be taking notes at all.

Notetaking should be both profuse and accurate if the subject is complex, or unfamiliar for the interviewer. For verbatim quotes, too, you must take *full* notes — or risk "I've been misquoted!" from a subject who sees you jot down but a few things. And, of course, notes should be taken if the interviewee insists on it — as some will.

Don Imus tells of the time a writer from *Newsday* came to the WNBC radio studios to do a story on the disc jockey. "He didn't ask many questions," recalls Imus. "While he sat watching me do my show he made occasional notes in a little book. Every time he went to the men's room I looked in the book. His notes showed that he was missing some important points. Every time he came back from the men's room I filled him in. As a result, the story he did on me was not too bad."

Subjects who fashion themselves as being clever will often advise an interviewer to "write it down" whenever a bon mot is served up. Be ready.

Afterward

When the interview is over, go through your notes and number the pages. Then go through your notes noting material that is likely to appear in the finished piece. Thus, if you have 12 pages of notes after an interview with, say, the city mayor, a breakdown afterward might include fragments like these:

Plans for reelection campaign (page 2)
Unemployment quotes (3,5,6)
Description of office (7)
Telephone calls — interruptions (8,9)
Quote on urban renewal — possible lead (10)

With an overview like this, it is easy to go into an outline for the article without having to thumb through pages of notes looking for a quote.

Another method of going from notes to outline is to xerox your notes, and then put away your original pages for safekeeping. Using the xeroxed pages, go over everything carefully, checking material that you will be using in the story. After you have studied your notes page by page in this manner, use scissors to clip apart all usable passages. Arrange these clippings into a rough outline, and you probably have the framework for your article. This system works just as readily if you have conducted several interviews. Just be certain you use a different-colored pen to mark the notes for each interview, so that you can keep your interview sources distinct when you bring the clipped materials together for your story.

Keep your notes for as long as possible — even after publication. Remember, a subject can holler "I was misquoted!" months after the interview has occurred. In fact, if the piece appears in a magazine, it is likely to be long after the interview has been forgotten. When the shooting begins, an interviewer's best defense is a full sheaf of notes — even if they are a bit yellowed around the edges.

Get a Move On

The key to good notetaking — and to too much else in journalism — is frantic speed. Set down the source's words quickly — abandoning one remark, if necessary, to alight on another more important;

transcribe your notes immediately after the interview, before the scribbles lose their meaning, like escaping gas. Then, you really ought to curry your notes into a rough draft for your article while the connections and overtones of your source's remarks are still fresh in mind.

Nothing is truly unforgettable. The sooner you commit the meat and minutiae of an interview to paper, then to article — the better. A good interview is too precious to allow to diddle away; in this business, haste *prevents* waste.

8. Tape Recording

No more pencils,
No more pad,
No more misquotes
To make you mad

—Lewis A. Harlow

There are two schools of thought on tape recording an interview: Yes and No. But there are no maybes about its popularity. In recent years, the use of a tape recorder for nonfiction writing has been promulgated almost to the point of suffocation. In book publishing, Leonard Shecter may have started the revolution when he talked baseball player Jim Bouton into "talking" a book, *Ball Four.* In the twilight of his knuckleball career, pitcher Bouton fed a recorder day by day during the 1969 season, sending the tapes to editor Shecter — who had a secretary transcribe everything. Bouton's pitch totaled some 50,000 words on 1,500 manuscript pages, which Shecter distilled into the tome that quickly became the most commercially successful sports book in publishing history.

Studs Terkel's *Division Street: America, Hard Times,* and *Working* are bestsellers made of straight-from-the-shoulder monologues distilled from taped interviews. "No journalist alive wields a tape recorder as effectively as Studs Terkel," says *Time,* "or is as adroit at eliciting from what he has called 'the man of inchoate thought' his most private fears and dreams."

The tape recorder has also been a successful conduit for "oral histories" — witness *Plain Speaking,* Harry Truman's deposition on history, as taken down by Merle Miller; and "oral memoirs" — such as the *Foxfire* books, produced by high school students in the backwoods of Georgia.

Still, many pros apparently feel that use of the tape recorder is strictly high school journalism. Of 234 reporters once polled on the two-headed beast, some 75 percent were agin' it. One reporter found the recorder "makes me less attentive to picking out the important details of an interview. Unless notes are taken, the whole interview has to be replayed — at least twice. A colossal waste of time and a lazy approach to news." Others complained that when the subject was into The Good Stuff, "in the middle of a sentence, the tape runs out and has to be flipped over." The final indignity: "I see no circumstance in which a reporter should use a tape recorder. If a verbatim report is wanted, send a secretary."

Many magazines, however, are sending a reporter with a recorder instead. "It's not that we've grown too lazy to take our own notes," says an editor at the financial magazine *Forbes*. "To most *Forbes* men, tape recorders are a tool of the trade as invaluable as the telephone and the typewriter. They give a man time to listen carefully to *everything* that was said, several times over if need be, to be sure that he understands exactly what was said. And generally that means better stories and more accurate reporting."

The New Wave

While old hands seem to prefer notetaking, a new wave of writers interview with microphone in hand. Today many public officials even give special attention to the electronic media. "A recorder works better than anything I know of for pushing into a crowd," says one writer. A sportswriter says he wouldn't be without his recorder: "In such environs as a locker room, it is almost impossible to get within six feet of the athlete you want to talk to. With a tape recorder, six feet is close enough."

"That a tape recorder may inhibit or intimidate unsophisticated persons is true," observes B. H. Liebes of San Francisco State University, "but the same can be said for a notebook. With today's audience, the TV news generation, a tape recorder, even a TV camera, is a commonplace."

"As a rule," says Stuart Bykofsky, a trade publication editor, "the more sophisticated the individual, the less static he raises about the tape recorder. Most seem pleasantly surprised." He adds: "Resisting the tape recorder is about as purposeful as resisting the telephone.

If used properly the tape recorder is infallible — which is a good deal more than can be said for scribbling notes on a pad. It gives the writer *proof* of the accuracy of his quotes."

Mike Fright

The key phrase: "If used properly." The debate comes down to whether or not an interviewer can use a tape recorder with the tact and style that will relax the subject and get the story — on tape.

Sophistication aside, Henry Kissinger was one sorry statesman after being interviewed by Oriana Fallaci: "Why I agreed to it, I'll never know." Fallaci's response: "There is only one person who is guilty of that interview, and it is him. Because he said what he said and he knows it. He knows that a tape exists and he said those words. So he should blame himself and nobody else."

Even celebrities who speak into microphones in their livelihood can be intimidated by a tape recorder during an interview — perhaps because they have seen too many of their own outtakes. Richard Warren Lewis recalls that when he began setting up a recorder in Johnny Carson's office, the comedian's "Adam's apple gulped, the grin turned to a troubled pout and he nervously lit a cigarette. Johnny doesn't like tape recorders. In the past, he said, unscrupulous journalists have taken his transcribed remarks out of context."

Carson asked Lewis, "Couldn't you just take notes?"

"Not and quote you accurately," Lewis replied. "I can't write that fast." After some further parrying, the comedian consented to the tape recorder — with Lewis's promise to send him a copy of the tape.

Not only are many subjects microphone-shy; many interviewers oppose the tape recorder out of principle rather than convenience. Gay Talese calls the tape recorder "an intrusion" that doesn't allow subjects to "be as frank or free with me as they would be if I were just there establishing personal communication without the presence of a third element. I avoid using a recorder so that I can achieve a more direct communication with the individual." Nora Ephron says she uses a tape recorder from time to time. "Generally, though, I think that there are very few people worth listening to twice." Also, she hates to transcribe. Martin Mayer is against poring over transcribed tapes altogether. "In general, I feel an obligation to make my first selection of what I may possibly use from an interview while I am face to face with my victim," he says. "I disapprove profoundly of the tape-recorded interview, which leaves the writer free at a later time to select from full text anything which serves his later purposes. If what a man says does not seem important enough to write down at the interview itself, he is entitled not to see it appear as one of the handful of quotes attributed to him in a finished piece."

There are situations, of course, in which the intrusion of a tape recorder would be unwise, if not impossible. "When you're talking to a man like Dr. Edwin Land of Polaroid," says Ken Schwartz, former editor at *Forbes* magazine, "the big thing is just to get in the room. You don't want to scare him off with a tape recorder. Or when you're talking to a man off the record on a touchy topic like stock manipulation, a tape recorder is impossible." "A tape recorder terrifies some people," adds JFK chronicler William Manchester. "Rose Kennedy told me that if I brought a recorder in the front door, she'd go out the back door — fast."

Alex Haley prefers a tape recorder. Yet when he was researching *The Autobiography of Malcolm X* — a book that required an intensive year of collaboration with his subject — he came away without a millimeter of recorded conversation. Why? "I noticed that with other people or a recorder, he changed," notes Haley. He recalls talking with Malcolm X one day when they were interrupted by a broadcaster who had come armed with a tape recorder for an interview.

"I watched how Malcolm, who with me had been going on and really flowing, sat down at the mike and gave the appearance of being on and emoting for the tape," says Haley. "Actually, he was very carefully editing what he said and saying only about half as much of what it sounded like. His pattern was one of saying something and then almost paraphrasing what he said. I could see that he was thinking what he was going to say next. . . . Malcolm had a particular caution about anything irrevocably recorded because he was one of these people who felt that a few words can mean a lot — good or bad — to other people."

Mike Like

Politicians, however, are often more comfortable with a microphone (although Mayor Richard J. Daley of Chicago once refused to talk with Hal Higdon because he had a recorder). Writer Henry Brandon showed up to interview John F. Kennedy, and the then-Senator had arranged for a breakfast of orange juice and poached eggs at a table on the patio. When Kennedy saw that there was no electric outlet for Brandon's tape recorder, he asked his valet to serve breakfast inside.

Some subjects will even supply the tape recorder themselves. When Jessica Mitford was researching her book on the funeral industry, *The American Way of Death,* she scheduled a series of interviews with undertakers in California. On one occasion, a group of morticians had their own tape recorder, just to be certain that an acccurate account of the interview would be available to them. As it turned out, Miss Mitford's recorder jammed — so she used the morticians' tape recorder as well.

Seven Advantages

How will a tape recorder help thee? Let us count the ways:

• *First, the interviewer can ask more questions in less time than the notetaker.* More questions mean fuller replies, which often mean a more thorough interview. In the foreword to his book, *I Get My Best Ideas in Bed,* Bill Melton observes that someone reading the interviews therein could doubtless "spot the few occasions on which I used a tape recorder." How so? By the extra length of those answers.

• *Second, taped interviews tend to have that crisp ring of truth.* When Haynes Johnson and David Broder of the *Washington Post* were interviewing voters and party pros during the 1972 Presidential campaign, they used the tape recorder extensively, reproducing large chunks of the interviews in sidebars to their main articles. "The suspicion of the printed word today is so immense," said Haynes Johnson, "if you do a lengthy series on some controversial topic, you find an enormous outpouring from people who don't agree with what you're saying and therefore simply don't believe that you've been there. So we used these transcripts to give the reader a sense of 'By God, whether or not I like it, *that's* what the man said.' "

• *Third, the interviewer can concentrate on the interview.* "The note-scribbling writer must juggle too much at one time," observed Robert J. Levin. "He must accurately quote the subject, keep his notes legible, avoid making the subject self-conscious as he writes, listen to what is being said and comment on it, plan his next questions, and skillfully guide the conversation. When it is all over, he knows — if he is honest — that he has lost some good quotes and others, which he will have to reconstruct, are necessarily secondhand." A social worker once conducted an experiment in which tape recordings of interviews were compared with notes taken from the same interviews. Result: distortions were found in the notes of one out of every three interviews because of "selective inattention."

• *Fourth, a taped interview is reassuring to an editor or publisher if the subject matter is at all controversial.* Insofar as possible, *Playboy* interviews are done with a tape recorder, and master tapes are kept at the magazine's offices. This minimizes the chance that an interviewee will claim s/he was misquoted. "Our attitude toward the tapes is In Case of Emergency, Break Glass," says Murray Fisher. "But we've never had to do that, really, because nobody's come to the point of suing us. Because they can't, finally." When Raquel Welch was interviewed by the magazine, she claimed afterward that she was misquoted. According to Fisher, Welch "caught so much flak from some of the more indiscreet and outspoken things she said in her interview that she felt she *had* to disavow the quotes, saying that we had distorted them. Of course, we had it all on tape." The editors at *Sports Illustrated* sure wish they had all of A. J. Foyt on tape before quoting him in their pages. The race car driver won a $75,000 law suit against *SI* when the magazine could not substantiate a quote attributed to him in which he was supposed to have said he was "gonna make a killing on those queers in California."

• *Fifth, a tape recorder frees the writer on the road.* Dero Saunders, who once lamented that "it takes three hours to transcribe an hour of taped interview," admitted after flying to France for an interview with Jean-Jacques Servan-Schreiber, "You can get it all on tape and then go on about your vacation." The interview on tape is money in the bank.

• *Sixth, when the interviewer's hands are tied, a tape recorder is of real assistance.* For instance, if a writer must interview a subject over lunch, a portable tape recorder can be set in motion and the conversation can flow without interrupting a bite.

• *Seventh, tape recorders can be used for recording lengthy documents.* If you are interviewing someone in his office, and you notice plaques with engraved messages on the wall, the recorder can be used for a fast, accurate copy of these materials by simply dictating them (including punctuation marks) into the microphone. It is best to do such dictating after the interview has ended, and with the subject's permission if he is in the room — though if he steps out, you might dictate in his absence and incorporate the testimonials into your article as color afterward.

At one point in my interview with Max Yasgur, the farmer on whose land the Woodstock musical festival unfolded, he referred proudly to a clock that the townspeople had given him to show that there were no hard feelings, in spite of the havoc that the media said the festival had created. I noticed that the clock, resting atop the fireplace mantel, had an engraved plate. When Yasgur left the room to answer a phone, I walked to the fireplace with my portable recorder and dictated the inscription (a quote from Shakespeare) into the microphone line by line. When "An Afternoon with Max Yasgur" was published, that particular inscription was even more significant — for Yasgur died shortly after our interview, and the townspeople's gift stood as a small monument to a big-hearted farmer.

Choosing a Recorder

What should one look for when buying a tape recorder? First, the convenience and flexibility of a portable recorder cannot be overemphasized. Author Art Fettig's portable paid for itself within 24 hours of the purchase. *"Archery World Magazine* had invited my wife and me to attend an International Tournament in Detroit," he recalls, "and I walked into Cobo Auditorium with my camera under my arm and my tape recorder in my hand." He noticed a crowd gathering around a young archer named Bob Brewer. "Although my knowledge of archery was meager," says Fettig, "I knew enough about it to realize that a perfect score in tournament competition was indeed a rarity. ... Quickly I pushed my way through the excited cheering crowd, extending my microphone toward the stunned archer ... then I went on to conduct my first live celebrity interview." Later, Fettig simply wrote a lead paragraph for the transcript of his conversation with Bob Brewer and sold it to *Archery World* for a fee "that more than covered the cost of the recorder." At the same tournament, Fettig recorded interviews with three other top archers, "all of which later found their way into print."

In addition to being portable, many convenient cassette recorders now come with built-in microphones. The interviewer merely points the front end of the machine toward the subject and starts the tape. The built-in mike picks up everything within ten feet or so, even adjusting its own recording levels. Thus, the risk of inhibiting a subject by setting up a mike in front of him — or jamming one in front of his face — is sidestepped altogether.

The journalist can use cassette recorders costing as little as $50. The main difference between the cheaper models and their $100-$150 brothers for interview use is reliability. The extreme miniaturization of cassette equipment makes it more liable to breakdown, which inevitably occurs at the most inopportune time. So the interviewer is advised to buy the best cassette recorder he can afford — though it need not be stereo, which is fine for stationary use but much too delicate to travel well. Stick with mono for interviews.

It is advisable, too, to use a cassette recorder with a digital counter, and to start the interview with a fresh tape and with the counter on zero. As the tape moves along, you might take some notes, jotting down the digital number whenever the subject lets fly a good quote. When the interview is over, you can use your digital counter jottings as an index to the tape's liveliest contents. The same system can be used for taking notes on the subject's appearance and attitude. If he assumes a striking pose while saying something lively, jot down the digital number — "353, leaned back, rubbed eyes, looked upward before responding" — and you can blend these descriptive details in with your quote for effective, dramatic writing.

Dr. Demento's Diagnosis

One tremendous advantage of the cassette recorder over a portable reel-type machine is the ease with which one can replace or turn over a tape. Select cassette tapes for your recorder with care, however. Many inexpensive brands are available, and if yours is a beginner's budget, they will probably suffice; but if you are able to consider the more expensive brands, you may find that the workmanship is worth the additional cost. One problem with cassette tapes, alas, is that if the tape becomes mangled or broken, it is nearly impossible for the average user to repair the tape without tearing the whole cassette apart. Because most cassettes (even higher-priced ones) are held together by a binding glue, this procedure often results in a pile of unwound tape, bits of plastic from the case, and a lost interview. A few quality brands, however — Maxell comes to mind — feature cassette cases held together by tiny screws instead of glue. Thus, the tape can be reached, spliced, rewound and repaired with a small effort and with a jeweler's screwdriver.

"Don't fall for the super-cheap cassette tape," cautions Barry Hansen, the Los Angeles freelancer aka syndicated disc jockey Dr. Demento, "particularly those 'assembled in Mexico from U.S.A. components.' Workmanship is low, and breakdown rate is high." Pay for reliability. Hansen also recommends that the interviewer abstain from the extra-long-play C-120 and C-180 cassettes in portable machines. "The extra-thin tape used in these cassettes tends to get jammed in the transport mechanism," he says, "ruining the recording and often the recorder as well." If you have a Sony recorder, you will find that Sony cassettes cause the machine to make an audible alarm signal when the recording time has expired — a feature that will save you many anxious glances at the recorder during the interview. Many a fine quote has been lost to posterity because the interviewer did not realize that the cassette had already ground uncomplainingly to a halt.

A wise investment (if it is not included as an extra) is an AC adapter for your cassette recorder. Batteries, however fresh at the outset, often wind down faster than anticipated; the adapter then is your lifeboat. In fact, if you know you will be doing an interview near an electric outlet, you should use the adapter — with an extension cord, if necessary — from the beginning. If you depend on batteries, and they begin to dwindle, say, after two hours, the third hour of that great interview may be captured on something less than the standard one & 7/8 inches per second that most cassette recorders maintain. A minor fall-off in power will not be reflected on the simplistic battery meters most lower-priced machines feature; and when you put in fresh batteries to transcribe the interview later, that final hour is likely to sound like Donald Duck in heat.

With a reel recorder, you will find that a reel tape's size and openness make repair work and splicing much easier. When the tape comes to a stop on one side, it is more evident to the onlooker as well. . In general, reel tapes range from .5 to 1.5 mils in thickness, and the thinner the tape the greater the likelihood that it will break. Many interviewers are reluctant to use a tape that falls below 1 mil, though if maximum playing time is required, a 7-inch reel of 1.5-mil tape — played at a speed of 3.75 inches per second — will provide two uninterrupted hours of playing time before it must be attended to. This is ideal for lengthy interviews that would suffer if there were interruptions such as the interviewer reversing the tape or putting a fresh reel on the recorder.

Handling a Mike

How should one wield a tape recorder during an interview? Most writers let the subject know in advance that they will be taping the interview. Some do not. "I don't mention it when setting up an interview," says Stuart Bykofsky. "My method of notetaking should be of no concern to the subject as long as the notes are accurate. I wouldn't mention my pad or pencil; why discuss this tool?" Nor does Bykofsky seek permission to use the recorder when he arrives. "After walking in and shaking hands, I simply set up the machine and test voice levels as I chat."

This attitude is likely to be dangerous for many interviewers. Equating a pad and pencil's presence with that of a tape recorder is like comparing a handgun with a howitzer and saying, "Well, either one can wound you." One is more awesome than the other — and most subjects know it. A source can deny the work of a pad and pencil; but a tape recorder leaves him no escape hatch. "If getting famous people to talk is exhausting," says Oriana Fallaci, "getting them to talk in front of a machine that is recording every pause and every breath is, in 50 percent of the cases, fraught with tension. . . ."

Don't assume that a recorder is OK with your subject. Ask beforehand. Even if he says yes, you may find that he is apprehensive when you arrive. One method for overcoming his misgivings is to talk about the machine as you set it up. Try to interest the subject in the mechanics of it. Loosen him up with reinforcement like "I've taken notes on some interviews, but I find that for 100 percent accuracy a tape recorder is imperative."

Still, be prepared for a change of heart. When I arranged to interview Max Yasgur, his first reaction to the use of a tape recorder was, "OK, I don't mind. I don't have much to say anyway."

About ten minutes into the interview Yasgur was obviously tense. Finally, he looked at me and said, "Would you mind turning that darn thing off?" I did, and he loosened up immediately. The interview moved along forcefully. I took notes furiously. Fortunately, my wife was with me, and she took notes, too. After the interview, we drove a few hundred yards from the farm, turned on the tape recorder and began going through our sketchy notes — fleshing them out on tape. Within an hour we had reconstructed everything of value while it was still fresh, and the article that resulted was rich in direct quotes from Max Yasgur.

After setting up your equipment for an interview, test everything to ensure a smooth run. Be mindful of background noises that your microphone may pick up and which may subsequently drown out your interview: street sounds, typewriters, music on a radio or Muzak system, a humming air conditioner, buzzing fluorescent lights. "Experiment to determine an appropriate distance and the required recording level for the room acoustics," advises Lewis A. Harlow in a *Popular Electronics* article.

If you have never recorded an interview before, you might practice the night before. Know how your tape recorder works — determine what the volume setting should be, and how sensitive your microphone is. Always bring more tape to the interview than you think you will need, and test the tape recorder for voice level before you start asking questions. Such testing may be a good icebreaker for the interview, in fact. (When Richard Warren Lewis clicked on his machine, Johnny Carson's test line was "Rose Mary Woods lives!")

Despite the best-laid plans, background noises and interruptions are bound to spoil some interviews. "I remember taping a breakfast interview with Harry Knight of Knight & Gladieux," says Tom Stevenson, former associate editor at *Forbes,* "and all you could hear for about five minutes was Mr. Knight stirring his soft-boiled egg!" Other noisemakers — and troublemakers — include iced water being poured into a goblet, and a phone ringing in the same room. If the microphone is placed on or near the recorder itself, it may pick up the recorder's motor sounds as well.

What sort of microphone should you use? Try an omnidirectional microphone when you're interviewing more than one person; it picks up sounds from all directions. A microphone with an on/off remote control switch is convenient, too; it enables the interviewer to stop recording with a mere flick of the finger on the hand-held microphone — and that minimizes the subject's awareness of the tape recorder. But: take care with a hand-held mike. In addition to being a distraction for sit-down interviews (you must constantly shift the microphone back and forth for question and reply), such mikesmanship might pick up that two-finger percussion performance that muffles words on the recording. "The best microphone position for most indoor recording is near the center of the room with the mike pointed away from the window to minimize background noise," adds Lewis A. Harlow. "The mike should be placed on a table approximately equidistant from each person involved in the interview."

When freelancer Gordon Fletcher was interviewing a member of the rock band Deep Purple, he established such good rapport that he was invited to view the group's show from a seat onstage. "And, incredibly, I was also able to interview Glenn Hughes while the rest of his mates performed," says the writer. "We talked about groupies and sex in the music industry, only I don't have any quotes because like a dummy I failed to realize that every word we spoke would be drowned out by the PA beside us." A good interview lost forever, thanks to sound on sound.

Pauses That Refresh

Occasionally, interruptions are helpful. They were for Bob Foy when he interviewed a busy zookeeper. "I wrote my questions out and read them to him and we recorded everything that was said," wrote Foy afterward. "But everything else that went on in the office came out on the tape too. . . . In between his answers was the telephone ringing, the zookeeper's instructions to a subordinate on how to feed the rhino, who to call when one of the chimps had a toothache, as well as a hilarious telephone conversation with a lady who thought she saw a snake in her kitchen." Of such interruptions are multiple sales made. Transcribing the tape was difficult, but Foy eventually sold three separate articles from the interview.

A common interruption in an interview is the changing of the tape. Replacing a cassette is easy; reversing a reel tape, distracting. "When the tape runs out and you can hear it flapping," suggests one writer, "show some concern, but make it appear that it would pain you if some important point in the interview were missed." Jot down a few notes for effect. When the subject has finished answering, excuse yourself and tend to the machine. Changing a tape represents a break in the interview, but with some forethought you can make the most of it. Turn it into a pause that refreshes. You might ask if the subject has any phone calls to make, or an answering service to check with. If refreshments are available, consider it a coffee break as well. Comment on the interview thus far. "I've got some fine material here." To warm up the subject, suggest that s/he repeat that last missed reply for the beginning of the new reel.

Make it seem important; people do not generally enjoy repeating themselves in such close order. If anything he has said thus far has been unclear, now would be a good time to speak of it. If you are interviewing a subject who is budgeting his time, and who may have an appointment in 45 minutes, acknowledge his timetable as you put on a fresh tape. "This runs for an hour, but I'm sure I can get everything I need in 30 minutes or so" is reassuring to someone whose voice is strained after an hour of talk, and whose eyes are bulging at that fat, fresh reel being wound into place.

Taking and Faking Notes

The interruption that interviewers dread most of all is the Complete Breakdown, which can — and will — occur at the worst moment. Rex Reed, who would later write that interviewing Warren Beatty "is like asking a hemophiliac for a pint of blood," showed up for the interview with two tape recorders — a special requirement — one a tiny Norelco cassette, and the other a large Wollensak. Both were broken before the interview began. Beatty puttered around for a few minutes, shaking them, holding them up to his ear, and finally gave up. "Forget the tape recorder," he told Reed. "I'll trust you." Reed got lucky.

So did Tom Burke, whose tape recorder began to make protesting sounds "at the perfectly wrong moment" in his interview with Kris Kristofferson for *Rolling Stone.* "If you tape interviews with celebrities, you must conceal your machine's crotchets at any cost," wrote Burke, "including a fake epileptic seizure or even, in extreme crisis, interrupting your subject, lest he perceive that his thoughts, usually dredged from the somberest levels of Reich, Janov, Reuben, L. Ron Hubbard and *How to Be Your Own Best Friend,* be lost." In this particular instance Kristofferson studied the broken recorder "as if its rudeness had restored his own good humor," and said: "Rose Mary Woods is lurkin' somewheres. Think we can fix it?"

With that, the subject manipulated the machine until it was working again.

Studs Terkel, who concedes that without a tape recorder his books would not be possible, says that whenever his recorder goes wrong, he swears at it. Terkel's subject inevitably laughs and seems "to feel more relaxed."

Gloria Steinem rarely uses a tape recorder for interviewing because of a deep-seated fear: "I don't trust it. I don't think it's working." And sometimes it's not. Consider Gabe Pressman, the TV reporter who once tried to interview Casey Stengel while the first Mets manager was sitting atop a float in a Thanksgiving Day parade. "As my camera crew rode alongside, I jumped aboard and climbed the steps to interview him," recalls Pressman. The interview complete, he jumped off the float — only to be told by the sound man that there was no sound. He chased the float, went through the interview again, and again: technical failure. When Pressman gave chase again, Casey bellowed, "You again! You S.O.B. How can I be sure you'll get it right this time?" Pressman got it right, and Casey was on the air that night — but few subjects would be so tolerant of mechanical breakdowns, unless trapped on a float with nothing else to do.

Moral: although the tape recorder may seem to be capturing everything on tape, stay alert and keep some notetaking equipment handy. An interviewer needs all the insurance he can get.

Hal Higdon uses a tape recorder for key interviews, but adds: "In many instances I also take notes and simply leave untranscribed an uninspiring taped interview." In view of the time and cost of transcription, this is efficient thinking. "Listening to someone talk isn't at all like listening to their words played over a machine," says Oriana Fallaci. "What you hear when you have a face before you is never what you hear when you have before you a winding tape. At times a flashing glance or a movement of the hands will make the most stupid remark meaningful, but without the hands, the flashing glance, the remark is left in all its disconcerting stupidity. . . ." A tape provides the quotes — and supplementary notes put them in perspective.

Author Morton Hunt finds it helpful to *pretend* to take notes, even though he uses the tape recorder extensively. While interviewing subjects for his book *The Affair* — which chronicles 91 ease histories — he found that "90 percent of those I interviewed had no hangups about talking of their affairs." His method was to "pretend to take notes so my subject would forget that a tape recorder was running." Result: "I carried a big box of Kleenex around with me because so many people cried." "Subjects like to feel that writers are writing," adds Stuart Bykofsky, also an advocate of taking notes while taking it all down on tape.

Wired for Sound

Of course, a tape recorder has a multitude of uses for the writer besides for interviewing. It can be used for recording lectures, television talk-show interviews, ideas in the middle of the night, library research, and flashes of inspiration which strike while you are driving a car with the recorder in the front seat. It can be used for recording captions to photos you are taking (particularly for group shots, when you must get a handful of names straight); on-the-scene notes for a nighttime event — a play, an outdoor concert, a police raid — when a notebook would be of value only to an owl.

The writer's recorder is also useful for a fast first draft of an article (that a secretary or an understanding spouse can transcribe while you move on to other areas of the project). "I find it difficult to work from sloppy handwritten notes taken during the heat of an interview," says Alvin Toffler, author of *Future Shock* and numerous articles. "I used to spend considerable time retyping these notes before attempting to organize my article. Now I find I can save time, avoid an unpleasant chore and telescope the whole process of organization by dictating the notes into my tape recorder and having a typist prepare them for me in a special way."

While researching *Westward Tilt*, a book on the migration to the American West since World War II, author Neil Morgan used the smallest of several recorders to interview himself. "I found myself talking into it as I drove or as I dressed in the morning," he recalls. "This gave me a reservoir of an almost subconscious stream of thought which otherwise would have escaped; it also helped me to recapture settings and moods for descriptive passages of the book which resulted." Today, he adds, he is "seldom far from a pocket-sized recorder into which I may confide. Talking vague ideas out on tape can help firm them into salable material."

Perhaps the best professional pocket-sized recorder is the Nagra SN, which weighs about a pound and three ounces (with batteries). It fits easily into a jacket pocket (or can be hidden in any book-sized object), is ruggedly built, and records with a quality that corresponds to the requirements of broadcast reporting. At this writing, it costs $1,916.10. (For information: Nagra Magnetic Recorders, Inc., 19 West 44th Street, Room 715, New York City 10036.) Television viewers have probably seen this recorder in action when they view a sporting event in which, say, a coach is "wired for sound." The recorder is located in a jacket or a hip pocket, with its microphone attached by clip to a belt, a breast pocket or an undershirt. Using extra thin tape at low speed in such a precision instrument will enable one to record up to 3½ hours of uninterrupted sound before having to change or reverse the reel.

Concealed Weapon

As tape recorders become smaller, their concealed use for interviews raises a question of ethics: does a journalist have the right to conceal a tape recorder during an interview? "Why should any honest person be willing to direct statements to a reporter's brain and notebook — and not to his recorder?" asks the Rev. Mr. Lester Kinsolving, an Episcopal worker priest whose weekly column on religion appears in more than 150 daily newspapers. Kinsolving often uses a concealed tape recorder for interviews, and defends the practice by saying he makes it "perfectly clear" that he is a working journalist before the tape recorder is turned on. He identifies his employer, and makes "careful note of any absence of any stipulation that the conversation was 'off the record' or 'in confidence,' which as a member of both the Fourth and Second Estates I am bound to respect," says the columnist.

Joe Hyams, on assignment for *Look* magazine to do a two-part series on Ava Gardner, had heard beforehand that the actress froze at the sight of a notepad. "Do you mind if I tape you?" he asked when they met. "Not as long as I don't know it," she replied. Hyams: "It was imperative that I get her quotes down accurately, and I didn't trust my memory, so I had laid careful plans. I was wearing a shoulder holster containing a small wire recorder; a flex ran across my back under my coat to a microphone disguised as a wristwatch." The actress didn't know it — and Hyams got his story.

"Neither editors nor reporters should fail to question the motives of those who are willing to direct statements to a reporter's ear, but not to his recorder," adds Lester Kinsolving. "And when the time comes when no editor will recognize such a sleazy distinction, there should be no further need for concealment of the recorder, which can be a reporter's first line of defense."

Robert J. Levin, whose personality profiles often appeared in *Redbook* and *Good Housekeeping*, used a hidden tape recorder for interviews. "I always tell a person that I am recording the conversation, but the fact that the machine itself stays out of sight has a telling effect," he said. "Everyone — myself included — forgets that a recorder is at work. Talk flows freely, spontaneously, sometimes vulgarly, almost always revealingly. The tape recorder liberates *me*. I can concentrate on what is being said, not on what I should remember; I can converse, not interrogate."

This approach, somewhat redolent of former President Nixon's taping apparatus in the White House, would seem to combine the best of both worlds for the interviewer who wants to record surreptitiously, yet satisfy his conscience. It results in a recorded interview without the risks of microphone fright or the drawbacks of cumbersome equipment. The result is a natural-sounding interview. "It allows me to capture speech patterns," added Levin. "In one case, for example, I tape recorded an interview with Mike Todd just a few hours before he took off on his fatal plane flight. Months later, his son commented on the article I subsequently wrote, impressed by the fact that the quotes sounded 'just like Dad.'"

That, of course, is the mainstay grace of tape recording interviews: that you will get down what was said in just the way it was said, without the lapses of pencil and pad and panicky notetaker. The trick is to keep your subject's mind on his opinions, and off your recorder. To that end, you should (underline one):

A.) Stash the recorder into your bra and the microphone into an alluring nosegay;

B.) Put the recorder on a chair and poke the subject with a pencil every time his eyes wander toward the whirring tape;

C.) Plop down the recorder wherever is handy and discreet, and carry on.

The answer is probably C. If *you* will forget the recorder is running, your subject will probably forget, too. Generally, a good interview is too absorbing to allow a subject to dwell on its mechanics. You only need to be sure that your recorder runs, and that your questions provoke.

Remember, the tape recorder is merely the insurance — not the ingredient — for a good interview. Treat it as a tool of your trade, not as a main attraction; and your subjects will do the same.

9. Hazardous Zones

There once was a writer from Treadline
Who interviewed drunks in a breadline;
They chewed on his legs,
Reduced him to dregs,
But his story came in right on deadline.
                            —Allan C. Scott

Neither rain nor sleet nor heinous handicaps shall keep an interviewer from making his appointed rounds. Routine impedimenta, however, can really get in the way at times. Consider:

• **Weird hours.** The time selected for an interview is extremely important. The interviewer should make an appointment at the subject's convenience, and be reasonably sure that the subject will have ample time to devote himself to the interview with a minimum of distractions. If your subject is a night owl, you may have to juggle your schedule accordingly. During one period in his career, Hugh Hefner was working for several days at a stretch without sleep. Life, in short, had no clock; and Hefner agreed to see writer Hal Higdon for a morning interview — at 4 a.m. "We talked for nearly five hours," recalls Higdon, "breaking our discussion only for trips to the refrigerator for Pepsi-Cola. When I finally staggered to bed, normal people had just begun to arrive to work. It took me nearly a week to recover."

• **Tardiness.** The watchword here is patience, unless you are a crusty publisher. Henry Luce, according to biographer W. A. Swanberg, was an arrogant soul accustomed to things running his way. When granted an interview with the Pope, he fumed because Pius XII was ten minutes late. "Goddamit, Walter," he growled to an aide, "where the hell is the Pope?" Fortunately, Luce never interviewed Marilyn Monroe, a chronic late-arriver. "Frequently, she would be an hour or two hours late for an interview," recalls columnist Earl Wilson. "And all the while the interviewer was waiting, she would be sitting in her bedroom continuing to work on her make-up or merely indulging the narcissist's love of looking at herself." Wilson found that one method of dealing with such a subject was to tell her in advance that you have another appointment for the same day. Make it personal, and make it urgent. The columnist once told Marilyn that he could not be late for a surprise birthday party for his wife later that day. "Marilyn was extremely proud of herself that day," he recalls. "She was only 15 minutes late."

A subject continually late for interview appointments can be fatiguing, but not nearly as fatiguing as someone who promises an interview, and then becomes evasive or "busy." Veteran Hollywood writer Joseph N. Bell spent more than a week following Danny Kaye through the preparations for a TV show. "I requested as much interview time as possible with Mr. Kaye," says the writer, "and was told to be patient and I would be worked in as quickly and as often as his schedule permitted." At the end of the week Kaye gave Bell "an eloquent monologue for a half-hour about why a performer of his stature would subject himself to the regimen of a weekly hour on television; then he abruptly dismissed me. The interview had ended." So it goes.

• *Interview Fatigue.* Boredom, tedium, and ennui on the part of the subject are usually tipped off by stale replies and restless eyes. When this happens, take five — or call it quits until another day. Psychological studies on perception have indicated that the most important element in our environment is change. A single setting for an interview, therefore, can have a narcotic effect. The subject becomes restrictive in the kind of information he wants to share, and he may be outrageously dull. Leonard Shecter wrote a book about the life and hard times of Roger Maris when the ballplayer began hitting a lot of home runs in 1961 (the year he broke Babe Ruth's single-season record). Maris agreed to cooperate on the book, and the writer began spending considerable time with him. "I found that after about an hour of interview," wrote Shecter afterward, "his attention would wander, even when he was talking about himself. So I spent about 40 separate hours with him over the next several months. He was friendly and amenable, talked with great freedom, revealed himself a lot more than he probably intended."

A change in time and setting, then, can mean a change in content — often for the better. The *Playboy* interviews work on this principle. A single interview will be spread over a period of several days, or even weeks and months. After Larry DuBois spent some six months with Hugh Hefner, the magazine's editors wrote: "He saw all of this complex man's facets and explored, more thoroughly than we dared hope, his thinking. The results are remarkable."

• **Hurry up.** Whether an interview is a minute or a month, let the subject talk on for as long as he wants. "Don't *ever* begin an interview by deadlining it: 'I've only got until 3:30, so I hope we can cover everything in an hour,'" advises Max Gunther in his *Writing and Selling a Nonfiction Book.* "If I sense a man or woman will be unusually helpful and talkative, I try to allow much more than an hour of time. In the case of a phone interview, I ask the source to talk to me in the evening, from his home, rather than from his office during working hours. People are generally more relaxed in the evening; their time is not so inflexibly scheduled as during the average day. I never tell the source in advance that I think the interview may last two hours, for that might frighten him. I simply make time for a long, leisurely interview in case it turns out that way. Similarly, in the case of face-to-face interviews, I like to make appointments for 11 a.m. or 4 p.m. This way, if we go beyond an hour and I want the source to go on talking, I can take him out for lunch or a drink."

• **Food forethought.** Interviewing a subject over a meal has its positive features, surely. "Men *always* talk best when they eat," observed pioneer interviewer Isaac Marcosson. And he liked to interview famous men over a meal. Do so with certain hazards in mind, however.

Actor Gary Cooper was a quiet man throughout his years of stardom, and also a legendary tough interview. "His press agents told me that no one had been able to get a publishable interview with Coop for ten years," recalls Charles Samuels, who eventually did get a story, but was nearly undone by the setting. He met the quiet actor for lunch at the noisy Warner Bros. commissary, "which is like trying to interview somebody during a hurricane," adds Samuels.

Oriana Fallaci gives storm warnings, too, regarding interviews over food. In her book *The Egotists,* she recalls the time she interviewed director Federico Fellini in a restaurant with her tape recorder. "I tried to talk him out of such an awful plan," she says. "My complaints were all to no avail. Either we did it in the restaurant ... or nowhere else and never again. So I looked for a table next to a plug, made room for the tape recorder among the plates and the glasses and the hors d'oeuvres platter, and started the interview, which, since we were constantly interrupted by innumerable telephone calls, proceeded as smoothly as a lame man running, against the clatter and noise of forks, glasses, and vulgar chewing." When she played back the tape, Fallaci heard phrases like, "With this movie I am trying to say ... Do you want the ham or the salami? I'll take the salami. People who talk about metaphysical dialectics ... No, I don't want any pasta, it's too fattening. A steak without salt, that's what I'll have ... It's so stupid to shut one's eyes to the mystery. ... Crack! Clink! Clink! ... The silence that surrounds you and becomes a gleam of light ... french fries! Why aren't you having any french fries?"

So it went. Useless. "Without a doubt it would all have to be done again," reflected the interviewer. And it was — but only after several delays, some cancelled appointments, and, toward the end, some hard feelings. "I used to be truly fond of Federico Fellini," says Fallaci. "Since our tragic encounter I'm a lot less fond. To be exact, I am no longer fond of him. That is, I don't like him at all." Or interviewing over food.

If an interview does occur at a restaurant, the writer should pick up the tab. An exception to this would be if a late afternoon interview appointment runs into a dinner reservation that the subject had made previously with some friends or family. If the subject wishes to continue the interview through dinner, and he invites the writer along, then the role of host dictates that the tab go to the subject. But neutral-ground hospitality should be paid for by the interviewer. Some publications will cover these expenses readily for the interviewer; other publications on smaller budgets will arrange for a higher fee, or for a follow-up assignment — or even let the writer absorb the costs. Work it out with your editor afterward. But pick up the tab.

For an interviewer to accept *anything* resembling a favor from the subject is considered dangerous, and is likely to be viewed as a compromise of the writer's integrity by an editor. Freelancer Elizabeth Mooney discovered this painfully when she wrote a profile for the *Washington Post,* only to have it turned down because she allowed a subject to pick up the tab for an unrelated lunch. "*Post* reporters do not accept as much as a cup of coffee from the people they interview," she said afterward. "It's a matter of freedom of the press. If you accept gifts, you're bought."

• *Can't You See I'm Working?* Business is business. When interviewing a subject who is at work, have respect for his situation. Red Barber, for instance, keeps certain "rules of thumb" in mind when he is readying for a baseball interview: "Never ask a pitcher who is starting the game to be your guest that day; one, he is warming up and should be left alone, and two, you don't want it on his mind or yours that he has a TV routine after the game." The Ol' Redhead also cautions against asking managers to agree to an interview after a game — "something drastic may happen in the ninth inning. Ask them for an interview before the game, when they have time, and when they don't know how the day will turn out. The manager is always a pre-game optimist."

Subjects doing an interview during business hours usually have little time to waste. They want to get down to facts fast. If an interviewer engages in too much chitchat, he may find that telephone calls or other appointments soon demand his subject's attention. Suddenly the interview is over, and he has not obtained the information he came for. Businessmen must consider business first. Irving Wallace found the painter Diego Rivera "resentful and brusque because I had interrupted his painting of a nude in his studio," but "later coming in the rain, sweet and cooperative, to submit to an interview in Mexico City's Ritz Hotel."

Curtis MacDougall suggests that a reporter might obtain an interview with a person difficult to approach by waiting out his subject, "accosting him in the lobby of the hotel or behind the scenes during a dramatic performance, concert or lecture." Magazine writers, however, have more luxurious deadlines; and most of them would probably find the Flush-'Em-Out Technique the worst possible approach for the wary subject. Todd Everett, for instance, approached Ian Anderson of the Jethro Tull rock group for an interview backstage at a television show. Everett left with no story, but with a valuable lesson. "I just sort of jumped at him," recalls the writer. "He didn't have the slightest idea who I was, so I introduced myself — I was working for *Record World* at the time — and I started asking him all sorts of questions. Anderson was between takes of the TV show, and he was rather abrupt with me. He was concentrating on his music and I was a distraction he didn't want. It kind of shook me up, too.

"A good time to interview rock stars is in the morning of the day of a concert," suggests Everett. "Usually they set up all their equipment in the auditorium or club or whatever then for a sound check to make sure everything is working. There is a lot of messing around, and it's largely dead time for the musicians. At this point, other people are doing most of the work that requires real concentration — checking the PA system and so forth. You can get the star's attention during this session in a way that you can't after the performance that night. After the show, the performer wants to get drunk, take a shower, go to bed — *anything* but talk to an interviewer. Sometimes the following morning, if the star is taking a plane in the afternoon, you can get in for an interview." In any case, be mindful of a subject whose mind is more on questions of the moment than on the questions of an interviewer.

• **Furniture arrangement.** If the interview is to take place in your office or living room, give some thought to how the room looks. (Even when the room for the interview is neutral turf, you may have some choice as to seating arrangement if you arrive first). Psychiatrists have found that even fairly sophisticated adults meeting for the first time are often more at ease if placed around a table rather than in a room with nothing in front of them. A desk or coffee table, therefore, may be helpful for initial rapport if carefully placed between you and your subject. Historians note that when Benito Mussolini had to face an interview, he usually did so from behind a vast desk deliberately set *higher* than the position of his seated interviewer. Impressed by the example, the late Hollywood mogul Harry Cohn did the same thing at Columbia Pictures and intimidated countless importuners. Unless your aim as an interviewer is to intimidate, though, keep such regal room arrangements out of sight.

Sometimes a subject will only consent to an interview in less than adequate conditions. When this happens, the writer must take the interview on the spot and make the best of it. Harry Truman used to allow reporters to join him for his daily morning walk along Pennsylvania Avenue — but he would not allow them to question him in his office (after some reporters spilled ink on the rug). Albert Goldman, author of numerous articles and a book on comedian Lenny

Bruce, tells of the comic's fascination with the bathroom. Bruce used the room for shooting up (he was a heroin addict) and cleaning up (he was a cleanliness freak); and "an interview with Lenny was usually conducted through a restroom door."

More recently, Rex Reed found himself in a ladies' restroom interviewing singer Bette Midler. Yes. The locales for Studs Terkel's interviews for *Division Street: America* varied considerably. "Frequently it was the home of the subject, or his place of work, or a quiet corner of the radio studio [where Terkel works], or my house, or a booth in the restaurant, or the front seat of a car," says Terkel. "On occasion, there was coffee or a can of beer or a shot of whiskey, or in the case of a gracious elderly lady, a memorable meal."

Generally, wherever two persons can gather, an interview can be conducted. But some places are *too* offbeat for an interview. Paul Cunningham's ingenuity went awry during the 1960 Presidential primary in West Virginia when the NBC reporter followed Sen. Hubert Humphrey into an amusement park. "How about doing an interview on the roller coaster?" asked Cunningham. "Fine," said Humphrey. All was arranged. As their car moved up an incline toward a plunge, Cunningham started the interview. "Senator, how does it look in terms of getting a big labor vote?"

"Well, Paul," began the senator, taking a look over the side, "EEEEEYYYAAAAAAAHHHHHHHH!!!"

"About the labor vote," persisted Cunningham.

"Well, said Humphrey, heading for another plunge, "YYYAAAAAAAHHHHHHH!!!"

Afterward the reporter wrote in *TV Guide,* "I still have the film, and it's one long scream. He was terrified! He'd never been on a roller coaster before." Um, avoid roller coasters for interviews whenever possible.

• *Third party hazards.* It's important that you be alone with the subject in a quiet place if at all possible. The presence of a third party may create interruptions and responses that are biased. A researcher writing in the *American Journal of Sociology* on whether or not elderly persons should live with their children found that replies were affected significantly, depending on whether the children were interviewed alone, the parents were interviewed alone, or the parents and children were interviewed together.

John Gunther encountered similar reluctance when he was invited to a small dinner in Cincinnati; during the meal he asked a few broad questions. "Who runs Cincinnati?" he asked. "What *really* goes on here?" An embarrassed silence was his answer. "Then I discovered that everybody who *did* run Cincinnati was right there in that room," said Gunther afterward, "but hated to admit that they ran it."

A clever interviewer can often play off the third party against another subject, and get what he came for anyway. (When the dinner party was over, a guest came up to Gunther and said, "I don't know about you, but I have learned more about Cincinnati tonight than I've learned in 20 years.") Author John Gruen was interviewing actress Barbara Harris more recently when her boyfriend wandered into the room. "Miss Harris became very still and grave," said Gruen afterward. Then, using a burlesque Russian accent, she said to the writer, "Tell me, Mr. Vulture Interviewer, can't you think of anything very, very serious, very, very deep to ask me? Don't you want to record my opinions on love, life, laughter and lox?" She was hamming it up, trying to unsettle the interviewer in front of someone who was now her true audience. Gruen responded by hamming it up in return, throwing subjects at the actress with lightning speed. In the article he reproduced the replies in effective checklist fashion:

On Women: "I like women. They make very good friends. I trust them."

On Men: "I like men. They don't make very good friends, but I trust them."

On Relationships: "That's relative."

On Competition: "I do believe in a little healthy competition, but I don't go along with whoever it was that said, 'To be successful is not enough — your friends have to fail!' "

On Rock Hudson: "Any movie star named after the *Hudson Review* can't be all bad."

On Love: "As Bruno Bettelheim says, 'Love is not enough.' "

On Medicare and the Tobacco Warnings: "I think it's a wonderful double bill."

"It was only after I had hit upon the idea of asking her to act out an interview that she began to communicate," wrote Gruen. "It would seem that within the improvisational framework of her theatrical background she can operate with distinctive humor and wit."

• **Press (and Pest) Agents.** An often-maligned intruder in interviews is the press agent. There was a time when a press agent's chief function was to manufacture publicity stunts in order to gain newspaper space for a client; but today the role of the press agent is one of protective assistance. In fact, many celebrities use the press agent, ironically, to stay out of the press and away from the inquiring writer. (A handful of PR biggies even make policy decisions for a celebrity, according to the "image" s/he wishes to project to the public.) No matter. For the interviewer, the press agent is often the third man in the ring.

"Usually in Hollywood there are three persons present — the reporter, his subject, and a press agent," says Bob Thomas, Hollywood columnist for the Associated Press. "The press agent's presence is not as insidious as it may sound. Only a few times have I heard a press agent caution a star about a statement — usually over something inconsequential. The professional press agents maintain silence, or sometimes they can help by drawing out a shy interviewee." Thomas adds that while he has had "some wowsers" tried on him over the years, the trick is in learning to use press agents for help. "They can be very helpful in letting you know when newsworthy personalities are in town, in making arrangements for interviews, in getting statements from their clients." And in Hollywood, where most stars have unlisted phone numbers, such assistance is invaluable.

A press agent can also help monitor the current mood of a temperamental star. "I caught Rex Harrison for a scheduled interview when he was in a black mood immediately after finishing work on *My Fair Lady,*" recalls Joseph N. Bell. "The press agent who took me to Mr. Harrison's dressing room on the Warner Bros. lot was decidedly uneasy. He told me that Harrison had just suffered through an interview by a female who wanted to talk only about his ex-wives, and a radio disc jockey who obviously hadn't read the studio biography and asked him such questions as: 'What was your last picture?' and 'Have you ever done any stage work before?' " Harrison, irked, was replying in monosyllables. The press agent warned Bell that he had better have some good questions as the writer went through his notes en route.

For openers, Bell asked the actor if he thought George Bernard Shaw would have approved of the ending of *My Fair Lady.* "The question intrigued him," wrote Bell afterward in the *Saturday Review.* "He relaxed, and we were able to establish some measure of rapport. His dressing room was pandemonium — phones ringing constantly, mercenaries moving in and out on such missions as the selection of booze for a closing party and travel arrangements for the Harrison family, scheduled to depart posthaste. Harrison moved through all this confusion with great aplomb, directing his platoons without passion as he fielded a succession of questions from me with grace, wit, and style. It was an impressive performance." Why? Because of a press agent's forewarning: beware of the moods of Rex, and have some damn good questions.

A press agent can be a pest, too. When Tom Nolan was interviewing Richard and Karen Carpenter for a *Rolling Stone* cover story, a press agent sat in on an interview one morning as the Carpenters exchanged harsh words. They had ordered some sound equipment that was months overdue, and Richard began to scold Karen because her boyfriend worked for the firm where the order was placed. The agent began to hum "Tea for Two" in a "strained and significant voice," according to Nolan, "as if to remind them of a writer's presence at the table."

Some intruders will not only sit in on interviews with their bosses, but will try to censor material gathered during an interview — and their judgment is not always in an interviewee's best interest. When Merle Miller was interviewing Harry Truman (for what would eventually become *Plain Speaking: An Oral Biography),* a small boy asked the former President, "Was you popular when you was a boy?" Writes Miller: "The President looked at the boy over the glasses that always made him look like an irritated owl. 'Why, no,' he said. 'I was never popular. The popular boys were the ones who were good at games and had big, tight fists. I was never like that. Without my glasses I was blind as a bat, and to tell the truth, I was kind of a sissy. If there was any danger of getting into a fight, I always ran. I guess that's why I'm here today.' " The candor of the response surely tells us more about the man than does his cowardice as a child. But afterward a pair of Presidential hoverers asked Merle Miller to make certain that the question and answer were removed from the tape. "Especially the sissy part," said one adviser. The writer refused, and we are surely the richer for it.

More recently, freelancer Christopher Buckley found himself in Las Vegas on assignment from *New York* magazine to do a profile of Frank Sinatra. "I knew right from the first moment," recalls Buckley, "that the only thing that Chuck Brown, the PR man for Caesars Palace, couldn't do for me was to 'arrange an interview with The Man,' and that the piece would be, of necessity, an Impression of a Scene." Thus, as the saying goes, Buckley had to work with mirrors. He caught a fleeting glimpse of Sinatra at the blackjack tables, spoke with the security guard who escorted Sinatra up to his room at night, with the girl at the front desk, with the singer's hotel valet, and with a Jewish couple from Fort Lauderdale who had memories of Sinatra stretching back to a morning in 1949 when the woman got up at six to get in line for tickets to a show. "When you're thrust into one of these peculiar situations," says Buckley, "the best way to work is to use other peoples' eyes. And to kiss proverbial ass. Still, I have this lingering after-taste of press agent flatulations, you know, like listening — seriously — to some dude who's being paid to give you this big shuck about how 'He still sends this tingly feeling down my spine. Always has. . . .' Zzzzzzz."

Buckley's first stop was Jim Mahoney, a public relations man for Sinatra, who sized the writer up, avoided him for two days, then (after Buckley followed him conspicuously from the poker table to the baccarat table to the blackjack table one night) consented to talk. "What a shuck that one was," recalls the writer. "I was playing it *very* low key. 'Mr. Mahoney' this, 'Mr. Mahoney' that. He warms up by buying me a beer and asking, 'Suppose you give me one good reason I should cooperate with you on this story?' Oh. I rejoined that I was not out to 'screw' Sinatra, that I was only interested in his emotions vis-à-vis another Las Vegas engagement. He let me babble on uninterrupted for what seemed the longest time, and then, sipping his Cointreau, cooled down: 'OK, let's get this straight. I'm talking to you tonight because of who you are and what you represent.' (Slight identity problem here; my father is a well-known, conservative sort of fellow.) So then Mahoney jives me around for an hour and a half, splicing Sinatra encomiums with such pearls as, 'I'll tell you what makes a lead paragraph: whatever you put up there makes it a lead paragraph.' Then Mahoney tells me the *only* reason he's speaking to me tonight (imparting the hot headliners that he is) is 'because when I was your age, I needed someone to say, "Hey you, kid, come over here." ' Thanks a load, Jim. Really." Thus, while Buckley was eventually able to file a devastating profile of Sinatra in action, he found himself after a few evenings with press agentry no closer to the story than he had been when he first got the call from *New York* magazine.

While press agents and other hangers-on may create obstacle courses for some writers, those who monitor interviews with high government employees may be even more intimidating. When Henry Morgenthau Jr. was Secretary of the Treasury, for instance, he never allowed Geoffrey Hellman to interview him alone for a *New Yorker* profile. "He always had an assistant on hand, who stayed around like a Burns detective," wrote Hellman. Robert McNamara as Secretary of Defense was even more protective: *all* Pentagon personnel were required to have a monitor in the room during interviews. The result? Subjects usually worry about what they say, and say a good deal less than they would otherwise. "Usually during a monitored interview the information officer sits there silently," writes Richard Fryklund of the *Washington Star*. "He takes notes. On some occasions, when it has turned out that my notes have been poor, I have borrowed his, and that has been very useful. If the person being interviewed gets into a ticklish area, usually he will be conscious of it and turn to the information officer for a ruling. Surprisingly enough, the ruling is often favorable. The news source tends to be a little shyer because he doesn't know what has been made public and what hasn't, while the information officer can tell him what has been talked about and what he can elaborate on. If the fellow says something that is truly classified, the information officer steps in and says, 'That's off the record,' and it is off the record."

• *Interviewese spoken here.* Occasionally, an interviewer may find himself in *need* of a third person in the room — an interpreter. John Gunther, for example, found Leon Trotsky extremely difficult to interview, "perhaps . . . because he insisted on speaking English, a language which he did not fully command, instead of using an interpreter." Such third persons in Russia, though, sometimes translate at their own risk. During an interview with Yuri Zhukov, the former editor of *Pravda*, the late columnist Bob Considine asked a question about England. The interpreter for Zhukov translated a reference to

Anthony Eden, calling the British statesman a "Conservative." But Considine's interpreter said, "Mr. Zhukov didn't call Eden a Conservative. He called him a Fascist." Recalled Considine afterward: "Filled with surprise, confusion and anger, Zhukov acknowledged that he had. Thereafter, we were minus our miraculous linguist during formal interviews. And by coincidence or design, he was ordered out of Russia some months later."

Which points out a real problem with dependence on an interpreter during an interview: you never know what you're missing. Consider the problems encountered by Stuart Byron when — are you ready? — press agents for 20th Century-Fox arranged for an interview with Luis Bunuel, the then-72-year-old Spanish film director, who was nearly deaf as well. How do you handle all the obstacles to understanding? Read on.

On this particular occasion Bunuel — whom Byron calls "probably the least-interviewed of the great directors" — had come to New York from his Mexican home to join his producer Serge Silberman in business conferences. "It is all *very* special, *very* delicate," wrote Byron afterward. "I am to report first to Silberman at another suite at the Hotel Pierre for a briefing on the do's and don'ts of talking with The Great Man."

"Luis doesn't like interviews," Silberman tells the interviewer. "So make it a conversation. He hears better with his right ear, so sit to his right. Can you speak French? A little? Good. Ask the questions in French, or in English and I'll translate. He will respond in French. Do not ask interpretive questions. He dislikes being asked what this means or what that means. He is an instinctive artist. He will bawl me out tonight for these interviews. Remember he is an old man. He gets tired easily. You will need no more than a half hour, no? I will signal you when I see he is tired, and then you will finish. But he is a kind, joking, generous man. You will love him. Come!"

Byron was about to discover that everything he asked the director had to be "1) translated, 2) simplified, and 3) shouted, sometimes more than once." During the introduction, Byron does not even hear words like press, journalist or interview. "I get a sneaking suspicion that Bunuel has not even *known* he was to see a stranger until that very moment," he writes afterward. "The disastrous pattern becomes established immediately. A *Question* which has a specific *Intention* is followed by an oversimplified *Translation* which produces an *Answer* of small news value."

Thus, the interview — which represented but a tiny closing section for the amusing *Rolling Stone* piece — came across as something like this:

Question: "How did you like working with each of the actors?"
Intention: What were the particular characteristics of each?
Translation: "Do you like actors?"
Answer: "Yes, even the bit actors. I love all actors."

And again:

Question: "There are three or four non-sequitur lines in the movie. Lines that seem to be pure nonsense. Like in the love scene between Rey and Seyrig. She suddenly says, 'The scars haven't healed yet.' That's never explained. I love that."
Intention: To discuss the use of such lines.
Translation: "He loves the Rey-Seyrig love scene."
Answer: "Thank you."

Other questions do not even reach the director. Translator Silberman doesn't consider them worthwhile. "And yet one sees that such a protective relationship is at the heart of the matter," concludes interviewer Byron, reflecting on the father-son relationship between the old director and his producer/protector. "One, ten, a hundred disastrous interviews are as nothing compared to a masterpiece like *The Discreet Charm of the Bourgeoisie,* a film that might never have been made had these two men never met." When Silberman thought the director was tired, he gave the signal, and the interviewer got up and left. A terrible interview, with third-party disturbances in an assortment of directions, but a memorable experience to write up later, for sure.

No hazard — short of bodily harm — can really prevent a determined reporter from getting his interview. Ungodly hours? He can meet them. Tardy subjects? Wait them out. Interviewee sick of interviews? Pique his curiosity. Interviewee locked in the bathroom? Use a remote microphone. Even an impaired interview — conducted through the fog of an interpreter, or in the presence of a wizened information officer — can be turned to the interviewer's advantage, if he has the wit and the wiles to adjust quickly to the interview on its own terms, and thence to convert what would have been a conventional "solid" piece into a revealing, offbeat article or TV/radio spot.

A blind and deaf subject would confound some journalists. Not Barbara Walters. The powerful television journalist and her handicapped subject communicated by his placing his thumb on her lips as she talked. "Of my nearly 11 years of interviewing," reflected Walters afterward, "this is the man who has made the most lasting impression." Yes. There are no handicaps for the interviewer who is resolute. Ye *shall* overcome.

10. Written and Telephone Interviews

Operator oh could you help me place this call
You see the number on the matchbook is old and
   faded ...

> —Jim Croce, "Operator (That's Not
>   The Way It Feels)"
>
> © *1971 Blendingwell Music, Inc. (ASCAP)*

Though a written interview — in which the writer sends his questions to the subject, then awaits a written response — is cumbersome today, there was a time when it was more common than a verbal exchange. For example, when Charles Lindbergh was one of the fliers gathered at Curtiss and Roosevelt fields trying to win the $25,000 price for the first New York-Paris flight, John Chapman of the New York *Daily News* was assigned to interview the contestants. "It was easy enough to get Admiral Richard E. Byrd and Clarence Chamberlin," recalled Chapman, "but Lindbergh said a flat 'no.' " For three days Chapman pestered the publicity man for the maker of the engine in Lindbergh's plane; finally Lindbergh dictated a statement to Chapman, asking him to type it up for approval and his signature. "But I did badly," Chapman later wrote. "The typing was atrocious and so were the spelling and punctuation, and somehow I had garbled the message. Pen in hand, I took it out to Lindbergh to be signed. He read it and said, irritably, 'This isn't what I want. Here — .' And he took my pen, using the tail of his plane for a desk, and wrote something on another piece of paper." Thus, while the pilot was over the Atlantic, the *News* published a longhand statement from Charles A. Lindbergh: "I am taking off for Paris with a combination of the finest aeronautical equipment in the world."

Columnist Sheilah Graham's first assignment was to interview George Bernard Shaw on the playwright's 85th birthday. Shaw generally refused to see journalists, but Graham was told by a secretary, "Of course you will have your interview. Just put your questions in a letter. Mr. Shaw will answer them and I'll post them back to you." The columnist hand-delivered the questions, and even showed up a few days later to pick up the replies. But the great man wouldn't expand on his written replies. "Don't add anything to what I have written," he warned. "You'll only spoil it."

Time $aver

Certain aspects of the written interview are ongoing, particularly when a subject is especially sensitive to the written word. E. M. Forster consented to an interview for *The Paris Review* only when the questions were sent in advance. Ernest Hemingway proofread and rewrote his famous interview with George Plimpton for the same *Review*. Frank Sinatra wrote out many answers to questions for his *Playboy* interview, and Bob Dylan rewrote his original *Playboy* interview completely after being dissatisfied with the transcript from the original taping.

While cumbersome, the written interview can be a timesaver. John Gunther, while doing research for his *Inside U.S.A.* bestseller (in the late 1940s), wrote to all 48 governors explaining his work and asking three questions: How does your state differ from all the rest? What does your state contribute to the Union as a whole? What led you into public life and what do you consider to be your chief accomplishment? The results: "Out of 48 governors, 47 replied." Thus, Gunther gathered useful information by mail for a book national in scope, without leaving his living room typewriter (though many miles of travel would follow).

Sometimes the only way a writer can get information is by framing careful questions and sending them to a government specialist. "Public servants will go far in the second mile with writers," says Larston Farrar — especially to questions by mail. "This is how I obtained an interview with Nobel Prize winner Glenn Seaborg during the height of the atomic reactor and ecology controversy," recalls Joseph Durso. "Seaborg saw the questions, and, disgusted with his staff for keeping me out, arranged for a personal meeting." Durso suggests that the writer ask a minimum of 30 questions in a written interview, and that tough questions be sprinkled in random order throughout. "Make your subject work to answer them," he says. "Don't let a written interview drift by a lack of tough and tight questioning; otherwise you will receive an envelope back full of unsalable platitudes that might be great to show your grandchildren but would hardly make a dent in a car payment."

Irving Wallace did some interviewing of former Nobel Prize winners by mail while researching *The Prize.* The novelist corresponded with a host of former Prize winners, and received lengthy replies from subjects such as Albert Einstein and Pearl Buck, resulting in some of the best material he was able to glean of the personal adventures of Nobel laureates.

The written interview, therefore, while risky, often ignored, and hopelessly out of fashion, can still be employed by today's interviewer with some success. And it is nearly always more economical than telephone or in-person interviews.

Some points to remember when using the mails for an interview:
• Don't just drop your questions in the mail. Preface your written interview with a written *request* for a written interview. Make it personal. Explain the nature of your project, the role the interviewee might play in answering your questions, the number of questions you have in mind, and the publication you are doing the article for.

If a fast deadline makes it necessary to use a questionnaire without a formal request beforehand, at least soften things. While researching a piece for *Rolling Stone* on the connection between writing and drinking, I sent a questionnaire to over 100 writers, covered by a form letter which was covered in turn by a short, personal note. The form letter explained at some length the nature of my project, so I could get answers to questions that were bound to seem personal, if not downright snoopy. The personal note, of course, was to take the starch out of receiving a form letter. It went something like this:

Dear Mr. Whatever:

I hope you won't find the enclosed form letter and questionnaire too personal or time-consuming, but I am researching a piece on writers who drink (and drinkers who write) and I am anxious to include your opinions in it.

In addition to being one of the leading writers in America

today, you have been quoted in *Time* magazine as saying that your first novel "was written in several East Coast taverns between divorces." Thus, my interest in you. My deadline is March 15, and I look forward to hearing from you?

Sincerely,

P.S. My phone is 513/984-0710 (collect, anytime) if you would prefer to talk about the questions.

Results: Of 110 questionnaires, 17 were returned (old addresses), 30 failed to reply, but the remainder came through — and I had some insightful quotes from many of the leading writers of our time. (Alas, the article never was published — due in part to rolling heads at *Rolling Stone.*)

The point is: know your subject. Do enough research to make the questionnaire and — in this case — the form letter seem pointed at a species, not at a genus. We all welcome interesting questions, even by mail. But no one likes to be handled like a statistic.

Other guidelines for guiding interviews through the mail:

• Always type your correspondence — neatly. If your request looks sloppy, the subject is likely to think your whole undertaking is less than stylish, and he might back away from the invitation.

• If you are using the same questionnaire for several subjects (many round-up pieces are done this way), have it mimeographed or duplicated on a good-quality duplicator — but always add a personal cover note when sending it out.

• On the questionnaire, draft questions thoughtfully and succinctly. Leave ample space between questions for the subject to insert answers. Remember, replies are likely to be brief — but the questionnaire format is more conducive to a prompt reply than a series of questions with no breathing space between them.

• Give the subject your phone number and tell him to call collect if it would be more convenient to talk; or if any of the questions on the questionnaire require clarification.

• Give the subject a deadline. Don't be stern in these matters, but make it clear that you need the answers in two weeks — 30 days, tops — so that you can meet your own deadline.

• Enclose a self-addressed, stamped envelope for a reply.

When you get a response, make a Xerox copy and store the original for safekeeping. Examine the answers on the questionnaire for possible follow-up questions that may be necessary or provocative — and, if this is the case, write at once. Make it a personal letter, with thanks and enthusiasm for the gracious cooperation — then ask your pointed questions. But unless you follow-up while the questionnaire is still warm, and while the subject is still mindful of your needs, you are not likely to get a reply. Old questions connote idle afterthoughts, not sincere curiosity.

If you receive no response from an interviewee within two weeks (allow three weeks for overseas mail), send a Xerox of your original correspondence (a Xerox or a neat carbon copy should be kept for your own files), along with a note suggesting that the original letter may have been lost in the mails — or waylaid by someone with an overloaded schedule and mailbox. "I still have a few days to meet my deadline, and would appreciate any information you might be able to jot onto the enclosed questionnaire" serves as a prod, without offending the beholder.

Tape Talk

An updated version of the written interview is the cassette interview — in which a cassette tape is sent to the subject with a spoken message and a series of questions. The increasing popularity of inexpensive cassette recorders — and the enduring popularity of monologue — makes it quite likely that the subject would be willing to take a few notes and freelance a reply on the unused side of the cassette. Again, it's a good idea to first propose the cassette interview in a note, lest you seem presumptuous to some subjects.

Many freelancers are discovering this portable interview. I once did a piece on the "underground" recordings of Frank Sinatra by interviewing Ol' Blue Eyes collectors via cassettes. I found that the network of Sinatra collectors circled the globe, and that several of the best-known collectors were in England, South America, Australia and Japan. People who have an interest such as this are enthusiastic and willing to talk, and anyone who is into music has some taping equipment. I found it easy to contact the collectors initially by letter, and then follow it up with a "talk tape" asking questions. The answers I got were revealing — and cooperation was 100 percent. In addition to appearing in two American publications, the article on Sinatra collectors was reprinted in England because of the 'round-the-world flavor created by the cassette interviews.

New York Calling

If the written interview has disadvantages for the writer, so too does the phone interview. "I have found that I get only about 50 percent of what I need when I phone or write," says Hayes Jacobs. Another writer adds: "How do you observe the twinkle in the eye, the glint of anger, or the reflective glance of a defense mechanism going into gear?" You don't. In fact, if the call is garbled, you won't even get the words right. This happened in the early 1960s when a reporter interpreted "shot in the head" as "shot dead," and wrote a wire service story saying that civil rights leader James Meredith had been killed.

Many celebrities are apprehensive about doing phone interviews, too. A disc jockey from a Toronto radio station once called up Richard and Karen Carpenter for an on-the-air phone interview that turned the Carpenters off of phone interviews forever. "We might as well bring it out," said the DJ. "I've listened to the lyrics of your songs. I know that Karen's singin' 'em to you. I know they're about incest. You want to talk about this?" Recalls Richard Carpenter: "I couldn't believe it. I was stunned. I tried to explain, absolutely not. Imagine – *I tried to explain!*" Afterward he threw the phone down. "That was the last *phone* interview we ever did."

If you have the time and the money, it's best to do an interview in person. "The important thing is the amount of money a publisher is willing to contribute to travel," says John Apple of the *New York Times.* "Because travel is the soul of this business. You've gotta be there, you can't do it all on the telephone." Yet Apple himself is a master of the telephone. "My all-time record is a hundred calls in one day," he says. "That was a story I did about five state conventions and a couple of territorial conventions or something. But I sat down at my desk at nine o'clock in the morning and got up at ten after seven. And I made about 25 of those calls trying to find out what happened in the Canal Zone. 'Cause I was determined I wasn't gonna have to write: 'A convention was also held in the Canal Zone, but we don't know what happened.' That's just a matter of pride."

The telephone interview is the McDonald's of journalism; it's not the best method of gathering information, but it's fast and serviceable. It is also the answer when a writer needs but one key interview to fill out a story, and the subject is too far away to visit before deadline. A good phone interviewer uses the instrument like a baton. Columnist Jack Anderson, for example, avoids the Washington cocktail circuit altogether (because of his religious beliefs as a Mormon, he abstains from smoking, booze and coffee); yet, he gleans information from carefully cultivated sources throughout the capital, employing four assistants and $10,000 yearly on phone bills for a column that grosses more than $200,000 in return.

"I've found phone interviews most effective in the roundup, where bits and pieces have to be gathered from scattered sources," says Theodore Irwin. Irwin once did a story on some pilots who had been wounded overseas. After speaking with a major in New York, he obtained the name of another veteran recovering at a hospital in Washington. "Since I had a tight deadline, I couldn't spare the day in Washington, so I conducted an hour-long phone interview with the man at Walter Reed," says Irwin. "In the bed next to him was another pilot. I interviewed him, too, and picked up the name and address of a third pilot in Alabama. It worked like a chain reaction. In all I talked by phone to eight men."

A telephone can get the attention of a subject at times when an in-person interview is impossible. A man will ignore a knock on the door if he doesn't want to be disturbed, but will answer the insistent phone in the room. A reporter from New York was once trying to get information on a Texas school explosion, so he phoned the town sheriff. "Now, you reporters got to wait," he heard the sheriff say. "There's a man on the telephone here calling all the way from New York."

The Smiling Voice

When making an approach by phone, remember that a subject is likely to be put off by poor or misleading telephone manners. And the interviewee has the power to end the conversation by simply hanging up. So when you are making a call, dispel any suspicion that you might be a salesman using an oblique introduction. Identify yourself at once, mention the publication you are doing the interview for, and be prepared to answer a few preliminary questions from a secretary who must screen the boss's calls. Even if you are working on a local story for a smalltown paper, it is to your advantage to personalize the introduction by saying "This is Charlie Williams from the *Tribune-Star,*" rather than merely announcing: "This is the *Tribune-Star* calling." That personal touch can raise conversation to communication. Sometimes it is helpful to write to the subject before calling him at the office. If the person you wish to reach is Really Big, with a large volume of daily mail, you might consider sending him a telegram announcing your hope of phoning in a few days for his decision on an interview. Don't forget the different time zones if you are making long-distance calls.

Some basic telephone manners should be observed throughout. Don't bang the receiver, speak curtly or carry on a side conversation about bagels during the call. "Put a friendly smile in your voice," suggests Dennis Murphy in his *Better Business Communication.* "Attitude toward your work shows up in your voice. A good telephone voice is low-pitched, pleasantly confident, cordial, and – alive. Nothing sounds worse than the dead-pan voice of an uninterested employee. Nasality and mannerisms are taboo."

One plus of phone interviews is that many subjects talk more freely when they cannot see an interviewer taking notes. Always have paper, pencils and necessary reference material nearby before phoning for an interview so you won't have to dig them up during the actual conversation.

If an interview is going to be lengthy, most interviewers ask for permission to tape it. "Taping is not a crime in *any* state as long as it's done with the person's knowledge," writes Art Spikol, *Writer's Digest* nonfiction columnist and executive editor of *Philadelphia* magazine. "The problem is not one of law. It is the fact that your telephone is a device normally made available to you when you comply with phone company tariffs." Why? Well, that brings us to the jungle of Ma Bell & Co. At this point it seems safest – and the most fun – to quote Spikol at length:

The front of your phone book contains some instructions on phone recording. These instructions vary depending upon where you live, but they *invariably* say something about a beep tone, the sound that the phone company is convinced that everybody will recognize as a taping signal.

Take Massachusetts. The Boston telephone directory says of its beep requirement, "... This signal is provided for your protection. Use of a recorder without Special Telephone Company equipment containing a tone-warning device is not authorized and is a violation of the Company's tariffs." The wording is important — it doesn't say that such recording is *illegal.* It does say that it violates the Company's tariffs. (**Warning:** If the directory *does* say that recording without a beep is illegal, be sure to check your state law. It just might be.)

Because of the reluctance of Bell's lawyers to give straight answers to questions regarding their employer's strengths and weaknesses, all investigations of this nature (sigh) are doomed to end up in Washington at the Public Utility Commission. As we look in, I am talking to a lawyer there:

"I'd like to know something about the regulations regarding tape recording of phone conversations. Tell me — are the phone company's tariffs the same as law?"

"Well, no. That is, not exactly. But you might say they have the force and effect of law. Would you please stop banging that thing in my ear?"

"That's my typewriter."

"I know. Can you write longhand?"

"It's a lot slower. But OK."

And so I wrote. Which is probably the best argument for taping. Unfortunately, I couldn't very well tape the guy before I found out if it was legal, since I knew that he would want to know where the beep tone was if I told him I was taping. Catch-22.

"You said force and effect," I said. "What does that mean?"

"Well, the tariff has the *weight,* but not the *strength,* of a law." He paused. "It's a nuance that only another lawyer could understand."

In other words, I couldn't. In fact, I wondered where they would find a jury of my peers who could. I said, "Can you be a little more specific?"

"Well, the adoption of a tariff is not quite the same as the passage of a law. But you *could* be taken to court for violating a tariff." He said it in the same way I say I *could* win the Nobel Prize in literature.

"OK. What would happen if I was taken to court for violating the tariff that says that I have to beep while recording, but there's evidence right there on the tape that I had told the person he was being taped. Would the fact that I didn't beep be a violation of law?"

"No, of a tariff. And I don't know how it would turn out. The court might well say that the person was warned that he was being taped and therefore had waived his rights. It's hard to say."

Well, that's what happens when you ask a question of someone who doesn't know the answer. It's like trying to use a marshmallow as a trampoline.

"Now," I asked the Washington attorney, "suppose I beeped every 15 seconds with that unit that Ma Bell sells, and when the thing comes to court the guy claims he didn't know what the beep tone meant. What about that?"

"Well, my response would be that what kind of person would hear a beep every 15 seconds and not have enough sense to inquire what it was?"

F. Lee Bailey he wasn't.

So what is the answer? Just this: if you want to be absolutely safe, use a Ma Bell beeper. But if you're satisfied with being reasonably safe, simply obtain the interviewee's consent for taping — and say (beep) to the beeper.

Says Art Spikol:

The question you have to ask yourself is, "Am I going to be a landmark case because I called up Mr. Miller at the butcher shop and taped him on how to pick out a good rib roast for the article I'm writing on meats?"

Then ask yourself:

How will the phone company know I'm taping?

How will they prove it?

They're not going to take me to court for it, so what *will* they do?

Do I have any intention of handing them my tape along with

a written confession?
If not, you have nothing to worry about.

If you think your subjects might be apprehensive about tape, "tell them it is just for accuracy and you will be happy to submit the piece to them for a final check as a courtesy," says Joseph Trento, former chief investigative reporter for Jack Anderson. "At no time indicate they will be able to censor their remarks."

Stuart Bykofsky finds the question academic. "I tape record conversations as a matter of course in gathering stories. I identify myself by name and magazine and explain I am working on a story. Having made it plain I am calling for business, i.e., editorial, purposes, I then pump the subject. Since I do not tell him that I am taping the conversation — and since there's no way in the world for him to know — the legal question simply never arises. When the interviewee sees the quote in print, he either thinks I am a good, accurate reporter — or he says that he's been misquoted. Depending on circumstances, I am free to tell him why I am certain he was not misquoted. It has never gotten that far."

Bone Up Before You Phone Up

A sloppy telephone interview is painful. It is even more painful than a halting in-person interview. Over the phone, your subject cannot react to any body language, clothing, mannerisms or surroundings that can gloss over deficiencies in your delivery or preparation. The subject cannot see you. The only impression he will have of you will be from your voice and your questions. And rapport, which can be maintained through breaks, silences, even minor catastrophes in the flesh, will vanish quickly whenever silence descends upon a telephone conversation. A winning smile, a charming manner, eye contact — all are lost as tools for the interviewer working on the phone. All he can work with are his tape recorder, his voice and his brain. Being skimpily armed, the phone interviewer concentrates on making both his questions and his delivery simple and understandable. Don't try to impress or "snow" a subject. Toadying, too, is risky — though a little flattery, deftly applied, might be all right. You will definitely do harm to the interview if you do not have questions prepared for quick delivery, if you aren't able to adjust to unexpected developments in the conversation, or if you haven't done the proper background research that allows you to fill in things that your subject is taking for granted.

Imagine trying to talk to Albert Einstein without prepared questions and adequate research into basic physics. "How large is the universe, Mr. E.?"

"Vell, it is either a positively curved parabolic positive infinity, vhich is open but yet unending, or it is a negatively curved, four-dimensional finite body that is yet unescapable and that is closed in upon itself in a finite infinity."

"Oh, uh, well, could you explain that a bit further?"

"Vhy, of course. Imagine yourself as a two-dimensional geometric form on the surface of a three-dimensional sphere of dimension of less than one micron according to the equation. . . ."

Out of control, immediately. The phone provides speedy access to the hard-to-get — but after that, it's up to you. The phone is a tool for transferring information, not for dispensing idle, uninformed chatter.

Handle numbers with care over the phone, too. Like Dr Pepper, stats and addresses are easily misunderstood. When possible, deal with numbers by correspondence, or in a person-to-person interview over a cocktail table spread with stat sheets. If you must draw out the data over the phone, type up your notes while they are still hot, then xerox and mail them to your source with a note along these lines:

Dear Mr. Milhous:

Thanks for your help over the phone yesterday. To ensure 100 percent accuracy, I've enclosed a copy of my notes from the phone conversation. Should you see anything here which needs correcting or updating, would you call me collect within ten days? Otherwise, I will assume that the material is accurate, and I will push through to meet my editor's deadline. . . .

Again, make clear to your source — politely, of course — that he is reading your material for *accuracy*, not for approval.

Names and titles can also be flubbed when taken by phone. Spell out names the Ma Bell way — "So that's S as in screwdriver?" Doublecheck even seemingly innocuous titles; your source may be vice president *for* — not *of* — student affairs at Poughkeepsie University, not University of Poughkeepsie.

Don't end a telephone conversation with "All righty" or "Okay doke" or "some similar moronic expression," warns Curtis MacDougall. Instead, reassure the subject that he will see the printed results of what he's been through. "Thanks for giving me your time and some great quotes," might be effective. "I'll keep you posted as things move along toward publication."

In sum: while the written interview may be precise, but canned, the phone interview is often spontaneous, but inexact. Use the two formats to complement one another. Gather your fresh quotes and anecdotes by phone, where you can egg your source on to the tiniest (and most revealing) details; but double-check your information by mail. Or, gather your dry information first in a written interview, then flesh out human interest material by phone. Double team your subject.

Neither the written nor the phone interview can approach the sparkle of an in-person interview; but when the two are skillfully orchestrated, they will yield precise and colorful material. Which is mainly what you want.

11. It's Over

*Now, Mr. Hellman, we want to have a nice
dinner, so we'll postpone discussion of your
article until after the meal is over. I will
say that after reading it I went to bed for
two days.*

—Mrs. Henry Morgenthau
to her husband's profiler

When is an interview over? When the subject has had enough.
Consider this exchange between *Cosmopolitan* interviewer Theodore
Irwin and Hugh Hefner:

Irwin: I understand you sleep in a huge, round bed?
Hefner: That's right.
Irwin: Where do you buy the sheets for this kind of round
bed, and what do they cost?
Hefner: I really have no idea.

When the courteous subject turns curt; when the knowledgeable
subject says he *doesn't* know—again and again: it's time to pack up
and bid your man Godspeed.

It's preferable, of course, to end the interview on a graceful note.
There must be 50 ways to leave your subject—and vice versa. Your
subject glances at his watch with a start, as if he has overslept, and
suddenly remembers an appointment. Or his intercom buzzes and
his secretary informs him of "unexpected" business. Or he asks, "How
much more time do you need?" Or he leaves the room "for a moment"
and doesn't return until late Thursday. Your interview with the
President of the United States is over when he stands up. Says William
Manchester: "You leave immediately."

If your subject is as hard-running as the President, you might have to conduct several short interviews rather than one extended one. When Lawrence Linderman interviewed Howard Cosell for *Playboy*, he observed: "The hectic schedule he maintains catches up with him by early evening. Whenever I stretched our taping sessions beyond an hour's length, his voice would begin to crack and there was no mistaking how tired the man was—to the point where his hands started to shake." *That's* when it's time to shake hands and close the interview. Until tomorrow, anyway.

The Same Old Answers

However you take your leave, try to leave your subject with the impression that *he* is ending the interview—even though you have called it quits in order to meet your deadline at 9 a.m. tomorrow. A question with a ring of finality can usually draw the interview to a fast finish. "One final question, Mr. Snavely . . ." might be enough to tell a subject you've got enough. William Manchester usually closes his interviews with, "Is there anything you think is important which I haven't asked?" Says Manchester: "Sometimes what they think is important is not important at all. But they should be given that opportunity, and sometimes it is very revealing."

"I always know when I'm through interviewing on a piece," says Gerald Walker. "It's when I feel bored stiff with the answers I'm getting; that is when I seem to be getting virtually the same old answers from everyone I question; and especially when I can't seem to think of any new questions to ask. If I'm out of town, this is when I grab a cab back to the hotel, start hurling things into a suitcase and call the airport for a reservation on the next plane home."

Another writer stops interviewing for a piece when he has ten good anecdotes. "This isn't as odd as it seems," he says. "Anecdotes are not easy to come by, and often by the time ten are in your notebook, you've amassed a great deal of information."

Your standard closing line should be polished and polite: "I think I have all the information I need, and you've given me some excellent material." Then close your notebook — but don't close your ears: at interview's end, a sphinxlike subject may lapse into his normal effusive, truthful self.

In one interview, Max Gunther was collecting a lot of "no comment"-type replies from an Army weapons officer, flanked by his watchful public information officer. So Gunther ceremoniously closed his notebook, put away his pen, and suggested that they all have coffee. The men laughed and relaxed.

"You know," the weapons officer told Gunther, "there are some things we're doing that I really wish I could tell you about." And he did.

"In a cab on the way back to my hotel," adds Gunther, "I took out my notebook again and wrote down everything I could remember of what he'd said."

Those golden few minutes at the end of an interview can also be put to less surreptitious purposes. This is the time to doublecheck figures and spellings, to ask about photos for the article, and to ensure the door is open for later questions. "When could I check back with you, in case any of my notes are unclear?" you might ask. "I want to be 100 percent accurate."

Your departure should be prompt but not hurried. The story is told of an activist Newspaper Guild reporter who refused to put in overtime, and who was midstream in a telephone interview 15 minutes before quitting time. "Well, I don't suppose you have anything more to say on the subject, do you?" he asked impatiently. The response: click.

Keep in Touch

Don't cut off your source — cultivate him. Send him copies of the published article, even if he is not directly quoted; in fact, in the course of extensive interviewing for a series of articles or a book, he should be told that his information may be used only as background, and that his name might not even appear in the finished product: an ounce of forewarning is worth a pound of disappointment. Keep him posted on readers' reactions to his printed statements. Tip him off to new developments in his field that you uncover in your research for articles. Court him shrewdly, with an eye toward your next article; like wine, a good source improves with age and occasional care.

"Don't make the mistake too many freelancers make — forget your subject once the assignment is in and the check is spent," says Joseph Trento. "These people did you a favor and they deserve your further attention. Chances are once an individual reaches a certain level of attention, he will be of public interest for awhile, so keep the channels wide open. Send him a Christmas card . . . . Keep in touch if you can. You can never tell when retirement comes and the VIP decides he needs a ghost for those memoirs; he might think back to that guy who writes the card every year."

Verification

Most likely, however, the journalist is not writing the VIP's memoirs; he is writing an article, and he wants to write the truth, so he carefully double-checks the VIP's information before he uses it.

"The reporter who believes all that he is told will not last long," says Neil MacNeil of the *New York Times.* "The competent reporter takes all the data he can get. He may ask embarrassing questions. He checks one person's statement against another's and against the known facts. . . . He makes certain that he has exhausted all available information before he writes a word of his story."

The problem lies in a temptation: to quote the man for his style rather than his substance; to unleash the Quote Fact, an opinion that becomes a fact because it resides between quotation marks. "When people sound knowledgeable, others believe them," writes Arthur Herzog, who coined the phrase "Quote Fact" in *The B.S. Factor.* "So much in modern life is guesswork and confusion that almost anybody who seems to know what he is talking about will be promptly smuggled between quotation marks."

How much of a source's information can you trust? It depends. You would think that you could trust the opinions of mothers on child raising — yet psychological investigators have found that some mothers' statements during a series of interviews reflected not the past, but their memories of the past. We remember best extremely pleasurable or extremely painful events, as well as those that support our pet theories. So the interviewer must be wary of selective recall, particularly if he is researching a piece on someone who is deceased; if his interviewees are elderly — and even if they're not — their remembrances are likely to be reshaped by nostalgia and the simple ravages of time.

Even respected writers sometimes fumble their memories. Budd Schulberg's description of the 1929 Rose Bowl for *TV Guide* prompted one reader to wonder if Schulberg had even been at the game. Schulberg wrote that Wrong Way Riegels had run some 60 yards, "with Benny Lom making a desperation flying tackle on the one-yard line." He continued: "The big man stumbled, with the little man holding on desperately. They, and the ball, fell together, exactly half a foot from the goal line." Actually, according to photos and text in Bud Greenspan's *Play It Again, Bud*, Lom caught Reigels on the ten-yard line and succeeded in turning him around on about the two. Then Reigels was tackled by opposing Georgia Tech players, and the ball was placed on the one-yard line. So much for Benny Lom's "desperation flying tackle" — and Budd Schulberg's memory 45 years after the fact.

Verify, verify. "Let it be known around town that just because someone says something — regardless of how big a star he is — you aren't necessarily going to accept it on face value," Humphrey Bogart cautioned a young Joe Hyams when the columnist started covering the Hollywood beat. Shortly afterward, Hyams interviewed Burt Lancaster, who said he wanted to do *Judgment at Nuremberg* even though he would be paid very little money, and would have but one good scene opposite Spencer Tracy, whom he greatly admired. When Hyams mentioned this to Bogie, however, the actor said, "Why don't you read Lancaster's quotes to Spence? You might get an interesting response."

Hyams traced Tracy to another set and read the Lancaster quotes to him. "Tracy snorted indignantly," Hyams recalls, "and informed me that Lancaster was going to be paid half a million dollars for his role. His scene with Tracy was seven pages long, during which Tracy didn't say a word. In addition, he was going to get star billing with Tracy." Hyams wrote the column — quoting both actors.

There are two ways to verify information from an interview: either point by point, during the interview; or immediately after the interview. Be flexible. If you think that a verification, however important, would distract the interviewee who is beginning to open up — hold back. But if your rapport is good, and your subject methodical, use the stop-and-go method; your man would probably be flattered by your close listening, and by your attention to detail.

Getting Under the Skin

Your attention to his body movements will afford you a glimpse into his mood. "The upper part of the body may appear quite at ease, but the interviewee's tension and anxiety will be evident if he is curling his ankles around the leg of the desk," says one child psychiatrist (his hints, presumably, would apply to adults as well). "The small muscles of the fingers and jaw often give similar information. Tiny changes in the eyelids are invaluable clues — a slight widening when he is frightened, and a slight closing when hostile or thoughtful. Skin changes should also be observed; these include slight flushing, pallor, and sweating."

Welcome, then, to the weighing of all flesh — body language. And it is not — like certain pursuits of the flesh — without social redeeming value. After experiments, Paul Ekman wrote in the *Journal of Abnormal and Social Psychology* that "body position and facial expression spontaneously shown during an interview are not random activity ... but have specific communicative value related to the verbal behavior." Ekman also says that "this relationship is not obscure or available to only the privileged few, but can be detected by untrained observers."

Well, *that's* for sure. For instance, everybody knows the telltale signs of anxiety: rushed speech, unfinished sentences, stutterings, a perspiring upper lip (if the subject is Richard Nixon), and "I dunno, I dunno, I dun*no*." Other gestures of anxiety, according to psychological testing, include putting one's hand to the nose when frightened; and grimacing, nodding, or raising an eyebrow (for which Spiro Agnew once chastised TV newscasters) — all indicating approval or disapproval of what the subject is saying.

Dr. Albert Mehrabian of UCLA has found that what a person says is but seven percent of what he *communicates:* 38 percent is conveyed by his manner of speech, and 55 percent by his facial and body movements. Frank Costello could have testified to that after his televised appearance before the Kefauver crime hearings in the fifties. "As he sparred with Rudolph Halley, the committee's counsel, the movement of his fingers told their own emotional story," Jack Gould wrote of the gangster. "When the questions got rough, Costello crumpled a handkerchief in his hands. Or he rubbed his palms together. Or he interlaced his fingers. Or he grasped a half-filled glass of water. Or he beat a silent tattoo on the table top. Or he rolled a little ball of paper between his thumb and index finger. Or he stroked the side of glasses lying on the table. His was video's first ballet of the hands."

Practically speaking, it is impossible to tell — by nonverbal evidence — whether a man is lying. Some liars have deluded themselves so well that they can fool nearly all of the people all of the time — no matter what the people may say. After Dr. Alfred C. Kinsey and his associates spent 15 years interviewing for *Sexual Behavior in the Human Female,* critics argued that the interviewees had exaggerated or covered up facts. How could Kinsey tell if his subjects were telling the truth? "Very simple," he replied. "I look them right in the eye. I lean forward. I ask questions rapidly, one right after the other. I keep staring them in the eye. Naturally, if they falter, I can tell they are lying."

Kinsey's reply was probably a convenient lie. Actually, a Kinsey interview would last one and one-half to three hours, and cover 300 questions. There was a formula for cross-checks to spot exaggeration or reticence in a subject. Some subjects were reinterviewed months later, and their answers were compared with their original replies for accuracy. So Kinsey's system for netting lies was a bit more elaborate than an eyeball showdown; and anyway, tests since Kinsey have indicated that a steady gaze is no guarantee of honesty. Subjects who were told to conceal the truth from interviewers did not avert their eyes any more than those who were completely truthful — although the responses of the concealers did tend to be shorter, punctuated with more silences and "no comment"-type replies.

Listen Up

Although liars cannot be stared down into confession, their deceptions can be punctured by skillfully scrambled questioning. "Do not ask your questions in logical order, lest he invent conveniently as he goes along," advises Francis L. Wellman in *The Art of Cross-Examination,* "but dodge him about in his story and pin him down to precise answers on all the accidental circumstances indirectly associated with the main narrative."

That, by the way, may not be the only bit of legal advice that you can get for free. The courtroom might well be the interviewer's classroom, as Richard Reeves notes: "The people we interview get increasingly sophisticated. We have an awful lot to learn from legal techniques, from courtroom techniques. In this area, I think we're a little simple-minded. We think that we are very clever because we have a good question. But if you watch good courtroom attorneys work, their questions are often in a long series. The answer to the first five questions may do nothing but box the person in, or they may even be meaningless. I think all reporters could be much more sophisticated about questioning techniques."

Watch him, cross-examine him, stare him down like a wrathful deacon — do with him what you will; still, your two best lie detectors are sticking out of your head. *Listen* to the man. Closely. Sift his words for glibness and double-talk. "Often men who are trying to conceal something will tip off the fact under direct and skillful questioning, when a reporter puts one statement against an earlier one and detects contradictions," note the authors of a popular journalism text. "When the questioner is able to challenge with, 'But a few minutes ago you said so-and-so,' he puts the evasive witness on the defensive and may obtain the facts he needs." He also puts the subject on notice that he is weighing every word; that alone will dampen an interviewee's enthusiasm for invention.

The Put-On

For some, however, that enthusiasm is all-consuming. Beware of the over-interviewed, for they may lie you blind. "I really like lying," says rock star Alice Cooper, who claims he lies to stay sane through his multitudes of interviews. " t's one of my favorite things, as long as it's creative lying, as long as it doesn't hurt anybody. *Vogue* magazine asked me what was the biggest lie I had ever told, and I couldn't think of one, so I lied about *that.* "

Lying is not a vice that begins or ends (well, few *do*) with Cooper. "Putting on interviews is a national pastime quickly overtaking both football and barhopping," explains Pete Johnson, an executive at Warner Bros. Records. "The trend can be traced back to 1964, when John Lennon was asked, 'How do you find America?' and he replied, 'Turn left at Greenland.' "

Put-on subjects are often quick change artists. "If it is their common practice to brush off small and idolatrous children, insult waiters, and saucer their coffee, they desist during the interview," Joseph N. Bell says of actors and actresses. "The interviewer can only deal in fleeting impressions, many of which are based on an image that a performer highly skilled in his trade wants to project."

When someone plays a role, or effects a pose, there is significance in that facade. If someone walks like a duck, sounds like a duck, hangs around ducks — he must *be* a duck; and that insight is useful to the interviewer. "I'm never flattered when people compare me to the roles I've played," actor Jack Nicholson told David Sterritt of the *Christian Science Monitor,* "although I'm from the school of acting that believes in using yourself, and believes that there's really very little difference between you and any character that you're going to play, when you get down to the essential values."

The verbal put-on is more wily, however. How can an interviewer tell when he is being put on with an elaborate reply? Sometimes the best can't. Certainly Clifford Irving put on Mike Wallace when the CBS newsman grilled him about his Howard Hughes autobiography. But often the put-on can be traced, with some meticulous backtracking. Irving's "essentially preposterous assertion that he had 100 interviews with Howard Hughes in less than a year could have been exposed by demanding the date and place of a single interview," said Gladwin Hill of the *New York Times* afterward. "And if he refused to give the information, asking *why* he wouldn't — and thereafter calling attention to his refusal. When he was belatedly inveigled into specifying a rendezvous . . . his story began crumbling."

When Irving was finally questioned closely, he mentioned meeting Hughes at the Holiday Inn in Beverly Hills. Hill: "It was inconceivable that Hughes, who had used dozens of sheltered rendezvous points around Los Angeles for decades, would have agreed to meet in such a public place. Indeed, investigation quickly revealed that while Irving and [his assistant/researcher] Suskind had been at the hotel in June, they had been preoccupied in telephoning all over town, brainpicking for tidbits about Hughes — utterly inconsistent with their having the man himself there to interview."

Thus, with the benefit of hindsight, a reporter suggests that a few pointed questions early in the interviews would have gone far in exposing Irving as a literary hoaxer.

A writer who saturates himself in a subject can usually evaluate his research for what is truth and what is put on. Richard Hammer found himself in an ideal position for doing *The Last Testament of Lucky Luciano,* for example, because *Playboy* magazine commissioned him at the same time to do a book on the history of organized crime.

"They didn't know about the Luciano book," the former *New York Times* reporter told freelancer Maggie Paley. "They had more or less just pulled my name out of a hat. Doing the two books at once, I would often come across conflicting versions of the same incident, and then I'd have to go by internal evidence to get at what really happened. If two stories go along the same line up to a point and then diverge widely, you have to decide which one — on the basis of internal evidence, in terms of what preceded it and what followed — seems more logical." Thus, Hammer had a convenient (and profitable) method of checking the accuracy of the information of Martin Gosch, Luciano's confidant and the book's coauthor. "Explanations that had been accepted by crime writers for years just fell apart," said Hammer. "Luciano was really leveling with Gosch."

Most put-ons have short life spans; then events and enemies overtake them. But an ill-prepared interviewer is always more susceptible. Loudon Wainwright, the longtime *Life* columnist, tells of a friend who had become "a little" famous and found himself interviewed by a reporter who "was under the mistaken impression that his interviewee had studied engineering in college." The subject obligingly engineered "a whole line of plausible but untruthful answers for him on the spot." Explained the slightly famous friend: "The reporter had this idea about me, and it might have shaken him to find out that he had it all wrong."

The best way to check up on a source is to check him out before you ask a question. If he suspects you've neglected your homework, he may exaggerate with little fear of being curtailed. Gloria Steinem reads everything of importance written about her interviewees, and talks to their acquaintances. Then she starts her interviews by asking her subjects what they think has been accurate and inaccurate in previous writings about them. "Writing from clips, I think, is a big problem since it makes for a lot of perpetual inaccuracies," says Steinem.

She adds: "I read things about myself very often written by people I've never met, and its very educational because you really understand how low the level of journalism is; you know what the facts are in this case, so you see how much of it is written from clips and how much of it is wrong. And it's repeated over and over.... And it probably turns up in your obituary."

Caution: Publicity Seekers Ahead

Beware, too, of the subject who *wants* to be interviewed. He may be like your brother's friend who wants to sell you his car, real cheap. Motives abound: prejudices, special interests, ego, income. Watch out. George Lincoln Rockwell, the late head of the American Nazi Party, riddled his replies with racial and ethnic slurs in a *Playboy* interview with Alex Haley, and explained to the interviewer: "In talking to you, I've used words like 'nigger' and 'kike' because this is a big interview in a national magazine, and I want to attract attention — to shock people into listening to what I have to say."

Publicity seekers can deliver sensational copy to an interviewer — but be prepared for a sensational denial if the subject gets cold feet. When Earl Wilson interviewed Marie (The Body) McDonald in the early days of her short-lived career, the starlet told him that actress Joan Fontaine wore falsies. The Body recalled a hot day when Miss Fontaine complained about the heat on a set and pulled out her bust pads and started fanning herself with them.

"I hadn't heard the tale," said Wilson afterward, "but in my capacity as a writer on entertainment, specializing at the time in physical culture, I was glad to learn about it." When Wilson's interview appeared in the *Los Angeles Daily News,* though, "there was hell to pay! Everybody involved jumped on Marie for exposing the inside bust information about Hollywood." So Marie denied everything. "Wilson's a goddamned liar," she said. "I never said any such thing. In fact, I never even saw him."

"The Body and I eventually patched up our quarrel," wrote Wilson "and I did several interviews with her over the years, and frequently reported her night club appearances and the various phases of her love life. The Body taught me, in the course of her promotional build-up, one valuable lesson: when interviewing an ambitious actress, always try to have a witness."

Watch Your Figures

"There are three kinds of lies," observed Disraeli. "Lies, damned lies, and statistics." Of that unholy trinity, however, statistics are the most convincing and the most fashionable tool of deception. And they lend themselves to more creative purposes than one would suppose. Humorist Henry G. Felsen, noting the bombardment of statistical claims from drug manufacturers, remarked that proper treatment will cure a cold in seven days — but left to itself, it will hang on for a week.

Fortunately, statistics can be easy to verify—if the journalist can spare the time. In the fifties, for example, Senator Joseph McCarthy made a speech in which he waved a sheet of paper that contained, he said, the names of 81 communists in the State Department. When he appeared on TV's *Meet the Press* shortly afterward, however, McCarthy lost face by failing to name names or to back up his statistics. "A guest may think he has evaded our questions," observed Lawrence Spivak, then moderator of *Meet the Press,* "but the evasion is an answer in itself."

A statistic can multiply like fishes and loaves when handed down by a press agent, and accepted as gospel truth by reporters. Take Richard Nixon's visit to Atlanta in the 1972 Presidential campaign. His press secretary, Ronald Ziegler, told reporters that at least 700,000 persons had turned out to see the President in Atlanta (pop. 497,421 in 1970); and that figure appeared in a number of stories—until Jim Perry of *The National Observer* did some routine ciphering. He estimated that 400 people a block, five rows deep, on both sides of the street for 15 blocks, had seen Nixon—or a total of some 60,000. He added 15,000 for side streets between blocks, and concluded: "I'd be willing to say that 75,000 people turned out to welcome Richard Nixon to Atlanta." So much for the New Math.

Commercial statistics — inventory, circulation and sales figures — are also remarkably susceptible to inflation. Listen politely to the disseminator of the statistic — then beeline for the statistic's *source.* When Nathan Cobb did a mildly investigative piece for *The Boston Globe* on the so-called underground press in his city, he was told by the publisher of *The Boston Phoenix* that the weekly's circulation was 110,000. That sounded high. So Cobb phoned the *Phoenix's* printer and spoke to the office manager, who told him the firm printed only 81,000 copies of the paper every week.

Like statistics, quotes from government officials have that crisp ring of authority — if not necessarily of truth. With public officials, there is often an Official Version of what happened, and an untold truthful version. What does an interviewer do if he wants to verify what seems to be a laundered version of the story? "In dealing with political events that are still going on," says Fred Freed of NBC, "you're not likely to get your best information from officials who are still in office. You're likely to get your best information from officials who have left office. They want to tell you what it was like when they were there and who double-crossed them." So double back. When NBC did a documentary called *Vietnam Hindsight,* for instance, Freed found that Roger Hilsman, a professor at Columbia University who had been assistant secretary of state for Far Eastern affairs in 1963-64, was willing to talk. "He felt that when he was in office he was not listened to when he was trying to give them advice," adds Freed.

Untangling My Lai

Material from discontented interviewees may produce lively copy — but the truth of the copy may later be challenged. Tandem interviewing — using two or more interviewers to question a subject — is useful in such touchy situations which place a premium on verification. The *Chicago Tribune,* for example, conducted an investigation on police brutality, and within five months a team of reporters had produced an eight-part series which *Time* magazine called "probably the most thorough examination of police brutality ever published in a U.S. newspaper." Because the charges were so serious and because the reporting team was denied access to files of the police department's internal affairs division (responsible for investigating brutality complaints), the series had to be researched with hundreds of interviews with policemen and the policed. Needless to say, many victims and witnesses were reluctant to talk. "People were afraid of the police department," said one of the writers. "We had to convince them that we were sincerely trying to pursue a social evil."

Whenever someone would cooperate with the reporters, every effort was made to verify the material obtained. In addition to giving key interviews to two newsmen, injured victims were asked to provide medical records, and to take lie-detector tests. Subjects with criminal records were dropped, as were witnesses whose accounts "proved to contain even the smallest inaccuracies."

Such interviewing is journalism of the highest order (and in this instance it resulted in indictments against three Chicago policemen, and investigations of others), but the point here is to conduct investigative interviewing with internal verification as you go. Double-check facts, screen interviewees, do your homework. Weigh one source of information against another. Interview subjects on both sides of an issue. Protect your flanks with careful corroboration. In a *Newsweek* piece on "jugular journalism" in the wake of Watergate, David Gelman says, "Scarcely a reporter in the country is now immune to fantasies of heroic achievement — and epic remuneration. Woodstein Envy is rampant, even among newsmen with enviable reputations of their own. On the whole, the affliction is a healthy one. Never before have reporters been so alert for official malfeasance, so reluctant to take bureaucratic handouts at their slippery word." But there have been slip-ups, too, in some reporters' search for wrongdoing. Rush jobs. "The point is to make your case," says Clark Mollenhoff of the *Des Moines Register*. "Getting evidence that's admissible in court is what it's all about. You can't always do it, but every time you neglect that, you cut into your credibility." Adds Gelman of *Newsweek:* "Whether investigations are big or small, there seems no substitute for dogged, unglamorous legwork." Motto: Verify before you villify.

A reporter with the doggedness of an evangelist can pull together conflicting stories into a Pulitzer-winner. Seymour Hersh did, with his My Lai story — and it had the craterlike impact on Vietnam that Kent State had on the National Guard. Although the massacre occurred on March 16, 1968, Hersh didn't get his phone tip until 19 months later. The Army was then trying to court-martial Lt. William Calley secretly, and it had tucked away the event so well that Hersh could only interview those witnesses and accomplices he could find.

He started with Calley, then expanded the story through other interviews. They "inevitably produced a maze of conflicting stories," Hersh later recalled. "Many of the men were unable to agree on details, especially when asked to discuss an event that took place nearly two years earlier and one in which they may have committed premeditated murder."

Hersh tried to arrive at the truth in three ways. First, he obtained access to the few transcripts of interrogations of key witnesses that already been conducted by the Criminal Investigating Division (CID) and the office of the Inspector General — the Army agencies which had already been investigating My Lai 4. Second, Hersh interviewed as many members of Charlie Company as possible "to find those facts and incidents that were generally agreed upon." He interviewed many Charlie Company members at least twice; most were contacted again (by phone) "to clarify conflicting points." Third, Hersh eliminated statements that "were obviously contradictory or could not be verified by other witnesses." When there was a conflict on points that Hersh felt were significant, however, he decided to describe that conflict as fully as possible.

Hersh used letters written by members of Charlie Company; a careful history of Quang Ngai Province; official communiqués, government letters and other background materials for verification. But he wrote the story almost exclusively from interviews — and without setting foot in Vietnam.

Evidence of Things Seen

Beyond corroboration is physical evidence. "There is still no man," says one legal writer, "who would not accept dog tracks in mud against the sworn testimony of a hundred eyewitnesses that no dog had passed by." Evidence of things seen, measured, or recorded — photos, statistics or letters — lend power and persuasion to the opinions of an interviewee.

But what if the interviewer himself is unpersuaded? Whom should he trust? "Well, you don't trust anybody, not when you're a writer of contemporary history," says William Manchester. "You weave into your interviews questions that you have asked other people, and you balance them out. When I was writing about the Dallas motorcade, on November 22, 1963, if there were six people in the car, I interviewed all six. If five of them saw something, I concluded that it happened. If only one saw it, I concluded that it did not."

Manchester adds: "I can tell if interviewees are telling the truth by first asking them questions I myself know the answer to. If they respond to these truthfully and without evasion, I feel I can trust their answers to other questions."

When Gay Talese gets conflicting reports, he plays them close to his vest. "I don't take chances in having someone else create fiction for me," he says. "I stay with what I can find out and believe to be as close to the truth as is possible. When it comes to reconstructing, if I have conflicting viewpoints on one point or another, I may just not even get into that area."

Sign Here, Please

There is, of course, an easy way out of the morass of verification: ship the story back to the source for checking. This is a humbling and risky business, but there is not always *another* way out ... particularly if you are a science reporter.

How else do you verify, for instance, a cancer researcher's painstaking explanation of his work in isolation? Or a story of the history of the electrocardiogram, when you can scarcely distinguish an electrocardiogram from a telegram? Yes, undoubtedly, the writer should never wade unprepared into unfamiliar waters. Yet science waits for no man: it strains ahead and performs miracles and swamps writers with its baffling new vistas. Any science writer with a sense of adventure must expect to get lost – over and over; and he'll probably have to turn to his sources to bail him out.

"Approved interviews are most important when it comes to dealing with medical men," suggests Waldemar Kaempffert, former science editor of the *New York Times.* "They may not be directly quoted in an interview, because that would be a violation of something called 'medical ethics,' but what they say can be stated in the third person. Medicine is about the most ticklish subject that a science writer is called upon to handle. Thus the word 'cure' must never be used by the reporter, but if the medico who is interviewed used the word, it is well to let the fact be known and say that it is his word."

The science interviewer should collect autographs as well as quotes, suggests author Helen Patterson: the interviewee should sign two approval sheets after he has seen the finished article, and one sheet should then be mailed to the editor. Patterson says the signed sheets "will protect the writer against later criticisms of the interviewee or the editor."

Not to mention legal costs. "A writer's practice of getting a release from a person he interviews is not a matter of ethics, but rather legal protection on his part," says Kirk Polking, Director of Writer's Digest School. "With the increasing number of suits for invasion of privacy (libel does not have to be the only concern), and the tendency of some people to say something for publication and then change their minds about it when they see their name in print, many writers stick with the signed release."

Not that the writer should stick *all* interviewees with releases.

"Obviously, who the interviewee is, what the subject matter of the interview is and its importance is all weighed by the freelancer in deciding whether to get a release," says Polking. "A doctor who's being quoted by name and whose reputation may be on the line is different from a smalltown grandmother who has invented some charming games to play with her grandchildren and is happy to tell the world about them."

Keep the language of the release form clear and concise:

_____ _____ has reviewed " _____ "
by _____ _____ , and affirms that he is accurately quoted in the manuscript.

Make *three* copies: one for your source, one for your editor, and one for your files.

Most broadcasting stations have a standard clearance form for interviewees — and it can cover a *lot* of ground. "It ties the interviewee to us for life," says Fred Freed. "The interviewee agrees that what he says can be used by us any place, any time, in any form, forever, and he won't complain about it in any way.

"You don't need a release when a news event is happening," continues Freed. "You have a right to cover it. When somebody talks to you and stands there and lets you film him, he's doing it voluntarily. With all of our gear, we can't exactly sneak up on people. But the legal department feels it's necessary to get signed releases. A lot of people are frightened by them, but we get them to sign."

Freed tells of a distinguished lawyer who was interviewed for a documentary on the decision to drop the A-bomb on Japan. The producer gave him the standard NBC release form. "I wouldn't allow any client of mine to sign one of these under any circumstances," he sighed. Then he signed it.

Sometimes a writer can net an interview with a Biggie only if he agrees to submit the transcript to him for approval before publication. And sometimes this will work in the writer's favor. One of Henry Kissinger's most famous interviews, for example, appeared in *Business Week* in January 1975. The secretary of state was asked, "Have you considered military action (against the Arab nations) on oil?"

"I am not saying that there's no circumstance where we would not use force," replied Kissinger. "But it is one thing to use it in the case of a dispute over price, it's another where there's some actual strangulation of the industrialized world."

It was a quote heard round the world, and Kissinger helped pack the powder in when he added the pointed "strangulation" phrase while reviewing the transcript. "He was a great editor of his own material," says Paul Finney, managing editor of *Business Week.* "We might even hire him if he decides to go into journalism."

So there are cases when it is helpful to submit a manuscript to that most attentive editor, your source. But some journalists would go beyond that; they would send release forms to all quoted authorities, like Christmas cards. Even *The Beginning Writer's Answer Book,* an often-helpful book using the Q&A format, says that if you quote authorities "specifically by name, then, yes, you do need a release on the material they give you."

Well, balderdash. Checking quotes with the quotee can be hazardous to your writing — unless your piece is highly technical, and the interviewee is your major source; or unless your key interviewee would agree to the interview only if he got a sneak preview of the ms; or unless the piece is steeped in facts, not human foibles, and an advance reading would be in the spirit of proofreading, not of retouching. Otherwise, submitting a manuscript to a source for approval can be like sticking your hand in Pandora's box to see if anything bites.

Just ask Frank Brady, a former *Playboy* editor who wrote a biography called *Hefner.* When he submitted the finished manuscript to his former boss for approval (in return, the author had received some photos and cooperation from Hugh Hefner), the publisher's lawyers threatened to sue Macmillan unless changes were made. In all, over 100 changes were demanded.

"The more people who read it, the more objections there were," said editor Fred Honig at Macmillan, as Brady's manuscript was passed around sternly at *Playboy.* Finally, a number of deletions were made to hold the lawyers at bay and to make *Hefner* libel-free. "If something was inaccurate or unsubstantiated or hearsay it was cut," said Honig. Which is OK. But which can also be capricious, troublesome and costly.

Tidying Up the Transcript

Checking with the source on the transcript of a taped interview is, however, a whole nuther ball game. We speak in fits; we plague our sentences with grade-school interjections, grammatical wreckage, aborted half-thoughts. To commit a man's inconstant speech to permanent print without allowing him to tidy up his syntax is cruel punishment; it is like shoving him before the TV cameras before he can get out of his pajamas. Don't let him tamper with the strength of his words, but let him streamline them; that will make them stronger.

When Rex Reed received the transcript of an interview he did with me, he went over it lightly with a pencil, and wrote in a cover letter: "I hope you will not mind the changes I have made, but they seem very important if the syntax is to be straightened out enough to make me seem like something less than semiliterate. . . . I don't think I have changed anything, just cleaned up my wandering Southern drawl a bit. Say anything you like about me in your intro, but allow me to crisp my dialogue a bit, OK?" His changes were grammatical, not substantial; the edited version was printed.

When returning your transcript to a subject, phrase that cover letter carefully. Ask for corrections, not for "approval." "*Correction* is the key word," says Murray Fisher of *Playboy*. "It has none of the freewheeling, pencil-happy connotation that approval does." And the interviewer should make clear that he is not bound to the source's corrected version. "I never commit myself to change what I have written on the basis of the source's suggestion," says Hayes Jacobs. "I will *consider* the suggestion, carefully, but I always remain free to disregard it."

The Replies, They Are A'Changin'

But you have to know when and where to give. Relinquishing even substantial control over a transcript can result in a better article occasionally. Bob Dylan thought he came off badly in the transcript of a 1966 *Playboy* interview; and Murray Fisher of *Playboy* thought the transcript made the protest singer look like "a disinterested cop-out" at a time when those who were truly committed to the protest movement had their bodies on the line. "He read the manuscript and was perceptive enough to realize this," adds the editor. "It was also a boring interview. We really didn't have his attention (nor did the protest movement), and he just didn't like himself in print."

Dylan told *Playboy*, "I'm not going to let you run this the way it is."

"There had been no stipulation for his approval of the manuscript as a condition of publication," recalls Fisher, "yet we gritted our teeth and said, 'Well, what are you going to do about it?' "

"I'll give you new answers to all the questions," said Dylan.

For the next week or so, Fisher received "bits and pieces of hand-drafted answers to the same questions we had asked originally, but this time they were really off the wall. It was a mind-bending, consciousness-raising editorial experience for me to have my precious copy subjected to this kind of ventilation, but it reached a point where it no longer mattered that things didn't follow. That became part of the interview's charm.

"The result was a far better interview—it went up from a C-plus to maybe an A-minus. Dylan himself came off as still uninvolved, but this time too hip for the movement rather than too square or too indifferent."

Moral? "I'll do anything if it makes the interview better," says Fisher, "if I've got time for it."

The trick, of course, is to *make* time for verifying and polishing an interview story—for the way one finishes an interview assignment is just as important as the way one prepared for it. So remember our motto here at camp: check out from the interview gracefully, and check out its facts diligently. All's well when you end well.

12. Pasting It Together

Writing is very easy. All you do is sit in front of a typewriter keyboard until little drops of blood appear on your forehead.

—Red Smith

Many readers, and beginning interviewers, think that once the interview is down on tape, the rest is easy. All you have to do is put the Q's and A's in front of the dialogue, right? Wrong.

Initially one must decide whether to even use the Q&A format, or to write the piece as a narrative spiced with quotes. Take a long look at your interview; its style may determine the article's form. "With somebody like Truman Capote, who is such a verbal person," says Gloria Steinem, "it seems less necessary to recreate the atmosphere in which that person is or to explain or to couch." Thus, Steinem's interview with the novelist ran in Q&A form — after a lively introduction. But Steinem took a different tack for her interview with Renata Adler of the *New York Times.* "If you recorded an interview with Renata, you would have long silences," says Steinem. "She's not a talker. You have to give the reader the experience of being in her presence by describing it because she's an enormously shy and vulnerable person."

As with art, the form of an interview article should suit the content. Of course, the editor may settle all that by deciding in advance that the piece should be a Q&A, which is particularly a popular feature in the men's and women's magazines. But don't put up your feet yet — even a Q&A manuscript demands much work. "Everything must flow," says Murray Fisher. "It must be logical, linear." *Playboy's* premier interview editor adds: "After a long process of trial and error, it's become clear to me that the eye is much more critical than the ear, and that the conversation that sounded fine while you conducted it (and would probably sound fine if it were broadcast on radio or television) is redundant, digressive, undisciplined, self-indulgent and boring in print. The ear passes over all these flaws and retains only the interesting parts; the eye, however, perceives everything. So what I try to do is to cut off the fat, like a butcher, and shape the meat."

Squeezing the Water Out

When Fisher sits down to edit an interview transcript, he begins by drawing a line across the page wherever he senses a jarring change of subject. He then rearranges the pieces of the interview, taping sections together so that one subject leads inexorably to the next. This usually means that long sheets of paper are hanging from Fisher's office walls. "For the Fidel Castro interview, which later ran as a book," he recalls, "my entire office was wallpapered with long sheets, which I then had to abstract into a manuscript of perhaps 20 or 30 columns that seemed to be of a piece, not merely a series of excerpts."

Fisher sifts an interview transcript into three categories: "A material, which must be used; B material, which is desirable but not absolutely necessary; and C material, which is expendable, to be used only if necessary for transitions or filler." The best interviews have only A and B material; but any transcript undergoes "a tremendous amount of processing, distillation, orchestration" before it is publishable.

After a Q&A has been edited for overall organization, the overseer must go through it line by line for clarity and comprehension. "Most people don't edit before they speak," says Murray Fisher, "so I have to do it for them. When I'm line editing an interview, I always have to clarify and distill, make what the subject says less undisciplined. This doesn't distort what a person is saying, nor does it make someone any more intelligent or articulate than he is. It just squeezes the water out of a conversation. It retains the verisimilitude of spontaneity — that unrehearsed quality — but, in point of fact, there's nothing informal about it."

Of course, Fisher is careful to edit "without doing an injustice to the essence of the original. We certainly have no intention of putting words in the mouths of our subjects. It's our practice, wherever there's any extensive juggling of material, where there's a chance of taking something out of context or of performing a linguistic blunder, to give it to the subject for him to correct."

Q&A vs. Interview Article

The Q&A form is most popular in magazines. Newspapers use it more reluctantly because it requires more space than the standard interview "story," and lacks the emphasis and selection of details that most newspapers prefer. Still, even newspaper editors have found it helpful as an impersonal device that gives readers precise answers to basic questions about complex issues. *The Wall Street Journal* used a Q&A to explain a business tax credit bill before Congress to its readers. After a brief introduction, the article assumed this format:

Q. Does the credit apply to investment in both new and used property?
A. Yes. But in the case of used property a businessman can claim the credit on only $50,000 worth of purchases in any one year.
Q. How is the tax credit calculated?
A. That depends on the useful life of the item acquired.

The Q&A form is ideal for controversial topics and personalities because it provides a clear window for the reader, free of the reporter's interventions. The subject speaks directly to the reader, and a lively Q&A is likely to have greater reader empathy than a profile.

While the Q&A is increasingly popular for subjects and personalities of national interest, most smaller regional publications prefer fact stories — in which writers interview for information; or people stories — in which the thoughts and opinions of an interviewee are the main interest.

Fact interviews are people interviews too, of course. But in fact interviews, people are less important than what they know. They are interviewed only because they can add some knowledge to the coverage of a current topic in the news. For example, when George Wallace was shot during the 1972 Presidential campaign, medical specialists were interviewed to determine whether or not the paralysis would be permanent. And when there was an oil slick off the coast of California recently, specialists in oil drilling, ecology and beach repair were very much in demand — as interviewees. Interviews such as this depend on insight, not on well-known names.

Variations on a Quote

But neither insight nor infamous names will make an interview story attractive to a reader if it lacks quotes — those brief, brilliant bursts of life. Many a successful story has been weaned off a rigorous diet of quotes and anecdotes. One problem facing the abundant notetaker, however, is what to quote and what to paraphrase. The writer's rule of thumb is to quote a subject only for effect — never for routine information that can be summarized into a tight, expository form. Most writers use indirect quotes to summarize long statements by the subject (elaborate anecdotes can often be condensed for greater impact). This is done by beginning the statement with the subject's name and then telling his story in your own words. Here's an example of an indirect quotation:

Hugh Hefner recalls growing up in an atmosphere that was highly puritanical, with neither drinking nor smoking allowed, and no movies on Sunday.

The same material handled as a direct quotation, however, would probably be more effective if attribution were held back until the end of the first sentence, or at least until after the first few words of the quote:

"I grew up in a highly puritanical atmosphere," says Hugh Hefner. "There was no drinking, no smoking, and no movies on Sunday."

"I try to use direct quotes when a quote captures the personality of the person who said it or if it would take me twice as long to say the same thing paraphrasing it," says Nora Ephron. "I can't stand writers who quote people saying very mundane lines like, 'I was born in 1934.' You read something like that and wonder to yourself why did he quote *that,* it doesn't take you anywhere, or show you anything that the writer couldn't have done himself in a more interesting way."

Gay Talese agrees, only more so. "I have gotten away from the direct quotation," says the man whose bestselling *Honor Thy Father* is some 90 percent expository writing. "People do not speak in sentences," adds Talese, "so if you are going to quote them directly, word for word, accurately, verbatim — you are going to find that people are not going to seem articulate. Almost without exception, you can say it better if you don't have to stay within the quotes that come out of this person's mouth."

Quoting directly, according to Talese, is not like writing: it's the easy way out. "It is much more interesting to read if you put it in your own words," he says. But like Nora Ephron, Talese will quote for effect. "People have to say things in such an original way, a unique way that would be so peculiarly their own that it would reflect so much of what they are, their style of speech, that I wouldn't attempt to imitate it. Obviously, if I'm writing an article about, oh, let's say the comedian Jonathan Winters, or the manager Casey Stengel — well, obviously, you'd have to use some of his language because that language would be so much a part of *him*." For Gay Talese, though, this is the exception — not the norm. "Why do we have to stick to other people's words?" he asks. "Particularly when we're the writers. Let's put the story in our own words — that's how we can communicate more fully and more accurately. At least, I can. That's why I got away from using direct quotes, although I always attribute material to the proper source."

Talese's apprehension about using quotes, and his fear of not being 100 percent accurate in quoting a person, are based upon a kind of perfectionism that goes back to his newspaper days at the *New York Times.* Many reporters, he found, settled for the gist of what a subject said — not a word-for-word quote; and Talese noticed that when he was on a story covered by other papers as well, the next day he would see differences in the quotations appearing in the *Herald Tribune* or the *New York Post* or the *Daily News.* "Sometimes we even matched quotes after our assignments were over," he recalls, "but even then I noticed there would be variations. Not intentional — no, we didn't change the meaning of the words out of the spokesman's mouth." But there were variations, and Talese has felt uncomfortable about using direct quotes ever since.

And now, the $64 temptation: can a writer put quotation marks around words that are not *exactly* those of the speaker? No and yes.

"Never use quotation marks unless you are certain that the words are precisely what was said," says William Rivers. "If it ever made sense to quote *approximately* what was said and to improve the grammar of public figures — once fairly common but dubious practices in journalism — it makes no sense today."

"Yes, if the phrase or sentence quoted reflects the meaning of the person quoted," says George L. Bird, professor emeritus of the Syracuse University School of Journalism. He gives this example: "One might ask, 'Do you believe in capital punishment?' And the judge might answer, 'No.' The writer would omit the question from his article and simply write, 'I do not believe in capital punishment,' said Judge Sebastian.

"When the writer can tell himself that the person interviewed would be glad to verify the accuracy of the quotations," adds Bird, "then he may feel assured he has done a good job of reporting."

'Tis a sensitive question, and it just might inspire livelier debate among writers around a bar than any controversy since the Dodgers left Brooklyn. Some writers are strict constructionists. "My practice is never to condense or alter a quote," says Sid Ross. "If it isn't usable as is, don't use it. This is out-of-context quoting in its worst form."

Yet, how do you handle the interviewee's grammatical bloops? With care. "The magazine writer who refines the rough-hewn English of Mayor Richard Daley of Chicago," says William Rivers, "creates for himself a credibility problem because his readers will contrast his version of Daley's speaking style with the reality presented by radio and television."

If the subject is not a public figure, though, the interviewer is in an easier position to handle grammatical lapses — and to decide whether he should reproduce the man's language fully, right down to the last ain't, or whether to touch things up, and make the subject seem more articulate than he perhaps is.

Many interviewers, of course, solve the problem by simply checking quotes with a subject for final approval before publication. The manuscript is likely to come back with penciled corrections that would make any grammarian proud. If the subject is supposed to be well educated, and if the clumsy syntax is an obvious slip, this double-check is helpful in avoiding unnecessary embarrassment.

Straightening Dialects

Dialects are often used more in the spirit of hilarity than accuracy, but they too pose a problem for the thoughtful interviewer. If used too faithfully, they become tedious and caricaturish. How would a Southern accent in a story about a beauty contest winner strike you after a few thousand drawling quotes: "Well, ah sho am glay-ed ta be tha winnah of this grand contest, ya heah?" Exactly. Better to play it straight, only occasionally bending the language for effect.

Always inform the reader when the subject is not speaking in her/his native tongue. "I like very much ice cream chocolate" may sound cute (with a wink) from Zsa Zsa or Charo; otherwise, it is disturbing, and can make the writer seem condescending. Once you have established that the subject has some endearing charms of speech, put your Mark Twain devices aside; stick to the King's English for maximum communication between reader and writer and speaker.

Holy Jesus!

In other circumstances, straightening out the grammar will harm the interviewer. If the subject has had a tough childhood, a meager education, and is now a heavyweight contender, it's ridiculous to quote him as if he were an Oxford don. H. Allen Smith was assigned to cover the Max Baer-Primo Carnera fight, for instance, and later reported: "Gaffers of my bracket may remember that Mr. Baer struck Mr. Carnera with great force and with great frequency about the face and head. When the Italian giant reached the dressing room he had large lumps all over his forehead, and his jaws were swollen. They took his ring clothes off and propped him up on a rubbing table, and he began looking around the room without apparently seeing anything. His handler faded back and left him sitting there. Nobody made a move to do anything, so I stepped up to him."

The following interview ensued:

> "Did he hit you hard?"
> "Holy Jesus!"
> "Do you want to fight him again?"
> "Holy Jesus!"
> "Do you think you could lick him if you fought him again?"
> "Holy Jesus!"
> "Does your head hurt?"
> "Holy Jesus!"
> "Do you think Baer can lick Schmeling?"
> "Holy Jesus!"

At this point Carnera's owners came into the room and the interview ended. "I was well-satisfied," reflected Smith. "It was one of the most revealing interviews I had ever had. I was quite astonished, however, the next day when I picked up the papers to see what the sports writers had to say about that scene in the dressing room. One of them quoted Carnera as having said: "Max's blows were very hard. He hurt me several times — I'll have to admit that. But I sincerely believe that I could defeat him and I would like to have another chance. I want to regain the championship."

When an interviewer wings a quote like that, s/he has gone beyond the customary bounds of good diction — and of good sense. But a sensible interviewer also knows that s/he can quote a man so accurately that he will appear incoherent. Journalists can take a tip from novelist George V. Higgins, known for his acute ear for authentic dialogue, who concedes that good dialogue isn't as realistic as critics like to suggest. "Style intervenes," says Higgins. "I put the false starts and pauses in, but I don't put them *all* in . . . . I read enough George Washington Cable — to wit, one book — to know that you can't do orthographic dialogue, the way people actually talk, because it's just too difficult to read. You *are* dealing in a different medium."

Out of necessity, the interviewer is sometimes an editor. "Play with the 'quotes' by all means — selecting, rejecting, thinning, transposing their order, saving a good one for the end," says William Zinsser, a former *Life* columnist. "Just make sure that the play is fair. Don't change any words or let the cutting of a sentence distort the proper context of what remains."

The ellipsis, for instance, can make the long-winded quote more compact, more meaningful, without altering the meaning. Use three dots to indicate a deletion in a sentence —

"I am . . . in love with you, and you might as well know."

— and four dots for a deletion at the end of a sentence; or a deletion that cuts through an entire sentence (or more):

"I am — make no mistake about it — in love with you. . . ."
"I carried the bucket to the edge of the field. . . . The coach saw me and guffawed."

Quotesmanship Rules

One thing that the writer should be able to handle effectively is punctuation — especially the use of quotation marks. A few rules worth repeating:

1. Direct quotes are indicated by double quotation marks at the beginning and the end of the quoted statements: "Many writers don't know double quotes from single quotes," says Rose Adkins.

2. Quoted remarks within already-quoted statements take single quotation marks: "Writers should remember that old axiom: 'Single quotes inside double quotes' — or else," admonishes Al Candia.

3. The period and the comma go *inside* the quotation marks perhaps 99 percent of the time: "Writers often put the comma or period outside the quotes because they are accustomed to seeing it handled this way in English publications," says Robert J. Prahl. "*American* English is different."

4. The semicolon (and colon) will often be found outside quotation marks, however: My neighbor said, "I wouldn't watch TV if you chained me to one"; apparently the color Sears set in her living room is for artistic purposes.

5. When a question mark or an exclamation point is part of the quotation, it stays within the quotation marks; otherwise it goes outside the quotation marks: "Did you go to school today?" asked Doug Sandhage. "You betcha!" replied Paula.

But: Did Jonathan really say, "Sex is not the English way"?

6. If direct quotations continue for more than one paragraph, they can run "open." This means that the first paragraph begins with quotation marks, but no closing quotation marks are necessary at the end of that paragraph. Instead, quotation marks appear at the beginning of paragraph two — to indicate the continuing quote. If the quote continues uninterrupted to paragraph three, again there are no closing quotation marks at the end of paragraph two. Only when the quote has come to its conclusion are the end quotation marks added. Here is an example of continuing direct quotations from an interview with actress Katherine Hepburn by Glenna Syse:

Indications of a positive mental attitude peppered [Miss Hepburn's] responses:

"Living is the important thing. It doesn't matter what you do, do it well. If you can't, you may as well get a gun and end it.

"I get satisfaction out of everything. I'd rather do one thing well than four things badly. I'm not much for trusting in luck. You don't get something for nothing in this world. I like to do things well."

7. Finally, quotation marks are not generally used in Q&A's:

WD: What are a few examples of how different celebrities work with press agents?

THOMAS: There are a few, strangely enough, who will not allow publicists present when they give interviews. ...

In Said's Stead

For indirect as well as direct quotes, the rule of attribution is as firm as the rules of grammar — and, fortunately, more often heeded. Every quote must have an attribution. Period. If you cannot attribute by name, then attribute by position (director of medical sciences) or, as a last resort, by cliché (a reliable source). "Someone in the crowd" will not do. As far as the reader is concerned, "someone in the crowd" might well be you.

Few devices are more annoying than attribution that intrudes with a sense of carnival variety. A manic writer can whip up a litany of attributives: he spat, he guffawed, he observed, he snickered, he stated, and on and on. One thesaurus-minded writer even drew up a list of alternate verbs for that trusty steed "said," and the list went well into three figures. Or so he articulated, anyway.

Strained word-searching such as this is bound to attract undue attention. Better the same passage should appear with a few "he said's" in succession. At least the reader is able to keep his mind on the quote rather than on the attribution. Sportscasters have the same hangup on the evening news during baseball season. Most feel they must give 20 scores without repeating a verb, and the result is silliness when simplicity would do just fine: Boston beat Cincinnati, Montreal squeezed by Philadelphia, New York ran away from Los Angeles, Chicago defeated Detroit, Peoria lost to Bowling Green, Kokomo eked out a victory over . . . nipped, clipped, bombed, ripped, topped, downed . . . .Just listen sometime.

Curses, Foiled Again

The writer who really wants variety, of course, can draw from the cornucopia of Anglo-Saxon zingers — at his own risk. We are well into the Age of Candor, but not yet into the Era of Anything Goes. How, then, can you handle the normal interventions of rough language? You have several options.

• *First, your publisher may not object to four-letter words, no matter what the four letters form.* This is true of most book publishers and many men's and women's magazines today, as well as numerous middlebrow and literary publications.

• *Second, if a publication does have a stylebook that prohibits four-letter words from its pages, remember that that is an editor's decision, not yours.* You would probably be expected to "tell it like it is," and to let an editor decide how to handle the tough stuff.

• *Third, euphemisms are part of a writer's arsenal, and they work both ways: telling the reader that tough language was spoken here, yet not rubbing his nose in it.* You can save a quote and get around the censor, for instance, by using the "expletive deleted" approach popularized by the Presidential transcripts of Richard Nixon. Dwight Whitney of *TV Guide* (with its G-rated audience) chronicled the conflict between Joseph Wambaugh, the cop-novelist and originator of TV's *Police Story,* and David Gerber, executive producer of the successful program. A running battle had developed between the two over how the show should be done, and Whitney stepped into the cross fire.

Whitney quoted one Wambaugh memo to Gerber as saying: "Are you people completely nuts? You are (expletive deleted) my cops!! Do you hear me?" Gerber to Wambaugh: "I still think at times you are a damn inflexible, hard-headed, volatile and mercurial SOB, perhaps with not as much patience as a maniac. But when it comes to writing, you know your business. And now that I've given your notes more than a cursory look, I love you again. Now go (expletive mercifully deleted)!" In the end, peace reigned and Wambaugh apologized in the spirit that Whitney had already captured: "I've come to realize that my remarks [to the press] are being drastically distorted . . . with you folks unfairly thrust into the role of insensitive lieutenants of the TV giant. . . . I've been an insufferable (totally unprintable expletive deleted) to work with."

A variation on this is the old &$!#!! ruse — using symbols from the exotic top row of your typewriter to indicate frustration, anger, and expletives you wouldn't wish on your Congressman. Eric Levin wrote a *TV Guide* piece on a detective who was the technical adviser to *Kojak*, called "A Cop Without a Gun Is Like a &$!#!! Streaker" — honest. The piece is peppered with these quotes:

"I blew my &%$# lid!"
"That kind of soft-hearted cradle-'em-in-your-arms stuff is strictly &%$#."
"The guy's *dead?* &%$# him. He's *dead.*"
"Personally, I could give a &%$# less about the public."

And so on.

Organizing Your Notes

The writer is likely, to unleash a few &%$#'s of his own after he completes several interviews and is mired in a pile of notes, wondering where to begin. Organizing interview notes — particularly if you have done several lengthy interviews — can be terrifying unless you develop a system. John Gunther used to clip all his notes apart, and then subdivide the notes into little piles covering a card table (or two). "For a chapter on the Sudan, as an example," wrote the travel writer, "I will assemble 30, 40, 50 small piles of scissored longhand scraps — broken down into Nile, politics, history, Gezira project, Khartoum, personalities, Gordon College, relations with Egypt, British attitudes, civil service, animals, Fuzzy-Wuzzies, whatnot." Gunther also kept a piled labeled "Not Using," another called "Future Reference" — and a final category, "Sources."

When cutting the original notes apart, Gunther placed a notation on each slip of paper indicating who told him what. "All this is tiresome," he conceded. "I have come near to yelling aloud in desperation when, having finished eviscerating one notebook, then another, then another, I find that there are still odd bits of paper to lay into fruitful formation. But somebody, I think Logan Pearsall Smith, once said that the true test of a person's love for his vocation was his capacity to tolerate the drudgery it involved." For Gunther, the drive behind an interviewer was "all very mysterious." But: "At last, when work on the notes is finished, when sources have been checked and essential reading has been done, it is time to write."

Ask yourself basic questions as you sort through your material. What kind of story are you writing? Is it intended chiefly to inform, or to entertain? Most important: what is the dominant chord you want to strike with this piece? The answer to that is probably your story's slant — and the details should then fall into place.

Too, it's a good idea to think in terms of three units: beginning, middle and end. Look for a strong quote to end the piece — along with something to begin it. "Beginnings are easy, I find," says Bob Thomas. "Usually I wait until the day after an interview before writing it up. By then my mind has sifted out the important elements. The lead might come to me in the shower or on the freeway. It's that final sentence that's tough."

When looking for a lead, remember O'Neil's Law, devised by the veteran *Life* magazine writer Paul O'Neil: "Always grab the reader by the throat in the first paragraph, sink your thumbs into his windpipe in the second, and hold him against the wall until the tag line." Will Grimsley, the veteran sports and feature writer for the Associated Press, adds: "A good writer is like a hypnotist. He gains the reader's attention with an enticing first paragraph and holds his attention until he gets his point across." The interviewer who has done his work well should have a rich assortment of lead possibilities.

Once the lead has been decided upon, the writer must bridge his opening with the body of his piece. The best transitions are ones that bring the reader into the story's midstream without his even realizing it. They're that subtle. Material in the body of an article is usually then arranged in an ascending order of importance — from items of less importance to information that is insightful and high in reader impact. Keep pulling the reader along with a narrative thread that builds in pitch to a climactic conclusion.

One organizational technique for using interviews that have occurred over a period of days or weeks is to compress everything into a more manageable time frame. Martin Mayer did this for a piece on hairdresser Mr. Kenneth, which appeared in *Esquire* — and which Mayer calls "the best piece of work I have ever done for a magazine." Mayer calls this technique a "bit of artifice," adding: "I spent several days hanging around Kenneth's scissors, and made a composite single day out of the best of the conversations."

This approach is similar to condensing quotes to make their meaning clearer; and it's usually acceptable if the article focuses on a single place. But it is risky if the subject moves from place to place, and the writer telescopes the action without tipping off the reader. Gail Sheehy, for instance, did a profile of "David the Pimp" for *New York* magazine, in which David maintained an incredible pace of living — so much so that skeptical readers were even more disbelieving when Sheehy later acknowledged that what she had made seem to be "a day in the life" was in fact several days of solid reporting. Likewise, when Sheehy interviewed scores of prostitutes, but created a composite character named "Red Pants" out of elements from several interviews, there was misunderstanding and criticism because the reader was not so informed. Whether this is journalism or cheating at cards is debatable, for sure.

Finally, the finale. Close with style — try linking the ending with the beginning, if possible.

Bob Greene used the full-cycle effect for a stylish profile of Frank Sinatra that began with a party scene after a Sinatra performance in Las Vegas:

> The little room was crowded, but like any room he walks into, there was no question that it was his room. He chose a table in the corner and picked up a piece of pizza from a tray. He bit into the pizza, a bit of cheese dripping from his mouth, and someone handed him a drink. The eyes began turning toward him, and the people began to say yes, he's here. If the man noticed all the attention he was attracting, he did not show it. He took another bite from his pizza, washed it down, and began to talk. "Well," said Frank Sinatra, "So here we are."
>
> That did it. The party had now officially begun. Before he had come in, it was just a room full of people and food and booze, waiting for something to happen. Now, with the entrance of Frank Sinatra, everything was right. . . .

After a few more paragraphs establishing the party scene, Greene shifts back to Sinatra's performance earlier in the evening — going through it chronologically, song by song, interweaving his own research on Sinatra's background with the events at Caesars Palace that evening: the blend of singer, songs, musicians, and audience. The show ends, but the profile continues. How to end? Return to the party scene which opens the piece. Now the party, too, is ending:

> He was out of the room and all of a sudden things got quiet. Just as the party starts when Frank Sinatra walks into a room, it dies when he leaves. . . .

With this echo from the lead, Greene moves into a concluding scene that shows Sinatra walking past the hotel bell captain's desk where a guest is trying to bribe his way into the next evening's Sinatra performance. The guest is so intent on pulling out two $20 bills (and reaching for a third one) that he doesn't even see the singer walk quickly past. Then Greene's conclusion:

> Sinatra did not notice the transaction. His day of work was over. He walked out through the casino, out the big doors, out of Caesars Palace, and he stepped into the waiting car, ready to go home.

Not a bad ending — and one beautifully organized profile from a flurry of notes for the *Chicago Sun-Times Midwest* magazine.

A popular ending device is to use a good quote for your kicker. The quote can be a declaratory statement, or it can be a question that entices and lingers in the reader's imagination. For his profile of actress Barbara Harris, interviewer John Gruen found himself in the role of interviewee as the piece came to this conclusion:

> "For our last question," said the actress, "could I ask *you* a question?"
>
> "By all means."
>
> "How do you like your eggs in the morning?"

Writing can only be learned by writing, not by reading about writing; and this book is mainly about interviewing at that. For more instruction and inspiration, and for answers to some of the most important questions that arise in daily writing, I recommend two great little books: *The Elements of Style,* by William Strunk, Jr., and E. B. White, and *On Writing Well,* by William Zinsser. (*A Dictionary of Contemporary American Usage,* by Bergen and Cornelia Evans, is a lively and readable guide to the wiles and potholes of grammar as well.)

Pangs of Collaboration

A halfbreed sort of article may come out of some interviews: the as-told-to piece. The writer who undertakes an as-told-to article may well feel that he is treading on eggs — or walking on air. Such an article can be a snap or a snag, depending on the teller. "If the subject is articulate and willing to talk freely," wrote Richard Gehman, "the as-told-to article is ridiculously easy to write. All the writer need do is ask the questions, prod the narrator's memory, then put the story into language that approximates the latter's and arrange it in logical or dramatic order." In his book *Writing and Selling Magazine Articles,* Gehman listed 11 steps for writing the as-told-to piece:

1. Read the clips on the subject.
2. Spend some time with him to become familiar with his manner of speaking.
3. Discuss the story in broad, general terms and make an outline.
4. Ask questions leading to details.
5. Make a first draft.
6. See the subject again for more details.
7. Write a second draft.
8. Sit with the subject and, if possible, read the story aloud, making notes of his corrections, alterations or additions.
9. Incorporate the changes.
10. Check with the subject again.
11. Get his initials on the manuscript — on each page, if possible.

This 11-step dance can be troublesome if one has an irresolute partner. "The most difficult subject of this kind I've ever had was Sid Caesar, the TV comedian," reflected Gehman — who had been asked by *Look* magazine to collaborate with Caesar on a piece called "What Psychoanalysis Did for Me." "We sat together for six hours while Sid rambled on about his problems and how he had solved them or failed to solve them," wrote Gehman. "The trouble was, he kept changing his mind. He would make one statement, then take it back; he would make another, then decide that the original was what he wanted to say. It was hard, exasperating work, made bearable only by his charming wit and his ability to laugh at himself. Finally I had enough material to do a draft, but when we sat down to go over it, I found that he had changed his mind several more times.

The piece that ultimately appeared in *Look* was not as strong as the one we originally wrote; it did not really get under the surface." Collaboration is not easy, warns Bob Thomas, who has done several as-told-to tomes. "You are often dealing with a person late in his life. His memory is sometimes hazy or has mellowed so that he doesn't want to revive old bitternesses. But sometimes they do — that makes it interesting.

"But, there again, you have to be wary because his memory may have become embittered over the years and you might be in danger of libeling someone. I don't think the collaborator should be in the guise of a policeman or an investigative reporter. Obviously, this person wants to tell his story. I think it's the collaborator's duty to tell it as artfully, as amusingly, as faithfully as he can."

Should the collaborator be faithful to the point of dispensing lies? "I can't recall any occasion when I have actually helped a person in a lie," says Thomas. "There are times when you use white lies in order to save the feelings of relatives, friends, co-workers."

For an as-told-to, the subject obviously has final editorial approval, but what about cash? "Some subjects insist on being paid," says Gehman. "Others are satisfied only with the publicity they get and with the amateur's thrill of seeing his name in print. One will insist on sharing credit with the writer; another will prefer that only his name appears. The professional writer should not care, one way or the other. He is not going to make a reputation with his as-told-to's, except among editors, and they will learn from other editors some estimate of his ability."

All of which indicates what a strange animal the as-told-to article is: not quite journalism, not quite public relations, and not quite satisfactory to the interviewer who wants to control his own work — who would prefer to gamble on his own skills, not on someone else's name; who is determined to sum up his subject's life honestly, not discreetly and effortlessly. For that interviewer — no; for that *writer*, two things are certain: the most stylish writing is crippled if it must bear bald spots in its research; and all the research in the world is lifeless if it is not written up with clarity and insight.

The writer is an interviewer first. That is how he obtains the critical mass for his articles, his books. And it is good that the interviewer pour weeks and months and years into his research. But he should know that while the writing comes second chronologically, he must write as carefully as he frames questions — lest the truth and color of his material leak away before reaching print. For when he writes with clarity and fire and light — with a piece of himself — he will not merely inform the reader, as any amount of research would. He will move him.

Onward.

A Short (Painless) History of the Interview

By our first strange and fatal interview,
By all desires which thereof did ensue. . . .

—John Donne
"On His Mistress"

While readers today take the interview for granted, its use as a means of gathering information to be published was "invented" — and not so long ago. Like other inventions, it passed through an initial period of scorn and skepticism, then an era of trial and error — only to emerge as the invaluable tool it is for the writer today.

Questioning has always been the chief form of learning and of satisfying curiosity for human beings. One of the world's oldest books — *Instructions of Ptah-Hotep* — is a book on how to talk. Written by a government official in Egypt over 4,000 years ago, it indicates that the craft of conversing, if not downright interviewing, has been a matter of concern since antiquity. In fact, the word "interview" (borrowed from the French "entrevue" and the expression "s'entre-voir," meaning to "visit with each other") in its early form did not necessarily imply that a writer recorded any quotations from a conversation. It simply meant that a meeting had occurred. Distinctions between social and fact-gathering encounters would come later. Much later.

The interview's infancy has provoked considerable disagreement and idle speculation. Some writers have wondered if historic figures such as Shakespeare would be a mystery today, but for the fact that such people were not interviewed. "Jesus Christ is an enigma," suggests one journalist, "because no interviewer got to him." Freelancer John Christie once remarked that the first interview to be printed was probably the Biblical account of Moses going up to Mount Sinai. "And, boy, did he get results!" adds Christie. "In addition to the Ten Commandments, he learned what God's name was."

Early variations of what would later be termed the interview appear in the Middle Ages and the Renaissance. *The Book of Marjorie Kemp,* for example, was written by a medieval housewife/mystic who was given to religious transports. The book contains "interviews" with popes, bishops and kings. Thomas More's *Utopia,* written during the Renaissance, likewise consists of "reports" of conversations delivered to More.

Interviews gathered momentum with the era of magazines and coffeehouses in seventeenth-century England. Daniel Defoe, in addition to being the creator of *Robinson Crusoe,* is generally acknowledged to be the father of modern journalism. His *Review,* a triweekly magazine published for more than ten years, featured "interviews" with numerous personages. While most were fictional, their success rested on an abundance of circumstantial realism that made them seem valid. Defoe's *Moll Flanders* and *Journal of the Plague Year,* for that matter, resulted largely from interviews.

Interview at End, Door at Hand

In England, taverns and coffeehouses were considered centers of communication before newspapers became popular — stressing once again the notion that Western communication is based on verbal skill. One of the wittiest talkers of this time was, of course, Dr. Samuel Johnson. Boswell's *Life of Johnson* is for all purposes a first-hand talk with a first-rate interviewee. "Why do you write down my sayings?" asked Johnson at one point. "I write them down when they are good," replied Boswell — a reporter who obviously knew a "good quote" when he heard one.

In 1836, Henry Taylor wrote a series of essays that were collected in a book called *The Statesman.* Intended to mock what Machiavelli did for the art of getting and holding onto power in *The Prince,* the book provided strategies for everything from writing a report to choosing a wife. There is even a chapter titled "Concerning Interviews." The placement of furniture was important in determining the success or failure of an interview, according to Taylor. "And in every case an interview will find a more easy and pleasing termination," concluded the author, "when the door is at hand as the last words are spoken. These are not frivolous considerations where civility is the business to be transacted." Uh-huh.

The Bed Afire

Of course, the interview and verbatim reporting had been employed in American journalism from the early years. A story on the death of Blackbeard the pirate in the *Boston News-Letter* for March 2, 1719, was apparently based upon an interview with a ship captain. But interviewing was only an occasional device until August 31, 1835, when James Gordon Bennett, publisher of the *New York Herald,* announced: "We mean to begin a series of Police Reports on a new and improved plan. The mere barren record of a person and crime amounts to nothing — to something less than nothing. . . . why not extract it and present it to the public in a new and elegant dress?"

Subsequent issues of the *Herald* featured two elements of the interview as we know it today: the use of Q&A verbatim reporting (reflecting the examination of witnesses in the courtroom), and the use of descriptive details to increase color and "human interest." Generally, this meant quoting a subject, and describing how he said something.

This new approach was soon dramatized by the *Herald* when Bennett decided to cover the story of a sensational murder that had occurred in a "house of ill fame" in New York in April, 1836. Ellen Jewett, a prostitute, had been killed, and Bennett went to the scene where he interviewed Rosina Townsend, the madame who had discovered the body. "His story of that visit," writes Bennett's biographer Oliver Carlson, "told on the front page . . . set the whole of New York rocking back on its heels. It just wasn't done!" One hostile critic compared Bennett's reporting with that "of a vampire returning to a newly found graveyard — like the carrion bird to the rotten carcass — like any vile thing to its congenial element." Well, now.

Bennett's question-and-answer method of reporting gave the reader a feeling of Being There, and the *Herald* — less than a year old at the time — was selling like never before. An excerpt from a typical Bennett story captures his technique:

> I knocked at the door. A Police officer opened it, stealthily. I told him who I was. "Mr. B. you can enter," said he, with great politeness. The crowds rushed from behind seeking also an entrance.
> "No more comes in," said the Police officer.
> "Why do you let that man in?" asked one of the crowd.
> "He is an editor — he is on public duty." ...
> "Mr. B. would you like to see the *place*?"
> "I would," said I ....
> "Here," said the Police officer, "Here is the poor creature."

A few days later Bennett published yet another story, this time in the Q&A format that is generally considered the first formal interview published in an American newspaper. Bennett prefaced the interview by saying he had a witness to the conversation who would vouch for its accuracy. He asked madame Rosina about Ellen Jewett's visitor that fatal evening. "I knocked at the door," said Madame, "and Helen said, 'Come in.' I opened the door and went in. — I saw Frank lying on the bed." Then Bennett, assuming the position of the magistrate, used his courtroom method of reportage:

> *Question:* What was he doing?
> *Answer:* He was lying on his left side, with his head resting on his arm in the bed, the sheet thrown over him, and something in his other hand.
> *Q:* What was that?
> *A:* I can't say.
> *Q:* Was it a book?
> *A:* I think it was — either a book or a paper. — I saw his face.
> *Q:* What did he say?
> *A:* Nothing. Helen said to me, "Rosina, as you have not been well today, will you take a glass of champagne with us?" I replied, "No, I am much obliged to you, I had rather not." — I then

left the room, as some of the other girls called me from below. — I neither heard nor saw anything more from that time. — The house was locked up for the night at 12 o'clock P.M. — I returned to rest. — About 3 o'clock A.M. I heard a noise at the front door, and found, on enquiring, that it was a young man who was in the habit of visiting one of the girls in the house. — I got up and let him in — after I had let him in I smelt smoke, and on going into the parlor I found the back door open, and Helen's lamp standing on the marble side table, by the door. I went directly to Helen's room, and found the door shut — I opened it, and on so doing, the smoke rushed out and nearly suffocated me. — I then raised the alarm of fire. — The watchman was called in, and he went into the room and found Helen lying on the bed and the bed on fire — she was burnt. — After the windows were opened and the smoke let out, the watchman discovered that Helen had been murdered, and then the bed set on fire. . . .

"Misquoted!"

Bennett received even more flak for this story. Benjamin Day, publisher of the rival *Sun,* called him a liar, claiming that Rosina Townsend denied the interview ever took place. The madame added that when Bennett and his colleague visited the house "Bennett uttered not a word . . . but appeared to be wholly engrossed with an examination of a picture and attempts at flirtation with one of the girls still remaining." Ah, yes.

"I did not make any attempts at flirtation with any of her girls," protested Bennett on the pages of his *Herald* with bemusement. "During the whole interview there was not a girl in the house with us. I have, besides, long since given over all flirtation — and when I did flirt, I never did so with such girls." Regarding the more serious charge of publishing an inaccurate conversation, he said that he and his witness would swear an oath to it. "It is exact to the word. I myself put the very questions there stated. It is probable that Rosina may have forgotten what she stated — she has been telling so many stories that it is likely enough she may be confused."

Bennett succeeded not only in causing all of New York to talk about the murder (and to buy the *Herald*), but also helped prove that the young man accused of the crime had not committed it. In the end, the defendant Richard P. Robinson was acquitted and soon vanished, reportedly to Texas. Madame Rosina Townsend also disappeared. The murderer of Ellen Jewett was never apprehended; and from the whole ordeal, only the interview has been passed along to posterity.

A Sovereign and Honor

Meanwhile, Henry Mayhew of the *London Morning Chronicle* was becoming the Victorian Studs Terkel par excellence. In fact, his main work — *London Labour and the London Poor,* a four-volume "Cyclopaedia of the Conditions and Earnings of Those That Will Work, Those That Cannot Work, and Those That Will Not Work" — surely outdistances Terkel's *Working* in both scope and ambition. Under "Those That Will Not Work," for instance, Mayhew listed the London criminal underground. "My vocation," he said, "is to collect facts and register opinions." He settled on the interview as a means of getting information from a representative cross-section of workers in a trade, and conducted important interviews with a colleague who took notes.

Mayhew's ability to inspire trust and confidence was legendary. In 1850, he arranged for a meeting with some young thieves, but the boys refused to talk on certain subjects for fear of reprisals. To gain their trust, Mayhew, declaring that no thief had ever cheated him, gave a sovereign to a boy who had gone to prison 26 times, asking him to return with the change. There would be no punishment if he did not return. "It was clear that their honour was at stake," he later wrote, "and several said they would kill the lad in the morning if he made off with the money. Many minutes elapsed in almost painful silence, and some of his companions began to fear that so large a sum of money had proved too great a temptation for the boy. At last, however, a tremendous burst of cheering announced the lad's return." Then the interview became "more rational and manageable," observed Mayhew, and several boys gave their life stories spontaneously.

The Cairo Connection

Back in the states, the interviewer gradually began to take the spotlight from the editorial writer. The *Herald,* for instance, sent Henry Morton Stanley to find Dr. David Livingstone, who had disappeared in darkest Africa, in 1869. Two years later Stanley found his man, interviewed him, and the news reached the world.

As the interview grew in popularity, it was attacked by some members of the press as being an unreliable, flippant reporting device. Many early interviews were indeed a bit quaint, if not openly humorous. When a correspondent for the *Herald* met the Emperor of Brazil in, of all places, Cairo, the 1871 exchange was published in this manner:

> *Correspondent:* I see a copy of *Galignani,* containing an interview with Mr. Seward, from the *New York Herald,* on your table. Has your majesty read it?
>
> *Dom Pedro:* I did, with interest. Mr. Seward has been a great traveler, and seems to have thoroughly improved his opportunities for observation. I shall not be able to go so far as he has done. By the way, I suppose I am now being "interviewed," which, I believe, is the term.
>
> *Correspondent:* Yes, your majesty; but I will with pleasure submit my manuscript to your secretary if there should be anything you may wish expunged.
>
> *Dom Pedro:* Thank you; but perhaps it will not matter. I have been in a constant state of "interview" all my life, and consequently say nothing I am not willing to have made public. It is rather novel, though, to find a correspondent of the *New York Herald* under the shadow of the Pyramids.
>
> *Correspondent:* They are very enterprising men, the *Herald* correspondents, and go everywhere.
>
> *Dom Pedro:* Well, you are an enterprising people, and deserve the great prosperity you enjoy.... But I must ask you to excuse me now, as I am engaged to receive the Prince Heretier at this hour. I wish you good morning.

The interview was considered an invasion of privacy rather than a news-gathering device, and a bit *too* intimate for many editors of the time. *Puck* ran a page of pictures in its March 1877 issue showing an interviewer forcing doors, rummaging in bureaus, wine cabinets, and going down chimneys and manholes after his victims. Others complained that stories resulting from interviews represented the writer's point of view more than the subject's. "This American interview," wrote the editor of the *Pall Mall Gazette* in 1886, "is degrading to the interviewer, disgusting to the interviewee, and tiresome to the public." Nor did James Russell Lowell think much of it as an American form of reporting. Looking back on a happier age, he reflected, "Let the seventeenth century, at least, be kept sacred from the insupportable foot of the interviewer."

Twain Feigns

Mark Twain was more whimsical about the matter. In 1875 he published a humorous account called "An Encounter with an Interviewer" in which a reporter from the *Daily Thunderstorm* came to interview the author. "You know it is the custom, now, to interview any man who has become notorious," the reporter told Twain.

"Indeed, I had not heard of it before," replied the interviewee. "It must be very interesting. What do you do it with?"

"Ah, well — well — it ought to be done with a club in some cases; but customarily it consists in the interviewer asking questions and the interviewed answering them. It is all the rage now. Will you let me ask you certain questions calculated to bring out the salient points of your public and private history?"

"Oh, with pleasure — with pleasure," replied Twain. "I have a very bad memory, but I hope you will not mind that." The following took place:

Q. How old are you?
A. Nineteen, in June.
Q. Indeed. I would have taken you to be thirty-five or six. Where were you born?
A. In Missouri.
Q. When did you begin to write?
A. In 1836.
Q. Why, how could that be, if you are only nineteen now?
A. I don't know. It does seem curious, somehow.
Q. It does, indeed. Whom do you consider the most remarkable man you ever met?
A. Aaron Burr.

   Q. But you never could have met Aaron Burr, if you are only nineteen years —

   A. Now, if you know more about me than I do, what do you ask me for?

   Q. Well, it was only a suggestion; nothing more. How did you happen to meet Burr?

   A. Well, I happened to be at his funeral one day, and he asked me to make less noise, and —

   Q. But, good heavens! if you were at his funeral, he must have been dead, and if he was dead how could he care whether you made a noise or not?

   A. I don't know. He was always a particular kind of man that way.

In the end, the interviewer left, perplexed. "He was very pleasant company," reflected Twain, "and I was sorry to see him go."

Shaving the Head of State

   Despite the amusement — and bemusement — of Twain, the interview trod onward. In 1875 a book called *Views and Interviews on Journalism,* edited by Charles F. Wingate, featured interviews with many of the leading journalists of the day, including Charles Dana, Horace Greeley, E. L. Godkin and James Gordon Bennett. A few years later, Joseph McCullagh devised a mass-interview technique while editing the *Globe-Democrat.* A group of Ohio editors arrived in St. Louis by train on June 21, 1879, where they were met by some 30 reporters wearing badges that said: "A Soft Answer Turneth Away Wrath, *Globe-Democrat* Interviewing Corps, With Malice for None and With Questions for All."

   Each editor was questioned in a poll-like manner, then given a yellow card for his hatband: "Pumped. Keep this check in your hat to avoid further disturbance." The following day eight columns of the *Globe-Democrat* carried the multi-interviews. The technique, a forerunner of the poll as we now know it, was used by McCullagh at subsequent political conventions, and soon other newspapers were imitating the approach as well.

   By the end of the nineteenth century, the interview had become an established tool for journalists. Speaking before the Columbia Historical Society in 1902, Francis A. Richardson recalled the sensation created by Joseph McCullagh, who President Andrew Johnson often invited to interview him. "The example set by the President of the United States excited not only sensation but strong criticism," he reflected. "It was not long, however, before his example was rapidly and widely followed, and interviewing became what it is today, one of the leading features of journalism in this country."

"After Grant," added Richardson, "no President up to the present time has been much enamored of the interviewing process, and Presidential utterances for the newspapers have been few and far between." A few years after Richardson's 1902 remarks, however, Theodore Roosevelt originated the press conference by inviting reporters to his office and briefing them on the day's events while he had a late-afternoon shave. All reporters were placed on equal footing. Roosevelt even set aside a White House room for reporters, and phones were installed. "Roosevelt's whole relationship with interviewers was unique," recalled Isaac Marcosson years later. "Although he would seldom allow himself to be quoted in an article, he talked with what sometimes seemed an almost incredible frankness. He bared the utmost secrets of state."

Relations between the press and the President have fluctuated dramatically from administration to administration, but the establishment of the Presidential press conference, and occasional private interviews with reporters (long considered an interviewer's peak assignment), gave the interview further power and prestige as a means of gathering information for stories. Some high-level interviewers became celebrities themselves over the years. Isaac Marcosson became so famous as an interviewer during the World War I years that it was once said, "A politician is just a politician until Marcosson interviews him, then he's a statesman."

Quote-Storing '20s

Marcosson, in his book *Adventures in Interviewing,* compared his work with that of a salesman. "Men often fail in business because they use the same arguments with everybody," he wrote in 1919. "They forget that each human being is a law unto himself. The more distinguished or famous a man becomes, the more distinct becomes his individuality. It would have been impossible to get next to Lloyd George with the same line of selling talk that you employed to make

Sir Douglas Haig break his chronic silence. Each of these remarkable men — and they are types — required an entirely different line of approach, based upon a knowledge of their work, interests, ambition and personality, together with a swift appraisal of the mood of the hour and the march of events."

"During the 1920s, magazine writers like Isaac Marcosson and Samuel Blythe developed newspaper interviewing to the dimensions of magazine pieces," says Maurice Zolotow, a noted interviewer himself. "Marcosson or Blythe would first bone up on the special field in which the subject was prominent. They would get ready a long list of specific questions. They would then meet with the subject, fire the questions, and take notes on the answers. The writer behaved in a purely passive way and kept his own personality out of the story as much as possible. And in talking to his subject, the writer kept on the acceptable conscious level. He never attempted to penetrate into the unconscious or undesirable phases of his subject's life or personality." Success was not always easy to come by. An interview that failed was sometimes known as a "water haul" — in the language of the police reporter of the 1920s, who used that term to describe a fruitless endeavor.

Personality Pieces

By the late 1920s *The New Yorker* had begun a series of personality pieces (called "profiles") which placed even more emphasis on interviewing. *"The New Yorker* profile writer was expected not only to question the subject, but also to pry into the subject's entire life — good and bad — and interview his friends and enemies," recalls Zolotow. "In the hands of Alva Johnston, Margaret Chase Harriman, Wolcott Gibbs, St. Clair McKelway, Geoffrey Hellman, the profiles became witty, polished, brilliant exercises in human nature." Hellman's profiles over the years were studies of extraordinary people — from publisher Alfred A. Knopf and architect Le Corbusier to artist Diego Rivera and author Somerset Maugham. The influence that *New Yorker* techniques had upon other magazines' personality pieces is inestimable.

The Paris Review, another upper-middlebrow publication, also boosted interviewing. The quarterly's Q&A interviews with famous authors started with the first issue in the spring of 1953. "The series of interviews was at first regarded as another device — more dignified and perhaps more effective, too — for building circulation," observed Malcolm Cowley in his introduction to *Writers at Work,* an anthology of the *PR* interviews. "The magazine needed famous names on the cover, but couldn't afford to pay for the contributions of famous authors. 'So let's talk to them,' somebody ventured . . . 'and print what they say.' "

Editor George Plimpton suggested E. M. Forster as the first author to be interviewed. Forster agreed — with the stipulation that the questions be given him in advance "so that he could brood over them." Adds Cowley: "The questions were submitted, and a few days later when the interviewers appeared, Forster gave his answers so methodically and slowly that his guests had no trouble keeping up with him. It was a simple interview to transcribe, and it furnished the best of patterns for the series that followed."

That pattern — a general introduction, followed by an in-depth Q&A exchange — became a format that other, more popular publications would follow, notably *Playboy* in the early 60s. As imitators of *Playboy* came on the scene, so too did more Q&A's. The format has been with us a long time (consider the *Baltimore Catechism*), but lately everyone seems to be doing it — from columns such as Dear Abby to books after David Reuben's *Everything You Always Wanted to Know About Sex but Were Afraid to Ask.* We even have the self-interview, in which someone of renown (Truman Capote in *Cosmopolitan,* Glenn Gould in *Hi-Fidelity,* etcetera) serves up the Q's to himself.

Today, the interview is so widely accepted that it has even been mechanized. In Chicago, a group of lawyers recently turned some of the interviewer's task over to a computer. The machine poses some 300 to 400 questions to a prospective plaintiff, instantly summarizes the answers, and rattles off a ready-to-file lawsuit. The computer is designed to base questions on previous answers. With further programming, according to the *New York Times,* "the computer would as readily prepare a will, draft a bankruptcy petition, put together a consumer complaint, and help with other standard chores."

While the computer may be a time- and moneysaver for attorneys, the writer's profession remains a cottage industry in comparison. Even Walter Rugaber, the *Times* reporter, had to use a telephone interview to get the story on computer interviews. But, unlike an earlier time when it was taboo and controversial, the interview is used today with a bravado that borders on the routine. Readers take the interview, in its many shapes and guises, for granted — and that is well and good, as long as *writers* never do the same.

Index

Other Books of Interest From Writer's Digest

Writer's Market, edited by Jane Koester and Bruce Joel Hillman. The freelancer's Bible, containing 4,454 places to sell what you write. Includes the name, address and phone number of the buyer, a description of material wanted and how much the payment is. 1,000 pp. $13.95.

Writing and Selling Science Fiction, edited by C. L. Grant. A comprehensive handbook to an exciting but oft-misunderstood genre. Eleven articles by top-flight sf writers on markets, characters, dialogue, "crazy" ideas, world-building, alien-building, money and more. 191 pp. $7.95.

The Mystery Writer's Handbook, edited by Lawrence Treat. A howthey-dunit to the whodunit, newly written and revised by members of the Mystery Writers of America. Includes the four elements essential to the classic mystery. A clear and comprehensive handbook that takes the mystery out of mystery writing. 275 pp. $8.95

A Guide to Writing History, by Doris Ricker Marston. How to track down Big Foot — or your family Civil War letters, or your hometown's last century — for publication and profit. A timely handbook for history buffs and writers. 258 pp. $8.50.

The Confession Writer's Handbook, by Florence K. Palmer. A stylish and informative guide to getting started and getting ahead in the confessions. How to start a confession and carry it through. How to take an insignificant event and make it significant. 171 pp. $6.95.

A Complete Guide to Marketing Magazine Articles, by Duane Newcomb. "Anyone who can write a clear sentence can learn to write and sell articles on a consistent basis," says Newcomb (who has published well over 3,000 articles). Here's how. 248 pp. $6.95.

The Creative Writer, edited by Aron Mathieu. This book opens the door to the real world of publishing. Inspiration, techniques, and ideas, plus inside tips from Maugham, Caldwell, Purdy, others. 416 pp. $6.95.

Handbook of Short Story Writing, edited by Frank A. Dickson and Sandra Smythe. You provide the pencil, paper, and sweat — and this book will provide the expert guidance. Features include James Hilton on creating a lovable character; R. V. Cassill on plotting a short story. 238 pp. $6.95.

A Treasury of Tips for Writers, edited by Marvin Weisbord. Everything from Vance Packard's system of organizing notes to tips on how to get research done free, by 86 magazine writers. 174 pp. $5.95.

One Way to Write Your Novel, by Dick Perry. For Perry, a novel is 200 pages. Or, two pages a day for 100 days. You can start — and finish — *your* novel, with the help of this step-by-step guide taking you from the blank sheet to the polished page. 138 pp. $6.95.

The Poet and the Poem, by Judson Jerome. A rare journey into the night of the poem — the mechanics, the mystery, the craft and sullen art. Written by the most widely read authority on poetry in America, and a major contemporary poet in his own right. 482 pp. $7.95 ($6.95 paperback).

Writing and Selling Non-Fiction, by Hayes B. Jacobs. Explores with style and know-how the book market, organization and research, finding new markets, interviewing, humor, agents, writer's fatigue and more. 317 pp. $7.95.

The Beginning Writer's Answer Book, edited by Kirk Polking, Jean Chimsky, and Rose Adkins. "What is a query letter?" "If I use a pen name, how can I cash the check?" These are among 500 questions most frequently asked by beginning writers — and expertly answered in this down-to-earth handbook. Cross-indexed. 168 pp. $7.95.

Writing Popular Fiction, by Dean R. Koontz. How to write mysteries, suspense thrillers, science fiction. Gothic romances, adult fantasy, Westerns and erotica. Here's an inside guide to lively fiction, by a lively novelist. 232 pp. $7.95.

Art & Crafts Market, edited by Lynne Lapin and Betsy Wones. Lists 4,498 places where you can show and sell your crafts and artwork. Galleries, competitions and exhibitions, magazines that buy illustrations and cartoons, book publishers and advertising agencies — they're all there, complete with names, addresses, submission requirements, phone numbers and payment rates. 800 pp. $10.95.

Photographer's Market, edited by Melissa Milar and Bill Brohaugh. Contains what you need to know to be a successful freelance photographer. Names, addresses, photo requirements, and payment rates for 1,616 markets. Plus, information on preparing a portfolio, basic equipment needed, the business side of photography, and packaging and shipping your work. 400 pp. $9.95.

The Cartoonist's and Gag Writer's Handbook, by Jack Markow. Longtime cartoonist with thousands of sales reveals the secrets of successful cartooning — step by step. Richly illustrated. 157 pp. $7.95.

The Greeting Card Writer's Handbook, by H. Joseph Chadwick. A former greeting card editor tells you what editors look for in inspirational verse . . . how to write humor . . . . what to write about for conventional, studio and juvenile cards. Extra: a renewable list of greeting card markets. Will be greeted by any freelancer. 268 pp. $6.95.

Writing for Children and Teenagers, by Lee Wyndham. Author of over 50 children's books shares her secrets for selling to this large, lucrative market. Features: the 12-point recipe for plotting, and the ten commandments for writers. 253 pp. $8.95.

Writer's Digest. The world's leading magazine for writers. Monthly issues include timely articles, interviews, columns, tips to keep writers informed on where and how to sell their work. One year subscription, $12.

(Add 50c for postage and handling. Prices subject
to change without notice.)
Writer's Digest, 9933 Alliance Road, Cincinnati, Ohio 45242.